The Countess of Longford CBE is a leading historian and well known as a woman of wide interests and numerous achievements. After her degree in *Literae Humaniores* at Oxford, she was a lecturer for the Workers' Educational Association in English, Economics and Politics. She has stood twice for Parliament in the Labour interest. Lady Longford was until recently a Trustee of the National Portrait Gallery, a member of the Advisory Council of the Victoria and Albert Museum and of the British Library, and is a Fellow of the Royal Society of Literature. She is an Hon.D.Litt of Sussex University. Her previous publications include *Victoria R.I.* (which won the James Tait Black Memorial Prize), a celebrated two-volume biography of Wellington, a much-acclaimed biography of the poet and traveller W. S. Blunt, *A Pilgrimage of Passion*, a biography of the Queen Mother, *Eminent Victorian Women*, and her most recent acclaimed biography of The Queen, *Elizabeth R.*

GW00673138

By the same author

# ELIZABETH LONGFORD

# Jameson's Raid

## The Prelude to the Boer War

*'I date the beginning of these
violent times in our country
from the Jameson Raid'*
Sir Winston Churchill

PANTHER
Granada Publishing

Panther Books
Granada Publishing Ltd
8 Grafton Street, London W1X 3LA

Published by Panther Books 1984

First published in Great Britain by
George Weidenfeld and Nicolson Limited 1960

*Jameson's Raid* was first published in 1960 under the
author's original name, Elizabeth Pakenham

ISBN 0-586-05898-2

Reproduced, printed and bound in Great Britain by
Hazell Watson & Viney Ltd, Aylesbury, Bucks

Set in Baskerville

*To Frank*

# Contents

## Part III: Probe

# Illustrations

# Introduction

'What! *Another* book on the Jameson Raid! Let's hope it will be at least an "astringent" one.' So wrote the South African-born poet and brilliant biographer of Rhodes, William Plomer, to a friend. I, too, hope my book will be astringent.

This new edition of *Jameson's Raid* (first published over twenty years ago) should certainly be rather more astringent than its predecessor. New material of a compelling nature has turned up since I concluded my researches in 1958. Nearly all the fresh evidence tells against the claim of Joseph Chamberlain, the Colonial Secretary, to have been guilty of no complicity whatsoever in the plot that became a raid.

Only one of the new discoveries supports the case for Chamberlain. This discovery was made by C. M. Woodhouse, the first historian to be given access to the Rhodes Papers at Oxford. In his joint biography with the late J. G. Lockhart (*Rhodes*, 1963), Mr Woodhouse reveals that one of the notorious 'missing telegrams' sent to Rhodes by his agent Harris – 'missing', or rather spirited away, because they would incriminate the Colonial Office – owed its main notoriety to what has proved to be merely a cryptographical error. (The messages were in code.)

But as if to balance this evidence for the defence, Mr Woodhouse virtually establishes the lethal nature of the controversial 'fireworks' telegram.

Lord Blake also has made a discovery that cannot but strengthen the prosecution. His chapter on 'The Jameson Raid' in *History and Imagination* (1981) is based on a hitherto unpublished letter from Rhodes's solicitor Hawksley to Rhodes himself, written on 22 May 1897, during the closing stages of the Select Committee on the Raid. (It was recently deposited by Rhodes's last surviving niece in her uncle's archives at Oxford.) Ingenious detective work by Robert Blake has enabled him to answer that elusive 'Who dunit?' Who spirited away the Telegraph Company's copies of the 'missing telegrams'? The answer is almost certainly Sir Robert Herbert, a director of the Telegraph Company and, even more significantly, a former Permanent Head of the Colonial Office, from which he had retired only four years before the Raid. This apparent liaison between the Colonial Office and the Telegraph Company over the cover-up, had it ever been exposed, would have proved most awkward for the defence.

The sympathies of both the above distinguished historians, Woodhouse and Blake, are normally with the Right. So are those of Mr St John Stevas. But in a witty review of the first edition of my book Stevas, too, had to give a verdict of guilty: 'perhaps the best verdict on Chamberlain is the theological one of culpable ignorance'.

Historians of the Left, writing either as reviewers of my book or to me personally, have all been strong believers in Colonial Office complicity. My radical friend A. J. P. Taylor reiterated only the other day his conviction that 'Chamberlain was in it up to the neck'. Another friend, the Liberal MP Sir Geoffrey Mander, wrote to me while the book was in an early stage:

I feel you are right in thinking that by the standards then existing J.C. [Joseph Chamberlain] was not really guilty. He, however, must have known quite well, unofficially, the sort of thing that Rhodes had in mind. It is also fairly obvious that the previous Liberal Government were to some extent mixed up with these events and nowadays, of course, such an attitude as taken up by J.C. would not be possible.

Exactly two months after these words were written came the Suez fiasco, and the Government's denial of collusion! Compared with this, the South Africa Committee's achievements in the way of cover-up look like peanuts.

Most recently, Richard Jay has written of Chamberlain's performance before the South Africa Select Committee: 'It was a superb, if disgraceful exercise in political survival.'

For the rest, I would like to pick out two pieces of information which reached me after the publication of my book.

The Colonial Office's intended 'fall-guy' was Edward Fairfield – or so Fairfield believed. His integrity has been staunchly defended in letters from his two nieces, my friends Dame Rebecca West and her sister the late Dr Letitia Fairfield. Dame Rebecca writes:

The story of his [Fairfield's] involvement in the Jameson Raid, as my mother told it to me and as I learned it from overhearing the conversation of my elders, was this, put briefly: Edward Fairfield admired Rhodes but feared his lack of scruple. He knew him well. . . . He loathed Flora Shaw, and objected to her peculiar position as a pet of some faction in the Colonial Office with which he was not in sympathy.

On hearing of the Jameson Raid my uncle was enraged and disturbed. As the weeks went on he told his two brothers and my mother that he was being faced with accusations of complicity in the Raid which were quite unfounded: and certainly there grew up at the same time a suspicion that Chamberlain had been guilty of complicity in the Raid.

It was a complete surprise to my uncle when he was told that he was to be made the official scapegoat for the Raid, and he then had a stroke. My father was overcome with anger and horror when he heard of my uncle's stroke, but neither he nor Arthur [his other brother] nor my mother were surprised – they guessed this would happen.

Another generous friend has sent me a copy of an unpublished letter from Cecil Rhodes to Alfred Beit, his fellow conspirator. It was preserved by Beit's secretary Mr Wagner. This long, passionate, virtually unpunctuated letter (I have punctuated it below) condenses into some eight hundred breathless words the whole of Rhodes's dream.

It is dated 'August 1895'. The original was handed to Wagner by Beit 'to avoid its being seen by the Parliamentary Committee of Inquiry into the Raid'.

Rhodes begins by asking Beit for a financial statement of his position with the firm Wernher, Beit & Co. 'I mean a simple statement which I can understand. I never know with carrying over where I am but you can send me an A.B.C. statement.' Rhodes was by now a sick and muddled man in a hurry. Beit was the financial wizard.

Rhodes goes on to mention details of their allegedly foolproof invasion plan, and the desperate need for Chamberlain's co-operation in getting the Bechuanaland Protectorate (or part of it) as a launching pad.

I hope you will arrange to send 2,000 or even 3,000 affairs [rifles]; they will get through all right; they will be supplied with necessary things to fill them. I do hope that after your telegram that Chamberlain will rise to the situation, for the Protectorate is essential, I assure you. If we have the Protectorate I do not feel one atom of doubt as to matter.

Next Rhodes emphasizes the urgency, due to Continental rivals.

As a last resource, if everything else fails, go yourself to see Chamberlain –
you are more convincing than most people – and show him the whole
position of England in the South [of Africa] depends on it, and that next
year may be too late. Our shares are going both at Johannesburg and
Charter to the French and Germans.

Then there is the problem of the House of Commons.

For goodness sake make him understand what it means, and the whole thing
may fail because he has not the courage to face Arnold Foster [H. O.
Arnold-Forster, an MP] and give us the Protectorate; and he has all the
assurances of his predecessors and Lord Knutsford [former Liberal Colonial
Secretary] in his hands, and can ask any guarantees he likes.

Rhodes now deals with the questions of guarantees for the Africans
and their Chief Khama, who are living in the Protectorate;
Gaberones being the proposed launching pad.

He [Chamberlain] might even keep his own resident with Khama. But we
must have the right of administration, to collect our forces at Gaberoones
[*sic*]; and I am told Chamberlain is a strong man and a farseeing one, and
we can give Africa to England if he will only take one step. If he does not, I
do not see how to do it, for 400 miles [from the Transvaal border] is too far –
from the other place [Gaberones] we can ride it in four days or even three,
and Johannesburg is ready.

I am willing to risk my whole position, and it seems to me that the
Secretary of State will not even risk a few unpleasant words from Arnold
Foster.

I may tell you that Khama is all right . . . but he is coming down with the
missionary Rev. Willoughby, and the rascal, who detests me, may change
Khama again on the road. Is it not awful to think that the whole future of
the British Empire out here may turn on a wretched Kaffer [*sic*] and a
Secretary of State who listens to some fanatic in the House of Commons?

The fact that I have got everything the world can give me, and I am
willing to risk it all, does not weigh one bit against the vote of one abusive
fanatic who happens to be a supporter. I wonder how the British Empire
has held together.

Finally Rhodes again underlines the vital meaning of it all for the
Empire.

You might say, 'Oh yes, [but] wait'. But as you know, we will wait too long;
and with its marvellous wealth Johannesburg will make South Africa an
independent Republic, which you and I do not want.

Now surely Chamberlain should see all this. He risks nothing; I risk
everything; and yet he will not budge an inch to help a big idea which makes

England dominant in Africa, in fact gives England the African Continent. I wonder again how the English Empire still retains so much of the world.

So here was Rhodes's big idea. But Kruger had his big ideas too: 'Africa for the Afrikanders'.

I need only add that in the story that follows I have made corrections or additions, either in the text or footnotes, in the light of new material now available.

Without repeating all the detailed acknowledgments recorded in the first edition, I would again like to thank those who have given me help either personally or through their writings or both, particularly Ethel Drus and Jean van der Poel; adding Dame Rebecca West, Lord Blake, the Hon. C. M. Woodhouse and Michael Trent, editor of *History Today*. I must also repeat my debt to those of the older generation who are no longer alive but who helped me at the time with their personal reminiscences: Mrs Carnegie (formerly Mrs Joseph Chamberlain), Miss Hilda Chamberlain, Alderman Byng Kenrick, Dame Lucy Sutherland, Miss Enid Moberly Bell and above all my mother, Katherine Harman, born Chamberlain.

I would like to think that the help given me by my son Thomas Pakenham over *Jameson's Raid* has proved mutual, in so far as the story of the Raid, being a prelude, may have stimulated him to produce his full-scale drama, *The Boer War* (1979).

It used to be said that the war between the British and the Boers ended with the peace of 1902. Later the true date of peace was seen as 1910, when the Union of South Africa came to birth. As the decades continued to pass, however, history seemed to write yet more 'last chapters' to a story that was once believed to be finished. The Anglo-Boer war is now thought to have ended in 1961, when South Africa resigned from the Commonwealth.

Yet today we are thinking more and more about the black Africans, whose position deteriorated with each chapter of that series of which the Raid was the first: the Boer War, the Peace of Vereeniging, the Union, the withdrawal from the Commonwealth, Apartheid. The consequences of the Raid are not yet exhausted. Some might say that Jameson still rides.

# Calendar of Main Events

| | |
|---|---|
| *5 November* | Sixth 'missing [flag] telegram'. Telegram from Rhodes – still missing. |
| *6 November* | 'Great Indaba' at Colonial Office. |
| *7 November* | Transfer of Protectorate; seventh 'missing [fireworks] telegram'. Drifts reopened. |
| *16 November* | British Bechuanaland annexed to Cape. Telegram from Rhodes – still missing. |
| *20 November* | Jameson visits conspirators in Johannesburg. |
| *21 November* | Moberly Bell appoints Younghusband *The Times* Special Correspondent in Johannesburg. |
| *29 November* | Harris and Beit sail for South Africa. |
| *30 November* | First contingent of mounted police arrive at Pitsani from Bulawayo. |
| *6 December* | Chamberlain confirms Robinson's plan for dealing with rising. |
| *7 December* | Uitlander leaders send first telegram to Jameson postponing rising. |
| *9 December* | Willoughby leaves Rhodesia to take up command at Pitsani. |
| *12 December* | Flora Shaw sends 'hurry up' telegram to Rhodes. |
| *15 December* | Transfer of Bechuanaland Border Police completed at Mafeking. |
| *17 December* | Rhodes receives second 'hurry up' telegram from Flora Shaw. Harris and Beit land in South Africa. |
| *18 December* | President Cleveland's ultimatum on Venezuela. Chamberlain's 'hurry up' letter. |
| *18–20 December* | Newton in Cape Town. |
| *19 December* | Interview of Fairfield with Maguire. |
| *20 December* | Eighth 'missing [hurry up] telegram'. |
| *21 December* | Telegram from Maguire to Harris – still missing. |
| *22 December* | Younghusband sees Rhodes. Rhodes quarrels with Bower. |
| *23 December* | Rhodes telegraphs Jameson, rising will take place as arranged. |
| *25 December* | Leonard Manifesto; rising postponed. |
| *26 December* | Uitlanders forbid Jameson to move. Chamberlain warns Salisbury of imminent rising. |
| *27 December* | Fairfield hears rumour of 'fizzle' of rising and of possible 'filibuster'. |
| *28 December* | Jameson receives 'Ichabod' telegram; replies 'Unless I hear to the contrary shall leave tomorrow evening'. Holden arrives at Pitsani. |
| *29 December* | Heany arrives at Pitsani. Chamberlain warns Robinson of possible 'filibuster'. Jameson invades Transvaal. |
| *30 December* | Chamberlain hears news of Raid; leaves for London at midnight. Boers order Jameson to retire. |
| *31 December* | Robinson orders Jameson to retire. Chamberlain repudiates Jameson. Reform Committee set up in Johannesburg. Rhodes offers resignation. |

### 1896

| | |
|---|---|
| *1 January* | Jameson again ordered to retire. Battle of Krugersdorp. *The Times* publishers 'letter of invitation'. |
| *2 January* | Surrender of Jameson at Doornkop. |
| *3 January* | Kaiser's telegram. |
| *4 January* | Robinson arrives in Pretoria. |
| *5 January* | Rhodes resigns. |
| *6 January* | Robinson meets Kruger. |
| *7 January* | Chamberlain promises inquiry into Raid. Reform Committee accept Kruger's terms. |
| *9 January* | Kruger arrests members of Reform Committee. |
| *11 January* | *The Times* publishes *Jameson's Ride*. |

| | |
|---|---|
| *21 January* | Raiders sent to England for trial. |
| *3 February* | Rhodes arrives in England; existence of 'Hawksley' telegrams disclosed to Colonial Office. |
| *6 February* | Rhodes sees Chamberlain. |
| *7 February* | Chamberlain publishes Uitlander dispatch; invites Kruger to England. |
| *11 February* | Opening of Parliament. |
| *13 February* | Chamberlain's 'fire-hose' speech. |
| *March* | Chamberlain visits Jameson secretly in prison. |
| *13–15 April* | Bower in London. |
| *27 April* | Trial of Reformers opens in Pretoria. Invitation to Kruger finally withdrawn. |
| *28 April* | Death sentences passed on Reform leaders. |
| *29 April* | Death sentences commuted. First instalment of 'Bobby White' documents published. |
| *8 May* | Parliament debates Transvaal disclosures. Rhodes prepares to quell Matabele rising. |
| *20 May* | Further reductions in sentences. |
| *30 May* | Publication of Transvaal Green book. |
| *June* | Robinson and Bower visit England. |
| *6 June* | Chamberlain sees 'Hawksley' telegrams; offers to resign. |
| *11 June* | Reform leaders released from gaol. |
| *15 June* | Jameson and officers committed for trial at Bow Street. |
| *17 June* | Telegrams returned to Hawksley. |
| *26 June* | Rhodes resigns from board of Chartered Company. |
| *17 July* | Report of Cape Committee of Inquiry into the Raid. |
| *20 July* | Trial of Jameson and officers opens. |
| *28 July* | Jameson and officers sentenced. |
| *30 July* | Chamberlain moves for Select Committee to inquire into Raid. |
| *14 August* | End of session; Committee of Inquiry lapses. |

**1897**

| | |
|---|---|
| *26 January* | Chamberlain sees Rhodes. |
| *29 January* | Committee of Inquiry into Raid re-appointed. |
| *5 February* | Inquiry opens. |
| *16 February* | First public session of Inquiry. |
| *28 April* | Death of Fairfield. |
| *June* | Queen Victoria's Diamond Jubilee; Kruger releases remaining prisoners. |
| *22 June* | Pageant and procession. |
| *2 July* | Close of examination of witnesses by Committee. |
| *13 July* | Report of Committee of Inquiry. |
| *19 July* | Debate on Colonial Office vote. |
| *26–27 July* | Debate on Report; Chamberlain's 'white-washing' speech. |
| *October* | Death of Rosmead. |

**1898**  Death of Meade.

**1899**

| | |
|---|---|
| *October* | Outbreak of Boer War; Chamberlain challenged to produce 'Hawksley' telegrams. |

**1900**

*January*   'Hawksley dossier' published in *L'Indépéndance Belge*; move for fresh inquiry into Raid.

**1901**

*March*    Markham case.

**1902**    Death of Rhodes. Destruction of 'Hawksley' telegrams?

**1946**

*January*   Opening of *Bower Papers* in Cape Town.

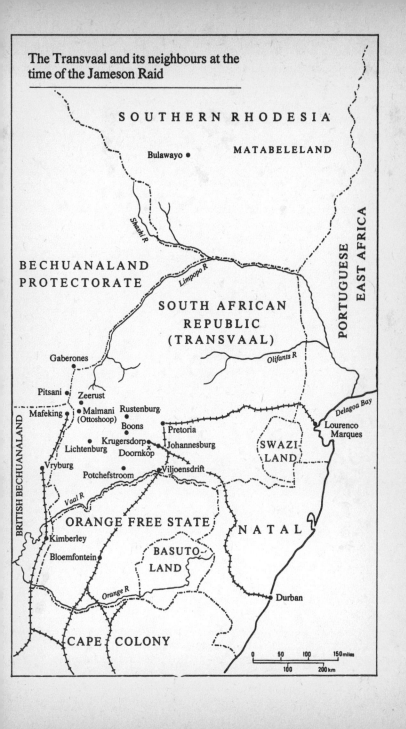

The Transvaal and its neighbours at the time of the Jameson Raid

SOUTHERN RHODESIA

MATABELELAND

Bulawayo •

Shashi R

BECHUANALAND
PROTECTORATE

Limpopo R

SOUTH AFRICAN
REPUBLIC
(TRANSVAAL)

Olifants R

PORTUGUESE EAST AFRICA

Gaberones •

Pitsani •   Zeerust •

Mafeking •   • Malmani
            (Ottoshoop)   Rustenburg •

                Boons •

                    • Pretoria

Lichtenburg •   Krugersdorp •
            Doornkop×   • Johannesburg

Vryburg •

Potchefstroom •   Viljoensdrift •

BRITISH BECHUANALAND

Vaal R

ORANGE FREE STATE

NATAL

Delagoa Bay

Lourenco
Marques

SWAZI
LAND

Kimberley •

Bloemfontein •

BASUTO-
LAND

Orange R

Durban •

CAPE   COLONY

0    50    100    150 miles

100    200 km

# PART I
## Façade

# 1

## *A Raid to Remember*

It was the year 1911. Percy Fitzpatrick, an attractive and popular South African, fifty-eight years old, was thinking of writing the life of the late Cecil Rhodes. He had already delighted the public with a book about a dog, *Jock of the Bushveldt*. But now he wished to hand down to posterity a story far more momentous but also far more intractable. After all, the worst crime of the bull terrier Jock was to seize his dinner before getting the order 'take it!' The human record-sheet was not nearly so simple.

There could be no life of Rhodes without the truth about the Jameson Raid. Dr Jameson was still living. He was now Sir Starr Jameson, the much loved Prime Minister of the Cape Colony. But to all South Africa he was still 'the Doctor' or more often 'Dr Jim'. Some of his traits seemed very like Jock's. Especially that tendency to 'take it' without waiting for orders and those 'browny dark eyes, full of childlike eagerness'. The famous Dr Jim would surely tell his friend the truth about the Raid.

But Jameson had no gift for revelation. Fitzpatrick had already tried and failed to get the story out of him several times. At one of these attempts Jameson showed by his emotional reaction that the subject was one he could not, rather than would not, elucidate. '"Oh, what's the use of talking?" he exploded. "Who knows the whole truth? Let it go at that!"' Later one night Fitzpatrick tried for the last time: '"Tell me, how much did Rhodes know when they [the raiders] started? . . . Was he with you? Or did you force the pace? And what did Chamberlain know? I want to get the whole thing straight."' At first Fitzpatrick believed he would succeed, for Jameson had been talking without reserve. But again he failed to extract Jameson's memories. Graphically he describes his friend's response:

Jameson nodded slowly and began quite calmly and deliberately, but in less than a minute he stopped and I saw the blood run to his face, and his eyes began to glow, and suddenly he leapt from his chair. His frail but intensely nervous frame shaking with the storm of feeling and with both hands clenched to his side, he blazed out, 'God in Heaven, what's the use of talking!' And in a second he was out of the room.[1]

'To get the whole thing straight.' That has been the ambition of many writers before and since Dr Jameson stamped out of the room. The object of this book, among other things, is to discover who 'knew' about the Raid and in what sense of the word they did so, though the historian is rarely given the privilege of getting the whole thing straight. The extraordinarily intricate nature of the material makes the process both difficult and fascinating. But eighty-seven years after the Raid it is no good saying, 'Who knows the whole truth? Let it go at that!' The truth must be worried out of it.

As a story, the Jameson Raid is in its own way unrivalled: dramatic action, high passion, famous participants, moral problems, complexity of events and lingering elements of mystery. At first, however, there was no widespread feeling that riddles were being propounded. Startling and shocking the Raid certainly was; sinister it only gradually came to appear. Even the sagacious Prime Minister, Lord Salisbury, received the first news of the Raid with philosophical calm and seemed to think there was a good chance of the whole thing blowing over. 'Fortunately no great harm seems to have been done in the Transvaal,' he wrote to his Colonial Secretary, Joseph Chamberlain, on 31 December 1895, 'except to Rhodes's reputation. If filibustering fails it is always disreputable.' Unfortunately for those involved in it, the sinister aspect in time came to eclipse all others.

Yet those occupying the front of the stage were not scoundrels. Dr Jameson, who behaved the most outrageously, was perhaps the most likeable man among them. Singularly unpleasant instincts were sometimes at work: ruthlessness, the craving for power and a selfish belief that the great man at critical moments must be allowed to burst the restraints of code, convention and law. But even so the fault lay as much in the ambiguous standards of the time as in the men and women who fell short of them.

Double-think appeared to be a necessary part of empire-building. It has often been said that the British Empire was acquired in a fit of absence of mind. We shall see that the activities of Cecil Rhodes and his Chartered Company of South Africa were made possible by an official policy of non-intervention. But the celebrated phrase about absence of mind by no means accounts for Britain's immense African dominions. There was a good deal of presence of mind in their acquisition.

Britain somehow won the lion's share in the great 'scramble for Africa'. In 1857 the Rev David Livingstone concluded a speech to members of Cambridge University assembled in the Senate House with these words: 'I beg to direct your attention to Africa . . . I go back to Africa to try to make an open path for commerce and Christianity; do you carry out the work which I have begun.' Then, transfixing his audience with a final burst of passion, he shouted in a stentorian voice, 'I LEAVE IT TO YOU!' Within forty years Britain had taken the best part of Africa.

Chamberlain propagated a new doctrine of imperialism. It involved twin duties: to extend the bounds and tighten the bonds of empire. Together they imposed upon the Colonial Secretary a further obligation: not to interfere with men like Rhodes. Non-intervention, however, in the affairs of empire-builders stopped short at naked aggression; for that was contrary to constitutional beliefs and practices.

When naked aggression does occur two things must be examined, the consequences and the occasion. The consequences are always disastrous. Those of the Jameson Raid are nowhere painted more vividly than by Sir Winston Churchill in the first few pages of his *World Crisis*. As a young officer in 1895 he lunched with Sir William Harcourt, the Liberal politician, and asked him the question: 'What will happen now?'

'My dear Winston,' replied the old Victorian statesman, 'the experiences of a long life have convinced me that nothing ever happens.' Since that moment, as it seems to me, nothing has ever ceased happening . . . I date the beginning of these violent times in our country from the Jameson Raid.

Abroad, the Raid had much to do with the outbreak of the Boer War, made its small but poisonous contribution to World War 1 and bedevilled the developments of a multi-racial society in Africa. People felt that the Raid had lowered British standards. This in turn poisoned the climate of morality all over the world.

If one looks for an occasion of naked aggression in British politics one might expect to find it in the act of some uncontrolled person.

Could the Raid then be put down to Jameson's folly? Not really. Or to the conspiracy of Rhodes? Only in part. If these had been all, the act of aggression could hardly have brought about the moral decline. The cause of moral decline lay in the belief that the whole British nation, through their Colonial Secretary, were criminally involved.

# 2
## The Colossus

When Mark Twain took another 'tramp abroad' in 1896, he found a
great shadow lying over South Africa from the Cape to the Zambesi.
It was cast by Cecil John Rhodes, 'still the most imposing figure in
the British Empire outside England', despite the Jameson Raid.
Twenty years earlier the shadow of Rhodes, though less vast, had
also been less black. His aim was the federation of South Africa. The
means he adopted were at first economic and political; a peaceful
method, if that worked. If it did not, he was always prepared to
switch over to stronger measures, whether against the black or the
white races who stood in his way. He became Prime Minister of
the Cape Colony in 1890. And he was a millionaire. Here was surely
the ideal opportunity to achieve his aims through 'peace and gold',
his own alternative to Bismarck's 'blood and iron'. But by 1895 he
had turned from peace to war and his motto was tainted with
Bismarck's. 'Blood and gold' was the slogan of the Jameson Raid.
Before reaching that moment of truth, however, it is necessary to see
how the darkening shadow of Rhodes crept up Africa.

In 1879 the real scramble for Africa began, with Britain, Belgium,
France, Italy, Portugal and a little later Germany staking their
claims, in much the same way as individual pioneers were taking
ship from all over the world for the new Eldorado. Rhodes, an
astonishingly youthful general, already had definite ideas on
strategy. It seemed to him that South African federation was not
developing fast enough. In some respects the goal might even be
receding. The Transvaal had not long ago been an integral part of
the Empire. Now those few thousand Boers were sitting pretty in
their independent Republic in the very heart of South Africa. They
had two sources of strength: the memory of Majuba, a spectacular
military defeat inflicted on the British in 1880; and their old
President Kruger, who had followed up Majuba with the Pretoria
and London Conventions of 1881 and 1884. The latter Convention
was a diplomatic victory for Kruger by which he extracted from
Gladstone's Liberal Government what amounted to independence

for his Boers. Joseph Chamberlain, who at that time was a radical member of Gladstone's Cabinet and as near to being a 'Little Englander' as he ever became, heartily supported a generous policy towards the Transvaal.

Not long after Majuba, West Africa was claimed by the Germans. What was to be the fate of the next territory involved in the scramble? Rhodes had already mapped the future of Bechuanaland. Britain's 'younger and more fiery sons', as he called the pioneers, must go out and take it. When the young and fiery had seized the land, the State could then step in. But not too soon. There must be no premature action from home. Bechuanaland was a thick neck lying between Boer and German territories to the east and west, and carrying the spinal cord of South Africa, Livingstone's great road, from south to north. Rhodes called Bechuanaland the Suez Canal to the interior: 'his' interior and 'his North'.

But Rhodes's ideas were not shared by the Imperial Government at home, nor by the mission stations. Interminable quarrels over the status of Bechuanaland broke out between Rhodes, the Cape Colonists, the High Commissioner, Sir Hercules Robinson, and Boer elements on one side, against the Rev John Mackenzie, Livingstone's successor, and Sir Charles Warren on the other. The Rhodes–Robinson combination ardently desired a southern Bechuanaland brought into the Empire only indirectly, under the Cape Colony: the Boers already settled there in those euphonious republics of Goshen and Stellaland were to co-operate amicably in the 'canal' zone, spontaneously accepting Cape government, in which their own nationals would have a part. Captain Graham Bower, a retired naval officer now serving under Robinson, led the first of five missions sent up to attempt a settlement in Bechuanaland. He put in a very favourable report on the Boer republics. But Rhodes, Robinson, Bower and the rest of the pro-Boer group were defeated. The country was annexed by Warren in 1885 and old Kruger kept saying that he was shut up in the Transvaal like a Kaffir in his kraal. In the course of this struggle Rhodes coined his famous term of abuse, 'the Imperial factor', meaning interference from Downing Street. At the same time he defined his idea of the correct imperial rôle: 'The government of South Africa by the people of South Africa with the Imperial flag for defence.' Rhodes would have liked the gun-boats without the governors-general.

The other side considered Robinson a poor substitute for Sir Bartle Frere, his predecessor in the Cape Colony, and stood for direct imperial rule. A politician who supported the Warren expedition was Joseph Chamberlain, spurred on by the Nonconformists. The Rev John Mackenzie, red haired and bearded, was 'Tau' the lion to his African protégés, among whom were Chiefs Khama and Montsioa. Ten years later Montsioa was to sell a vital strip of his land to Cecil Rhodes.

A year after Rhodes saw the gateway to his northern empire secured in Bechuanaland, though not in the manner he wished or could regard as permanent, he found himself building up an astonishing new empire right in the middle of the Transvaal. He rushed from the diamond mines of Kimberley to the goldfields of the Rand and in 1887 founded a huge gold trust, the Consolidated Goldfields of South Africa. 'The Great Amalgamator' was the nickname he earned from his monopolistic triumphs. As he journeyed into the last decade of his life he firmly believed that the final amalgamation he planned (a far-reaching political one based on Johannesburg) must be supported and impelled by the irresistible power of gold.

At the moment, however, the prospect of another gigantic amalgamation was absorbing his attention. After Bechuanaland, Matabeleland. Again the Transvaal Boers, with their itch to trek, were rivals for these northern farmlands, rich with the celebrated herds of the magnificent Matabele. King Lobengula's cattle and kraals had not yet come under the 'protection' of any European country but in 1887 infiltration began. Pushing back the occasional Boer 'raiders' and circumventing or amalgamating rival concessionaires, Rhodes secured an option from old 'Lob' on the mineral wealth of Matabeleland. This time Sir Hercules Robinson tried to withhold his sanction. He thought Bechuanaland was enough. But Rhodes wrung from the High Commissioner a tepid blessing: 'Well, I leave you alone.'[1] Another slogan of the imperial phrase-maker now came into operation: 'Philanthropy plus five per cent.' He must turn his northern enterprise into a Chartered Company. For this purpose the British public must be made to see his pioneers as purveyors both of civilization and of cash.

In 1889 Rhodes came to England determined to rally the friends and scatter the enemies of his proposed Charter. Among the friends were two journalists, W. T. Stead, apocalyptic editor of the *Pall Mall Gazette* whom Rhodes had seduced from a former allegiance to Mackenzie, and Stead's assistant, Flora Shaw. In the City there was Lord Rothschild who introduced Rhodes to that sharp critic, Chamberlain. Rothschild's son-in-law, Lord Rosebery, used his good offices on the political side. The main enemy was still the mission world whom Rhodes savagely dubbed the 'negrophilists of Exeter Hall', the Nonconformists' HQ, while the London Chamber of Commerce was scarcely more friendly. Chamberlain, from his position on the South Africa Committee appointed under Mackenzie's inspiration to inquire into the question of the Charter, strongly attacked all the ways of colonial syndicates, from the introduction of firearms among blacks to the buying of concessions for an old song. Radical politicians, like Labouchere and Bradlaugh, went for the Charter hammer and tongs, accusing Sir Hercules Robinson of being under Rhodes's thumb.

But the Charter was granted. Contrary to Chamberlain's advice, his friend Albert Grey joined the Dukes of Abercorn and Fife on its board. The Duke of Fife delighted Rhodes by declaring at board meetings that no other company in the world had been thus honoured by his presence. Rhodes, however, did not really need such compliments. He was perfectly aware that 'Chartereds' was unique and he was 'Chartereds'. Everyone, from Robinson, the High Commissioner, to Fife, the son-in-law of the Prince of Wales, was under his thumb.

The 'amalgamation' of Matabeleland went ahead. King Lobengula gave Rhodes land as well as mineral rights. More rival concessionaires were swallowed up, including the Lipperts, German cousins of Rhodes's partner Alfred Beit, while the concession hunters from another syndicate were kidnapped by the Administrator of Bechuanaland, Sir Sydney Shippard, on Rhodes's behalf. Minerals and land being already under Rhodes's thumb, it was the turn for Lobengula himself. The instrument for his liquidation was to be Dr Jameson. The king whom Jameson had earlier 'cured' of gout with morphine, suffered defeat at Jameson's hands in the most ignoble of colonial wars and died, while fleeing from Bulawayo, of smallpox.

In Matabeleland, Rhodes was supreme. How long would he have to wait before the next plums fell into his lap? In the following year,

1894, he was made a Privy Councillor by Lord Rosebery and Lobengula's kingdom became by proclamation 'Rhodesia'. To the conqueror it was 'like giving a man the whole of Australia' and Rhodes, the agnostic, admitted that it was a warming sensation to be sure at last of immortality. In a hurry for more, he sent an emissary to England in the summer of 1895 to discuss with Chamberlain, now Colonial Secretary, the handing over of Bechuanaland. Where the great Lobengula had failed, surely the Bechuana chiefs would not manage to thwart him? He intended to give Chamberlain the honour of adding yet other 'Australias' to the empire of Rhodes.

Not that all the continents of the world could ultimately satisfy the Colossus. 'I would annex the planets if I could,' cried Rhodes one evening, looking up in irritated frustration at the then inaccessible void.

# 3
## Golden City

The plot was hatched in Johannesburg. People called it the Golden
City. It had, in fact, been named after Stephanus Johannes Paulus
Kruger and Johan Rissik. Ten years before the Jameson Raid there
was no Johannesburg. Then the rumour that gold was to be won on
the Rand drew a motley crowd of strangers into the 'heart of
Kruger's pastoral republic. The Boers always referred to them
sternly as 'Uitlanders'. Literally, the word simply meant 'outsiders'
from the lands beyond the Transvaal, that small Boer republic
planted boldly in the middle of the South African veldt. But the
word had a pejorative overtone. The ancient Greeks would have
understood it and frankly called the Uitlanders barbarians.

Kruger and his farmers were deeply shocked by this crude new
civilization in their midst, with its soulless shanty-towns and its
morals of the mining-camp. The Uitlanders returned the dislike,
regarding the Boers as dirty, uneducated peasants with a tendency
to slyness and deceit. One side read the Bible; the other read *The
Cape Times*, *The Johannesburg Star* and *Tit-Bits*. Two centuries, two
different ways of life had met in head-on collision.

At first it looked as though the farmers' heads would prove the
harder. For the town's beginnings were precarious. While Kruger
was visiting England in 1884 he invited financial aid for the settlers
from the mother country. He saw no reason why these difficult
stepchildren should not pay their way with the help of their own
blood relations. A few years later he visited Johannesburg in
response to urgent demands for assistance. The profits from gold-
mining were still hazardous. The people felt raw, desperate, bank-
rupt. Kruger promised help in the form of railways. When he got
home to quiet, domesticated Pretoria he confided to his Boers
exactly how he felt about the foreign zoo. 'They remind me of the old
baboon', he said, 'that is chained up in my yard. When he burned
his tail in the Kaffirs' fire the other day he turned round and bit me –
and that just after I had been feeding him.'[1] His Boers knew what he
meant. Furious Uitlanders had torn down the Transvaal flag, the

*Vierkleur*, right under Kruger's nose. Curiously enough Frank Harris, who as editor of the *Saturday Review* interviewed Kruger immediately after the Jameson Raid, described him as looking like a 'maddened baboon'.[2]

But it was not Kruger's kindly 'feeding' which suddenly caused Johannesburg to spring, in five years, from contemptible, unrelieved shantyism to a gold and glittering Vanity Fair. Indeed, after the railways were built, rail freights took a prominent place in the Uitlanders' growing list of grievances. Their blossoming into opulence, if it can be credited to any one human being, was probably due to 'Cyanide James', a Cornishman who discovered that cyanide would make deep-level mining possible on the Rand.

From then on England sent more and more miners; Germans flocked in, and American engineers. People came from all over Africa and almost from all over the world. When the Uitlanders set up a reform committee of sixty-four to deal with Kruger at the time of the Raid, it was a 'miniature United Nations'.[3] There were 23 Englishmen, 16 South Africans, 9 Scots, 6 Americans, 2 Welshmen, 2 Germans, 1 Irishman, 1 Australian, 1 Dutchman, 1 Canadian, 1 Swiss and 1 Turk.* Kruger's zoo grew, in his disapproving eyes, more foreign and more corrupt every day. Baboons at one moment, a short while later they had graduated into thieves and murderers. 'People of the Lord!' he addressed a great meeting called to celebrate the Transvaal's independence won at the Convention of 1881: 'You old people of the country, you foreigners, you newcomers, yes, even you thieves and murderers!' Kruger, it must be admitted, afterwards denied that the 'thieves and murderers' had any connection with the newcomers. He just added them in case there happened to be any thieves or murderers at the meeting. All the same, he had some reason for his distaste.

The Uitlanders travelled light into the promised land, carrying no heavy moral baggage. Their wives and children were generally left behind. Their God was money. Their manna was dug out of the earth instead of falling from heaven. Aaron's rod they would have

---

*Their occupations were: 10 mineowners, 9 solicitors, 9 dealers in shares, 7 company directors or managers, 7 doctors, 6 merchants, 3 stockbrokers, 3 engineers, 3 mine managers, 2 barristers, 2 soldiers, 1 sanitary inspector, 1 journalist, 1 secretary.

despised unless it caused liquor for the grog-shops to spout from the reef.

An unaccompanied woman journalist, quite a phenomenon for those days, visited Johannesburg in 1892. This is what she thought of it:

Johannesburg at present has no politics. It is much too busy with material problems. It is hideous and detestable, luxury without order; sensual enjoyment without art; riches without refinement; display without dignity.[4]

The journalist was Flora Shaw, later to play a spectacular part in the Raid drama. Alfred Milner, High Commissioner for the Cape after the Raid, is said to have stated bluntly that South Africa bred a special bacillus nourished on whisky: the habit of telling lies. The oddest rumours were always flying about. 'In South Africa,' wrote Sir Graham Bower, Imperial Secretary to Milner's predecessor, 'it is necessary to be incredulous.'[5]

The physical aspect of the City of Gold matched its moral climate. No doubt its centre was spacious and imposing with palatial office buildings, clubs and places of entertainment as in the capital cities of Europe. But the wealth of the centre changed suddenly into the squalor of the suburbs. Straight, dusty roads ran between blocks of shanties roofed with corrugated iron and built of biscuit tins, each block aridly similar to the next. In them lived a white population of speculators, businessmen, clerks and miners for whom politics meant little. They had less loyalty to the Kaiser or Queen Victoria than to King Midas. Once they had arrived in the Golden City, they were transformed into a hurrying, scurrying, hustling, bustling colony of gilded ants bent on carrying home as much money as possible in the shortest possible time. Kruger, indeed, hoped that they would soon work out the gold seams altogether and take themselves and their 'civilization' home again for good. Everything in Johannesburg seemed to grow quickly. Trees, like wealth, shot up to immense heights after only a few years. The crowds of homeless grew too, hundreds of them sleeping in the streets at night, while round about the town stood the gaunt skeletons and winding-gear of the mines where they worked by day.

Judged purely on their own merits there was nothing to commend Johannesburg rather than Pretoria, Kruger's capital, to a British statesman. In Pretoria one found a settled homeliness, flowers, trees and music; whereas in Johannesburg, as Flora Shaw remarked, there were not a dozen men who knew the difference between a violin and a vegetable. If national interests had not existed it is possible that 'Oom Paul' (Uncle Paul Kruger) would have appealed more than the 'Randlords' to Chamberlain's latent Nonconformism.

Not that the British accepted the reports of Kruger's evangelical piety without a pinch of salt. It was said that he had made a point of being seen, whenever he descended from a train, with his head buried in the Old Testament. Those assembled on the platform to greet him would be kept waiting until the President had finished with the Book. When H. W. Nevinson, a distinguished journalist, called on Kruger he was informed that the President was engaged – in prayer. Kruger belonged to the Bible-reading Calvinistic sect of Doppers. His own way of life was simple. There were no lavish meals; his wife would brew coffee for guests and serve it on the stoep of their modest dwelling, whose only sign of grandeur was a pair of marble lions presented to the President by Barney Barnato after the Raid, as a *douceur*. But it was widely believed among the British that he was hoarding a vast personal fortune, extracted in taxes from the pockets of the Uitlanders.

General Piet Joubert once described how Kruger unfailingly worsted him in argument. He combined single-mindedness with a wide range of emotional gambits which it was hard to withstand:

I know he is wrong and I tell him so. But first he argues with me and, if that is no good, he goes into a rage and jumps about the room, roaring at me like a wild beast, and I cannot hear myself talk. And, if I do not give in, then he fetches out the Bible and – *ach du liebe Gott!* – he even quotes that to help him out. And if that fails he takes my hand and cries like a child, and begs and prays me to give in . . . Who could resist a man like that?[6]

Kruger's appearance was rugged, primeval, grotesque; both his body and mind were elephantine. His face was large and pale. His beard and whiskers were like a fringe of sea-weed fanning out round the edge of a great rock. On formal occasions he wore a gold chain across his waistcoat with a heavy gold fob and a top hat like a weather-scarred chimney-pot. He had shrewd, keen, rather small black eyes with saurian lids and enormous bags under them. He spat. One interviewer recalled his difficulty in dodging the presidential expectorations. Kruger himself told a story suggesting that in some ways he and his simple Boer farmers were more at home with the indigenous tribes of Africa than with the 'outsiders' from the world of industry, commerce, hygiene and patent medicines. Owing to a hunting accident Kruger's thumb had to be amputated. He did it himself with his hunting knife. Later, gangrene set in. So his women-folk, says Kruger, 'killed a goat, took out the stomach and cut it open. I put my hand into it while it was still warm.'[7] This was a Boer remedy which the Boers themselves admitted they had probably learnt from the Africans. Altogether, there was a corrugated grandeur in the old Transvaal President. But the majority of Englishmen who met him saw only what Milner saw – 'a snuffy, mendacious savage'.

As a boy of ten he had gone on the Great Trek. This was the heroic occasion when his people deliberately tore up their roots in the south and sought freedom from the English across the Vaal river. After a strenuous life full of physical hazard, Kruger reached a high position in the Boer state. Elected President of this small, proud Republic in 1883, Kruger made it his aim to bring even the relics of British influence, surviving in the London Convention, to an end. He therefore frowned upon the Dutch who lived in the Cape Colony. Through their political party, the Bond, these men of Kruger's own race insisted on co-operating with the British. Young Boers coming up from the Cape were aggrieved to find neither welcome nor jobs up to expectations in Pretoria. Instead, Kruger imported 'Hollander' officials from Europe. The British feared that he would be bringing in Germans next. All these strains and tensions between Boers and British were played upon by Rhodes.

As soon as Chamberlain took office Johannesburg presented him with an obvious political challenge. It was not long before the challenge had formulated itself to his inner mind as an opportunity for political creativeness. The public, however, did not yet know this part of the story. What did the general public know of affairs in Johannesburg before the Raid?

The answer to that question will form the first part of an attempt to tell the Raid story in a manner which preserves something of its original excitement and intrigue.

The reader will at first follow events as nearly as possible through the eyes of well-informed citizens who knew the latest facts and rumours, but not the full pattern of the jigsaw as it was to be revealed, bit by bit, over a period of some eighty years. The troubles in Johannesburg, the Raid and its immediate effects will be described as they seemed to happen. Many of the secrets which were at first hidden will remain so. But piece by piece the missing details will be restored to their correct places, and the contradictions explained as analysis gradually takes over from description. Finally the Committee of Inquiry will round off the story, and an answer will be given to the question, Who were the guilty men?

# 4

## *Ferment*

During the year 1895 South African prospects were the subject of increasingly lively gossip in England. Every visitor from that continent was sooner or later asked, 'How is the Transvaal revolution getting on?' Over the past seven or eight years people had heard many tales of disturbances. Petitions were presented and flouted. There were rumours of a plot, if all democratic means failed, to force democracy upon Kruger. Sometimes they would read of demonstrations getting distinctly out of hand. Everyone would remember those last two occasions when the British High Commissioner at the Cape, Sir Henry Loch, went up to the Transvaal. In 1893 he got a rousing reception in Johannesburg. Next year, at Pretoria, it was more rousing still. The place was in an uproar over the commandeering of Uitlanders to fight against African tribes.

His train reached Pretoria station at 8.30 A.M. but the crowd was already there to meet him: red, white and blue ribbons, *God Save The Queen* and all. Visitors from South Africa would recall what a lark it had been when old Kruger got entangled in the Union Jack, which someone had hoisted at the last moment over the presidential carriage. Our fellows pulled the carriage all the way to Loch's hotel, singing *Rule Britannia*. Kruger did not say anything, but if looks could kill . . . ! Of course officialdom had to frown on that sort of thing. They would not let the High Commissioner go again to Johannesburg in case of more trouble. Even Rhodes expressed regret in Parliament. But a year had passed since these events and everyone now felt sure that Kruger could not last much longer – or so the visitors said.

The public in England would have had, too, a rough idea of Uitlander grievances. Heavy taxation discriminating against the mining industry. A scandalous dynamite monopoly held by Germans. The commandeering system. In Boer schools, British children taught in Afrikaans or not at all. These and other injustices on top of the worst sin of all – no vote. In his homely way Kruger compared the Uitlanders who demanded the vote to a man who went up to the driver of a wagon. 'Give us the whip and the reins,' says the man; '*our* stock, *our* property, *our* interests, *our* homes are also in this cart.' 'Yes, that is all very fine,' replies the wagoner. 'I admit your belongings are also in the cart. But where are you going to drive me? And how do I know that you don't intend to upset me?'

Kruger saw the numbers of the foreign rabble rising in a scummy tide. A dam was needed, he explained, to keep the muddy water outside from fouling the pure water within. Then the water outside could be filtered in, drop by drop, leaving the mud behind. But the vote 'drop by drop' was not good enough for the Uitlanders. As Rhodes put it without any false modesty: 'The Uitlanders had all the wealth and all the intelligence while the Boers were just an ignorant minority.' Kruger was getting rich at the expense of those he despised. In the words of J. L. Garvin, Chamberlain's official biographer, Kruger 'wanted the gold without the diggers'.

The dream of empire by the end of the nineteenth century was no longer the pipe-dream of a few. It was a fashionable philosophy poised between old-fashioned, unacquisitive liberalism and socialism's coming international challenge. Even some of those who would least welcome its implications were unwittingly contributing to the imperialist theme. Bradlaugh and Labouchere, for instance, favoured empire demolition rather than empire-building. But as atheists they joined forces with the successors of Darwin, who were using *The Origin of Species* to demolish religious belief; for the doctrines of the survival of the fittest could be used to oust Christianity from politics as well as from metaphysics. It could justify empire-builders in wiping out backward races like the Matabele and backward nations like the Boers.*

During the winter of 1894–5 Rhodes visited England to sell his imperial dream to the public. He found the going easier than when he fought for his Charter. *The Times* was now an imperialist crusader. Significantly, Flora Shaw, who had become its colonial

---

*Darwin, the prophet of evolution, appealed more to Rhodes than Isaiah, the prophet of Christianity. Many Liberals, on the other hand, were suspicious of the effects of evolutionary theories on sociology. Morley and Asquith once discussed whether the discovery of evolution made people more or less merciful. Morley agreed with Asquith that since evolution had become generally accepted, States believed in 'Justification by Success' and 'the God of Battles'. (Morley's *Recollections*, p. 370.)

expert, succeeded in changing the title of her column from *Foreign &
Colonial* to *Colonial & Foreign*. London was at Rhodes's feet. The
Queen received him in audience at Windsor and Rhodes received
society in audience at the Burlington Hotel in Cork Street, where he
rented a permanent suite in that discreet establishment. A conversation between himself and Queen Victoria was reported by Rhodes as
follows:[1]

*Queen Victoria*: What have you been doing since I last saw you, Mr Rhodes?
*Rhodes*: I have added two provinces to Your Majesty's dominions.
*Queen Victoria*: Ah, I wish some of my Ministers, who take away my
    provinces, would do as much.

The Prince of Wales listened with a distinguished gathering in the
Imperial Institute to Dr Jameson expounding his friend's hopes for
Rhodesia. *The Times* said afterwards that Jameson had described
Rhodesia as 'a happy combination of Canaan, Ophir and the Black
Country'. Next month, in the less august but still ample confines of
the Cannon Street Hotel, Rhodes told the shareholders of the
Chartered Company that they should vote at the next election for
the man who would go in for empire preferences. The public were
ready to be convinced that nothing stood between them and a vast
extension of empire but a few Liberal scuttlers in England and a
handful of Boers led by one uncouth, impossible old man.

It seemed a far cry from the days when Rhodes put his case for
holding Uganda to Gladstone, only to be told: 'Our burden is too
great. We have too much of the world, and as it is I cannot find the
people to govern all our dependencies. We have too much to do. Not
that I blame you, Mr Rhodes, you never give us any trouble.' *You
never give us any trouble*. Those words were spoken three years before
the Jameson Raid. By the year of the Raid, 1895, it seemed that no
burden could be too great in so great a cause as the Empire. The
imperial task all over the world was soon to be elevated to a title of
nobility, the White Man's Burden. People like Flora Shaw, intelligent and sophisticated, would see nothing funny in that famous
phrase.

On 25 June 1895, Joseph Chamberlain supplanted Liberal Lord
Ripon at the Colonial Office, with Lord Selborne as Under-
Secretary. At first the public were more puzzled than impressed.

They looked upon the Colonial Office as a musty, third-rate branch of the Foreign Office and had expected 'Pushful Joe' to seize a bigger plum – the Exchequer or War Office. They did not realize what an astute journalist like W. T. Stead spotted at once, that Joe intended to direct British foreign policy from the Colonial Office. Nor had they quite caught up with the fact that the new Minister had been for some years an emphatic 'Big Englander'. Chamberlain, to do him justice, made every effort to explain himself. In a speech on 11 November he enunciated his faith in unmistakable terms: 'I believe in the British Empire and I believe in the British race.'

The immediate result of Chamberlain's appointment was a marked change in Colonial Office atmosphere. Maps were brought up to date, candles of antique design were replaced by electric light. (This was four years after the Lord Mayor of London had done the same for the Mansion House; the Randolph Churchills put electricity into their house as early as 1882.) The whole place began to look less like one of the old Inns of Court and more like a businessman's headquarters. Chamberlain became known as the 'Chief' and the 'Master' where his Liberal predecessor, Lord Knutsford, had merely been good old 'Peter Woggy' – the one who looked after the Wogs.

The next thing the public knew was more dramatic. Three Bechuana chiefs arrived in England on 6 September and were shepherded round by the Rev Edwin Lloyd and other missionaries.* Something big was afoot at the Colonial Office. During July Rhodes's agents in London had been talking about the promised transfer of Bechuanaland from direct imperial rule to that of Cape Colony and Chartered Company. The Liberal Government had made the promise and the Conservatives were to carry it out. The Cape, with Rhodes as Prime Minister, was to get the 50,000 square miles of British Bechuanaland. The Chartered Company, with Rhodes as managing director, was to get 275,000 square miles of the Bechuanaland Protectorate. The politically knowing ones pointed out that the Liberals would never have promised so much, except that Lord Rosebery was an imperialist and he was Prime Minister at the time. Rhodes was devoted to Rosebery and Rosebery

*One of these was the Rev. W. C. Willoughby of the London Missionary Society, who had been Labouchere's correspondent on *Truth* during the Matabele War. Fairfield of the Colonial Office called him 'the *enragé* missionary'. (C.O. 417/145, 15 August 1895.)

called Rhodes a 'new Elizabethan'. The observant would have seen many friends of Rhodes going up and down the steps of the Colonial Office during the month of August. They were conducting the negotiations for the transfer. The attractive one, every inch a gentleman, was Earl Grey. Another was Rhodes's agent, Dr Rutherfoord Harris.

Now the missionaries were really getting busy. Loudly the three chiefs protested against the transfer of their territories: 'We wish to be ruled by our Mother, the Queen, only.' 'We had peace and rest during the Protectorate and we cannot agree to be thus cast away.'[2] They would surely be 'killed and eaten by the Company'. Let them remain 'children of the Great Queen'. Everyone knew by now that they had come to England at their own expense to beseech Her Majesty to save them from Lobengula's fate and their country from being ruined by liquor shops, as in Bulawayo. 'We are living nicely without the white man's brandy,' cried old Montsioa from Bechuanaland. The three chiefs visiting England were called Khama, Sebele and Bathoen; all excellent fellows and making a wonderful impression (though a rumour was circulating that Sebele was not personally averse to the bottle).

Chamberlain put himself out to entertain them. He arranged for them to see Birmingham, his own 'Protectorate' and the city which exported to them so much desirable hardware. On 13 September they visited him in his office. He received them in 'a kindly and sympathetic manner',[3] explaining once again that the Protectorate must be handed over because Rhodes wished to extend the railway from Mafeking in British Bechuanaland to Bulawayo in Rhodesia. It would run through the Protectorate, as near as possible to the Transvaal border. For that was the shortest route to the north. It happened to be Chief Bathoen who owned the land nearest the border – that piece with the queer name, *Gaberones*. If Rhodes must have land for his railway, the public expected Chamberlain to carve out of it large native reserves. Chamberlain listened to the chiefs and to public opinion, as was his wont. For the present, he urged the chiefs to try and settle with the Company themselves.

Then everyone went on holiday. The chiefs toured England. Chamberlain set off for the Mediterranean and Spain where he remained until the end of October. Rhodes's friends made for the grouse moors.

# 5

## The Drifts Crisis

October brought bad news from South Africa. Kruger was up to his tricks again. Traders, both British and Dutch, had for some time been dodging the Transvaal rail freights on goods coming from the Cape into the Rand. They saw Kruger's main purpose in imposing these duties as an attempt to divert the rich goldfields' traffic on to his own newly opened Netherlands railway, driving the Cape and Free State lines out of business. But the British retaliated by unloading their trucks at the river Vaal, crossing the drifts (fords) at Viljoens Drift and elsewhere by ox wagon, and continuing thus into Johannesburg. At the height of the previous summer as many as one hundred and twenty wagons crossed a day. What a tribute to Kruger's twisted genius! He had forced a great industrial community back to the pace of the ox. Now he made a new move in the transport war. On 1 October he closed the drifts. Surely, everyone was asking, Britain would not lie down under this deliberate provocation, this flouting of the London Convention? Besides, the Netherlands railway had not enough trucks to cope with the extra traffic and goods were piling up. Many Cape Dutch sympathized with the Uitlanders. And how would the Colossus take it?

Rhodes was about to bring off a masterly *coup* in neighbouring Bechuanaland. On 18 October the High Commissioner issued a proclamation putting that strip of the Protectorate through which the new railway would be built under the administration of the Chartered Company, 'in the interests of Peace, Order and Good Government'. In the same issue of the *Gazette Extraordinary* appeared an announcement that Dr Leander Starr Jameson, CB, would be Resident Commissioner at Pitsani in the strip, and Major the Honourable Robert White would be Magistrate. How like that brilliant man Rhodes to have got part of the Protectorate already, despite the obstinacy of the local chiefs encouraged by those missionaries and the Colonial Secretary. It was by now common knowledge that Rhodes had sent Dr Rutherfoord Harris hot-foot to London to frustrate Khama. The slick doctor realized what he was

up against. 'You know the way Khama will play the old gooseberry
with the blessed British public,' he told his friends. And now here
was the first sign that Khama would be dished and the Colossus, as
usual, get what he wanted.

It had not taken Rhodes long to persuade two minor chiefs left
behind in Bechuanaland – Ikaning and Montsioa – to sell out to the
Chartered Company behind the backs of their absent brethren. Of
course it was really due to the irresistible charm of Cecil Rhodes's
elder brother Frank, who was in Johannesburg. The public could
not guess that Frank Rhodes's charm was ably supported by semi-
official pressure from Sir Sydney Shippard, Administrator of
Bechuanaland; that Fred Graham, one of Chamberlain's officials,
described Shippard as 'a creature of the Chartered Company';* that
Chief Ikaning tried to change his mind after the deal and that
Montsioa changed his every time he met a new white 'adviser'. Nor
did they know that a draft letter, dated 11 October, from Sir Robert
Meade of the Colonial Office to Chiefs Sebele and Bathoen lay in the
office files, explaining that the Chartered Company *must* administer
this strip of land because 'a Railway is a thing which attracts to its
neighbourhood a population who are not always of a law abiding
character'. Therefore let them support the concession of Ikaning and
Montsioa, which was only a 'little word' between the chiefs and Mr
Chamberlain, compared with the 'big word' over the whole Protectorate. In the light of future events, Meade's justification of the
'little word' is sufficiently ironical.

While on holiday, and between fascinating conversations with the
Queen Regent of Spain, the Colonial Secretary ratified this first
stage in the great take-over bid. Cruising about the Mediterranean
among the scenes of Nelson's triumphs, he looked forward to a
coming triumph of his own. As for Rhodes's success, the public
recognized it was only a strip that he had acquired so far. But it was
just enough to allow him to continue the railway from Mafeking to
Bulawayo. The moment the Company could make terms with
Khama the rest of the Protectorate would follow. Rhodes would be
in charge of thousands of miles of Africa. Kruger was more or less

---

*After the Raid, disagreeable rumours forced Shippard to write to *The Times*
denying that, in acquiring the Pitsani strip from Chief Ikaning for the Company, he
had had an ulterior motive.

encircled. If he did not climb down over this drifts crisis, surely it would come to war?

But Kruger did climb down, after an ultimatum from the British Government backed by a show of force. Troopships sailing to and from India were temporarily diverted from the Suez Canal route and told to call in at the Cape. It was Chamberlain's first test as Colonial Secretary. He passed it with flying colours. The public were not to know for some time that he had even lined up the Cape Government and made them promise to fight if necessary. A peremptory message went from Chamberlain to Rhodes on 1 November. If, in reply to the urgent requests of the Cape Government, Britain were to intervene against Kruger, it must be a joint effort. The expedition would not, 'like most previous Colonial wars, be conducted at the entire cost of this country'. Rhodes must give 'a most explicit undertaking in writing' that the Cape would bear half the cost and furnish 'a fair contingent of the fighting force, so far as its resources in men may suffice'.

Rhodes perforce gave the undertaking. Whereupon Chamberlain delivered to Kruger an ultimatum which, polite though firm, compared favourably with the truculent attitude adopted towards Rhodes.

It is perhaps not altogether fanciful to see in the very different tone of Chamberlain's two messages a reflection of the hidden drama now being enacted between the Colonial Secretary and the Cape Prime Minister. The nagging demands of Rhodes for the Protectorate were at this moment reaching their peak. One of the Secretaries at the Colonial Office wrote to Chamberlain on 4 November that he was 'very keen' to get it and had been 'telegraphing all day to this end'.[1] When Chamberlain sent his imperious message of 1 November it was as if he were asserting his authority over Rhodes for the last time. A few more days, and Rhodes would be on the Transvaal border, free from Colonial Office controls, with Kruger, as both he and Chamberlain imagined, soon to be delivered into his hands.

On 6 November 1895, one day before the drifts were reopened, Chamberlain transferred the rest of the Protectorate to the Chartered Company. The African chiefs got their reserves and christened Chamberlain 'Moatlhodi', the man who puts things right. In the evening, while excitement over the drifts was at its height, Chamberlain made his first public speech since taking office. The 'spread eagle' speech, it was called. It seemed to focus men's eyes on 'that Empire – that world-wide dominion to which no Englishman can allude without a thrill of enthusiasm and patriotism – which has been the admiration and perhaps the envy of foreign nations'.

By the end of November the stage had once again been cleared. The chiefs sailed for Africa, followed shortly by several of Rhodes's friends, including Dr Rutherfoord Harris, his agent, and Alfred Beit, the gentle millionaire. Each side was well satisfied with the result of the negotiations. After a strenuous five weeks, most successfully concluded, Chamberlain departed for Highbury, his home in Birmingham, on 9 December, to digest the contents of his red boxes more tranquilly than for some time past and to collect his thoughts. The stage for the moment was empty; only a handful of people knew what was being prepared in the wings.

Who among the general public could have believed that Rhodes's second *coup* was only three weeks distant? After the reopening of the drifts on 7 November, excitement had abated. No one imagined, of course, that Johannesburg was still anything but resentful. The other grievances remained to be settled. But the Uitlanders' secret had been well kept. The arms for the rising were securely hidden. Certain troop movements in the surrounding regions could not be concealed. These included the strengthening of the Rhodesia Horse by a vote of the Chartered Company's shareholders in London, who were quite unaware of how the increased force was intended to be used; the sending of part of this body of horse, in the interests of health and economy, to Pitsani, the village near the Transvaal border in the Company's new railway strip, which Dr Jameson was now brought down to administer (he was Administrator of Rhodesia); the disbanding of the old Bechuanaland Border Police and the absorbing of about two hundred of them into Jameson's Rhodesian force.

Not even Kruger himself linked these troops on the Transvaal border with the trouble known to be brewing on the Rand. Jameson and his men were understood to be guarding the railway against Africans not yet wholly appeased by 'Moatlhodi'. There was a particular chief named Linchwe whose activities had been picked out and publicized by the plotters. They hoped that his troublesome behaviour, insignificant though it was,* would be enough to catch and hold the attention of any too inquisitive government. Almost everyone believed the well-circulated story that it was Linchwe whom they feared: the Governments of Natal, the Free State and Cape Colony; Kruger; the British authorities in the border zone and all Rhodes's colleagues at the Cape.

Not that criticism of Jameson's border force was entirely absent. On 28 September, W. H. Surmon, Assistant Commissioner for Gaberones, protested to the High Commissioner: 'In my opinion there is no necessity for any such force to be sent to protect the Railway, its presence in the country would be more likely to cause than to prevent trouble, especially if it be a force of Europeans.' Surmon spoke more truly than he knew. A month later the High Commissioner received a worried telegram from Sekhome Khama: 'Please let me know what is the meaning of their coming. I and my people are anxious to know.' It was a leading question, to which the official answer, as so often at this juncture, was ironic – 'to preserve order'.[2]

If the Linchwe scare was trumped up, there were other, genuine signs that someone was fishing in troubled waters. These were not always signs, however, which the uninitiated could read. Ever since September the behaviour of that shaky financial undertaking, 'Chartereds', had been odd. A sudden, disastrous fall in share values occurred at the end of the month. Who were selling and why? Could it be that the Rhodes group were bearing 'Chartereds' for a rise after the revolution? Then in October came the drifts crisis. 'Chartereds' soared far beyond their true value. This time everyone knew the reason – the prospect of war. Should the drifts crisis lead to war, Kruger would be swept away and Rhodesia find itself a prominent part of a federated Union of South Africa. 'Chartereds', standing at £9, were a measure of that hope. Five years later the German, Siemens, was to say in the Reichstag: 'The one pound share is the basis of British Imperialism'. It was also the barometer.

But when the drifts were reopened, the fall in 'Chartereds' began

*A Colonial Office minute of 8 August 1895 by the African expert, Edward Fairfield, exposed the trumped-up nature of the Linchwe scare. In approving the reduction of the British Bechuanaland Police to a total strength of 350 men, he wrote: 'This is quite enough in these peaceful times.' The real danger of disorders was in Matabeleland, whence troops were removed shortly before the rebellion!

again; this time the cause seemed to be not rumours of war but rumours of revolution. On 20 November 1895 Mr Lionel Phillips, mining magnate and Chairman of the Johannesburg Chamber of Mines, performed the opening ceremony of the institution's new building in bellicose vein. His 'violent attacks on the Government', as Kruger called the Chairman's remarks, sent the already stalling 'Chartereds' into a spin. They remained in a precarious state until near Christmas, when once more the mysterious climate changed. Why? Some of those whose interests lay in the City seemed to have a clue. At any rate, they went about twitting the Company's personnel in London with the latest rumour. Johannesburg's famous revolution had fizzled out. Though supported by many great financial interests, the revolution was far from popular with certain other magnates. As a symbol of this group's relief from anxiety, 'Chartereds' again stood at the excellent price of 105s.

Not all the influential people in London, however, seemed to be quite so happy about the future. *The Times* newspaper gave an unseasonable jolt to its readers just before Christmas by printing an ominous leading article against Kruger:

*16 December 1895*
The time is past, even in South Africa, when a helot system of administration, organized for the exclusive advantage of a privileged minority, can long resist the force of enlightened public opinion.

Many readers must have wondered whether the helots of Johannesburg would be content to rely solely on the rather anaemic kind of force which *The Times* declared to be on their side – public opinion; or whether *The Times* was not preparing the public for a liberation of the helots in the usual historic way.

The public might have settled down to making their preparations for Christmas in a state of nothing worse than uncertainty. But two days after the 'growl of editorial thunder' from *The Times*, a far louder detonation came to drown all other mutterings. A quarrel over the boundaries of British Guiana and Venezuela had been in progress for some time. It had caused the United States to rise up in all the majesty of the Monroe doctrine. President Cleveland offered arbitration. The Prime Minister, Lord Salisbury, like Lord Rosebery before him, declined to accept it. Thereupon President Cleveland replaced his offer with an ultimatum. On 18 December England suddenly found she was facing the incredible prospect of an Anglo-American war.

Such a disaster could not be tolerated. *Punch* called it 'An Unpredicted Storm' and issued a gloomy meteorological warning:

A storm of unusual violence coming from the United States struck the British coasts on the 18th ult. The usual storm warning from New York had not preceded it. It was accompanied by loud thunder and blustering winds, and seemed likely to cause great damage.

The British people, however, had no intention of letting the storm rip. Within a week they made it clear that arbitration, rejected in their name, was more than acceptable. Eventually all ended happily. But that first week of shock and horror was enough to drive the affairs of South Africa into a remote corner of the political picture. 'I do not know any people from whom we can afford to accept a kicking,' wrote Joseph Chamberlain, of the American crisis. England escaped a kicking from her powerful sister nation, but within a few days was to receive a devastating humiliation from a people very much smaller and weaker than herself.

A fortnight after President Cleveland's ultimatum the storm over the Atlantic was petering out while the unregarded cloud over the Rand had changed British and world history.

# 6

## One Man's Madness

The public got their first stunning news on the last day of the old
year. Dr Jameson, they learnt, had made a dash across the border
and was even now galloping towards Johannesburg. Journalists
reported that the Raid 'electrified' the world. Jameson and his
filibusters had gone in on Sunday night; now it was a case of 'ride,
ride together, forever ride', until they reached Johannesburg. For
the world it meant hours of suspense.

In London delicious excitement prevailed. This feeling soon
spread to the provinces and within a short time the whole nation was
living at the highest pitch of emotional intensity. Would Jameson
succeed? Would Johannesburg be liberated and old Kruger smitten?
*The Times* on New Year's Day provided a vivid pointer to the
sympathies of educated people. In its leading article the Doctor's
action was admitted to be 'technically incorrect'. But the writer
went on to point out that 'the sense and feeling of the nation will
recognize that technicalities could not have been suffered to stand in
the way where the lives and property of thousands of their fellow-
citizens were at stake'.

What was this threat to the lives and property of thousands? In
the same edition *The Times* published a heart-rending 'letter of

invitation' from the Uitlander population of darkest Transvaal. Dated 28 December, it purported to have been sent the day before the Raid to their gallant saviour 'Dr Jim' on the frontier. It became notorious as the 'women and children' letter. 'What will be the condition of things here in the event of a conflict?' asked the sponsors of this appeal:

Thousands of unarmed men, women and children of our race will be at the mercy of well-armed Boers, while property of enormous value will be in the greatest peril . . .

The circumstances are so extreme that we cannot but believe that you and the men under you will not fail to come to the rescue of people who will be so situated.

We guarantee any expense that may reasonably be incurred by you, in helping us, and ask you to believe that nothing but the sternest necessity has prompted this appeal.

Five prominent Johannesburgers signed the document: Charles Leonard, Chairman of the National Union (the Uitlanders' instrument for achieving their political and economic rights), earning £10,000 a year as a barrister; Lionel Phillips, Frank Rhodes, John Hays Hammond, a distinguished American mining engineer, and George Farrar, a mining magnate. It was an impressive list.

Overlooking the mundane transition in the last sentence of the letter from the sublime to the petty cash, the heart of the British people paid immediate tribute to the purity of Jameson's crusade. For them the word 'filibuster' did not exist. Jameson was a hero, a knight-errant, a sacred vessel from which they prepared to pour their most precious libations to romance and jingoism. There was only one villain of this melodramatic piece – the spoilsport Colonial Secretary, Joseph Chamberlain.

The Colonial Secretary promptly repudiated Raid and raiders. *The Times* informed its readers that Mr Chamberlain went to the Colonial Office on 31 December at 10 A.M. and stayed till 7.30 P.M., before going home to Prince's Gardens. He had arrived in London from Birmingham during the small hours of the morning of that same day. At 11.50 P.M. on the previous night, 30 December, before he himself had even reached the capital, he sent off the strongest possible message to the High Commissioner ending with the words: 'Leave no stone unturned to prevent mischief.' During the course of

New Year's Eve he committed himself irrevocably to the side of law. To four key people, together with the directors of the Chartered Company in London, he cabled or wrote his denunciation of the Raid.

He cabled the High Commissioner, Sir Hercules Robinson, at 2.10 P.M.:

. . .It is an act of war or rather of filibustering. Had the Government of the South African Republic been overthrown or had there been anarchy at Johannesburg there might have been some shadow of excuse for this unprecedented act.

To Rhodes and the Company he pilloried the Raid as 'an act of war', 'filibustering', 'marauding'; adding that if the Company turned out to be involved its Charter might be revoked. Kruger received a cable sent to him direct, *en clair*:

Regret to hear of Jameson's action. Sir Hercules Robinson has sent messengers to call him back. Can I co-operate with you further in this emergency in endeavouring to bring about a peaceful arrangement which is essential to all interests in South Africa, and which would be promoted by the concessions that I am assured you are ready to make?

Chamberlain's last words showed that he hoped to make a little hay even though the sun, to put it mildly, had ceased to shine.

He wrote to the Prime Minister:

*Colonial Office, 31 December 1895*
I am sorry to say that the Transvaal business has entered on a more acute stage. Having failed to get up a revolution in Johannesburg, Rhodes . . . has apparently sent in Dr Jameson who has crossed the border of the Transvaal with 800 armed police.* This is a flagrant piece of filibustering for which there is no justification that I can see in the present state of things in the Transvaal. If it were supported by us it would justify the accusation by Germany and other powers that having first attempted to get up a rebellion in a friendly State and having failed, we had then assented to an act of aggression, and without any grievance of our own, had poured in British troops. It is worth noting that I have no confidence that the force now sent, with its allies in Johannesburg, is strong enough to beat the Boers — and if not we should expect that a conflict would be the beginning of a race war in South Africa . . .

---

* Chamberlain was no better informed than *The Times*, who reported 700 men with Jameson. In fact there were about 478.

This strong condemnation of the Raid was clearly intended to furnish the Prime Minister with ammunition against Tory jingoes. It is far from indicating, as has been suggested, that Chamberlain 'had coolly weighed the question of supporting the Raid and had decided against it merely on grounds of expediency'.[1]

So Chamberlain took his decision. No action could have been more unpopular. *The Times*, without committing itself too far, frowned on his harsh correctitude and implied it would be better to wait and see if the Doctor won through. The Colonial Secretary could be justified in recalling Dr Jameson, it felt, only if positively no rising had taken place. But suppose there were bloodshed? Then Chamberlain would be to blame.

Ballads and cartoons were rushed out, singing the praises of Britain's hero. One magnificent poster depicted the smiling ghosts of Drake and Nelson supporting a harassed Jameson between them. The lines beneath the picture give a pretty clear idea of the emotions which Chamberlain was flouting when he condemned Dr Jim:

*Shade of Nelson*

Shiver my timbers, Jimmy, my lad,
    Hold up your head, now do.
'You disobeyed orders?' Well, that's pretty bad,
    Though I did the same thing, too;
But, of course, there's a world of difference –
    I had a run of LUCK!
So England wink'd the other eye,
    And called it BRITISH PLUCK.

The music-halls which held high carnival for Dr Jim, execrated Joe. But if one single action ever saved a man's career, Chamberlain's condemnation of the Raid, while its issue still hung in the balance, was that deed.

# 7

# Revolution by Consent

In Cape Town the news of the Raid caused consternation. The mixed white population of Boers and British gathered in tense groups on the streets. The noisy mirth of coloured troops celebrating the passing of the old year 'jarred terribly'.[1] (One remembers that Wilfrid Blunt, the diarist,* found in those same coloured races the only beauty and laughter left in the world.) On New Year's Day excitement was prodigious. Foreboding mingled with reckless optimism. One fellow-doctor, inspired by fraternal loyalty and the poetry of medicine, was heard to prophesy that 'Jameson will go through the commandos like a dose of salts'.[2] The High Commissioner issued a proclamation condemning him. Racial hatred, hitherto miraculously dormant in the Cape, revived. There was even a rumour that Jameson shot some young Afrikanders for refusing to invade the Transvaal with him.

As for Rhodes, no one knew exactly what was going on behind the panelled walls of Groote Schur, his home at the foot of Table Mountain. On the first day he avoided his office in town, hiding indoors or riding along the hydrangea-bordered paths in his woods. Later, when the inevitable consultations began, friends noted his changed appearance and acute distress. Even if they did not yet know all his thoughts, it was quite plain that he must have been deeply implicated in the Raid. Rhodes offered to resign before the Raid had failed. The Colonial Office were much relieved, for it was feared that this incalculable desperado might even now be planning a new raid from Bulawayo.

Boxing Day in Johannesburg had been the last day before the storm. Everyone was at the races. Percy Fitzpatrick, then a prominent member of Eckstein's firm, wrote to his family: 'The whole place is as gay as can be now, and the races were an immense success.'[3]

---

*Wilfrid Scawen Blunt, contemporary writer of inexhaustible wit and vigour, was born into the aristocracy but driven by the whips of his genius into bitter hostility to the grandiose dreams and dogmas of his age, and into passionate love for the small and weak. The British Empire was anathema and his enemies attributed to him the astringent motto, 'My country always wrong'.

In less than a week he was to become secretary of a revolutionary committee. Ten days later he was in prison.

It was at these races that many people got their first whiff of danger. Two political leaders from the Cape, Johannes Albertus Faure and Sir Thomas Upington, both heard reports of an imminent rising, and from now on alarmist rumours began to circulate. Soon a crowd of non-combatants was swarming out of the Transvaal, amongst them many of those same racehorses which had so lately brightened this exceptionally happy Christmas, but whose owners were unwilling to see them carrying military packs for Boers. A new gold rush started, away from the Golden City. 'Wealthy gold bugs', as a contemporary called them, put on false beards and hid under the seats of the jammed railway carriages. One packed train ran off the rails on the way to Natal, killing and injuring fifty-two refugees.

A battle of words was already in full swing. Charles Leonard, the Chairman of the National Union, issued a manifesto and called a monster meeting for 6 January. Kruger abandoned his Christmas tour of the country districts. Followed by General Joubert, he reached Pretoria on Boxing Day, to be at once bombarded with petitions. A deputation of highly respected Boers earnestly advocated reform. Another group of burghers demanded sterner measures against the 'rebellious element'. To them Kruger replied with one of his famous parables:

You must give the tortoise time to put out its head before you can cut it off.

Next day the Johannesburg papers burst into flaring headlines: 'Ferment on the Rand' – 'Sensational Rumours'. By 30 December these pressures had wrung from Kruger a favourable response. A proclamation calling for law and order was changed into a promise of redress to the orderly. Kruger's 'zarps' (Boer police) increased his anxiety by sending in exaggerated reports of the Uitlanders' armament. Other unmistakable signs of incipient revolution were present – the breaking down of social barriers as miners' families sought protection in the sacrosanct buildings of the Wanderers and Turf Clubs; khaki uniforms, rifles, bandoliers and 'smasher' hats on the streets; the town cyclists, 'a large and athletic body', forming into a Women and Children Protection Brigade; refugees given the traditional send-off with white feathers; and a run on the banks. There was also a run on food. The price of the one-pound loaf doubled.

As Kruger sniffed the revolutionary breezes, his first reform went through. Food duties were abolished. If loyalty and order prevailed, more reforms would follow; the vote, lower railway charges, schools. It looked as if a 'bloodless revolution' was about to crown the Uitlanders' hopes. At this crucial juncture came the news of Jameson's bolt.

Kruger received the news in the midst of a session of his Executive Council, resplendent in tall hats, frock coats and brown boots. A new deal for the Uitlanders was in process of being debated. He must have felt, as he had felt so often before, that Providence was behind 'the old people of the Lord'. In the nick of time Jameson rode in. On heroic rescue bent, it was Kruger's régime which he succeeded in saving.

The fervid old Dopper spontaneously burst into the sixty-eighth Psalm:

Pour out thy indignation upon them: and let thy wrathful anger take hold of them.

When Leonard Courtney, an English radical MP, heard of Kruger's pious thanksgiving, he said that he would have gladly joined him. Upon which a sardonic foreigner remarked: 'You never kick an Englishman but you hear a Psalm.'

Two sensational telegrams broke the news to the Uitlander leaders. The first came at midday on 30 December from Cape Town:

The Veterinary Surgeon has left for Johannesburg with some very good horseflesh and backs himself for seven hundred.

The second, arriving at 4.30 P.M. the same day from Mafeking near the Transvaal border, confirmed their horrified suspicions. The bearer of the evil news threw down the telegram before a group of fellow revolutionaries with the words, 'It is all up, boys. He has started in spite of everything. Read this!' They read:

The contractor has started on the earthworks with seven hundred boys; hopes to reach terminus on Wednesday.

This was Monday. But the only terminus he ever reached was the one that ended their hopes.

The people of Johannesburg would have been hard put to it during those three days of suspense while Jameson and his filibusters were still at large to know what kind of game their leaders inside the town were playing. They hoped and believed that Jameson would succeed. After all, he had seven hundred men, or so they thought, and Captain Charles White, brother of two other Whites serving in Jameson's force, who was with the conspirators in Johannesburg, told them it was enough. Had not the dashing Doctor conquered the whole of Matabeleland with only a few hundred more than that? It was an encouraging myth.

On the other hand, the leaders regretted the 'women and children' letter. They prayed that the Doctor might have heard false reports of massacre in the town, which would give him more excuse than their own letter furnished. In the extreme confusion, they hourly changed what plans they had. On the first day the whole town was throbbing with nervous tension. All the shops were shuttered. The stifling heat was what Hays Hammond, born in California, called 'earthquake weather'. The crack of a rifle (a recruit letting off his gun by mistake or a horse being shot) would set everyone a-quiver. Yet there was no outbreak, not a single shot fired in anger. They spent Monday in unpacking and cleaning the smuggled rifles, most of which still lay in their cases. A few more were rushed in by rail under layers of coke. Two Boer peace envoys, Malan and Marais, were allowed to address the Reform Committee. One of its members, George Farrar, cheerfully apologized for arriving late with oil up to his bare elbows; he had been unpacking the guns! There was a fundamental lack of revolutionary ardour, for the Leonard Manifesto had definitely postponed any action until after the first week in January.*

On Tuesday the atmosphere improved. The town was recovering from the shock caused by the first news of Jameson's ride. More and more volunteers began to enroll in the defence forces. Germans and Americans, whose political allegiance had at first made them

---

* The last man to join the Reform Committee, W. H. S. Bell, admits that he was no revolutionary, scarcely a reformer; he only supported the movement because he hoped it would mediate between Jameson and Kruger, thus clearing up the mess made by the leaders. (W. H. S. Bell, *Bygone Days*, p. 205.)

repudiate this British adventure, were now joining the reform movement. The Mercantile Association called for volunteers: 'WANTED 400!'* Another notice ran:

VOLUNTEERS
(For Town Duty)
THIS AFTERNOON
Report At Once
At The Office Of The
Australian Association
AEGIS BUILDING

But there were still no signs of the situation getting out of control, and on the Wednesday a special edition of the *Johannesburg Star* (which strongly supported the reformers) looked forward to a compromise with no 'tumult', despite the fact that one and all confidently expected Dr Jim to ride in at any moment.

Aided by the Uitlanders' own inner desires, Kruger managed to change their rising into a revolution-by-consent, by *his* consent. A Reform Committee was appointed and something like a provisional government was set up by the reformers, but with the tacit agreement of Kruger. They ran their own police and court of justice, but only after Kruger had tactfully removed his zarps from the streets and confined them to barracks. Trenches were dug round the town manned by volunteers. A relief fund of £80,000 was raised to house refugees from outlying districts. A man named McClelland was appointed cashier to the Reform Committee. His cash book, afterwards presented to the British Museum by James Hall of New York, records donations of £5,000 each from Eckstein's, Howard Farrar & Co., Barnato Bros.; £2,000 each from Abe Bailey and Lionel Phillips, and numerous other smaller sums. Among the expenses were £25 for rations for Bettington's Horse, £9 13s. 0d. for 'towels and salad oil' and £1,343 10s. 0d. for a 'detective agency'. The account, opened on 31 December, broke off on 3 January, and 125 of its 150 pages were unused.

The Uitlanders' headquarters were in the Goldfields building, only the flag they flew was not the Union Jack but Kruger's flag, his 'dear *Vierkleur*' with its four colours of red, white, green and blue;

---

* One humorist put up a placard saying, 'WANTED A CROMWELL'.

albeit flown upside down to symbolize the revolution. When the reformers found that Kaffirs were being thrown out of work by the crisis, they bought up stocks of liquor in 'bad' areas and destroyed it, closing the canteens – with Kruger's permission. Picturesque uniforms of the Australian, Irish, Scottish and George Washington corps jostled one another on the streets, but the Reform Committee accepted the High Commissioner's repudiation of Jameson, continued to treat with Kruger and forbade any demonstrations against his Government. Never had rebels been more co-operative nor the authority rebelled against more accommodating.

The truth was that neither side wanted civil war. And while Jameson rode and all was uncertain, each side needed to keep more than one policy in play. But before the Raid was over, Kruger, with typical adroitness, made sure of cornering the Reform Committee once Jameson was captured. Having 'entertained' them with 'insincere negotiations',[4] he required a deputation to furnish their credentials. Obligingly they handed over the list of all their sixty-four members. Later Kruger used this list to arrest every man jack of them. Indignant and incredulous, these prominent citizens were rounded up in batches and dumped in Doornfontein gaol, where earlier arrivals welcomed them with cheers, jeers, sandwiches and whisky. When the 'bag' was complete, Boer guards marched them to the station, Kruger's zarps carrying their luggage. A disagreeable term of imprisonment awaited them in Pretoria.

From the start Kruger was not taking any chances. He believed that the reformers had 20,000 rifles. (In fact their total was only 3,000.) As the Uitlanders ostentatiously maintained their military bluff and a succession of alarms, most of them false, continued to reach Pretoria, Kruger ordered his old white horse to be kept saddled and slept with a loaded rifle by his bed. According to his wife he had not been 'across a horse' for many years. Nevertheless the President was ready for a fight; or, as the Uitlanders preferred to believe, for flight.

# 8

## *The Raiders*

The time now goes back a few days to Saturday, 28 December 1895. Jameson's part in this story has so far amounted to no more than the assumption of an administrative post at Pitsani in the Protectorate where a force of Chartered Company police was stationed to make sure that when the railway construction began it would not be hampered by marauding tribesmen. But to Dr Jameson, guarding the railway was a very minor part of his duties. One hundred and eighty miles away across the veldt the Johannesburg pot was due at any moment to boil over. His own brother Sam was there, the brother of two of his officers and Rhodes's elder brother Frank. When they and their friends summoned him he was to go in and help. This very Saturday had originally been fixed for the rising to start. But it had not started. The summons had not come.

Jameson and his men felt that they had waited at Pitsani long enough. It was a wretched place even for a soldiers' camp, treeless and barren but abounding in flies. Jameson's first contingent had arrived on 30 November, having been six weeks on the road from Bulawayo. A surprising proportion of the rank and file were scarcely out of their teens. They were impatient to sally forth on their quest, though few of them knew what it was. Their knowledge of riding and shooting was equally uncertain.

Jameson's officers, too, were more remarkable for gilded youth than for military genius. Among them were three honourables and a baronet, besides well-known names like Villiers, Grenfell and Cazalet, and a Captain Gosling, son-in-law of Sir Sydney Shippard, Administrator of Bechuanaland! One of the honourables, Major Robert White, was believed afterwards to have distinguished himself by bringing along a dispatch case which was later captured by the Boers, and became famous as *de trommel van Bobby White*. It contained his diary, the names of the Uitlander leaders and other secret documents in code. Most conveniently for the Boers, his case contained the code key as well. Without this treasure-trove the full enormity of Jameson's adventures might never have been discovered. Was there ever such a farcical case of 'conspiracy by double entry'?

But in truth the catastrophe was not due to the much-maligned Bobby White. It turned out to be the fault of his commanding officer, 'Johnny' Willoughby, who has been described as 'a wonderful transport officer';[1] on this occasion he lost his magic touch. Bobby White did not even know that his dispatch case had been taken along with the raiders. The first thing he heard of it was when his brother Harry came up to him in Pretoria gaol with a breezy reference to the captured diaries: 'Bobby, old boy,' said he, 'your facile pen has got us into trouble.'

Why did Sir John Willoughby omit to see that all incriminating documents had been destroyed before his troops crossed the border? The answer was given thirty-six years later by J. B. Stacey-Clitheroe,[2] another of the raiders, who shared No. 9 cell with Bobby White in Pretoria. The *trommel* was with Willoughby, who was stationed at Mafeking in charge of another part of Jameson's force. Stacey-Clitheroe had been detailed off to pack Willoughby's staff cart, ready for the ride. Having finished his job, he brought the cart up to Willoughby's tent in case there were a few last things to be added. To his amazement he found Willoughby busy packing White's case including the code books. A remarkable exchange followed; Clitheroe agitated, Willoughby imperturbable:

*Stacey-Clitheroe*: Good heavens, you are not going to take in this box with us?
*Willoughby*: I am.
*Stacey-Clitheroe*: Surely you could send it round with your servant by rail?
*Willoughby*: I shall want this box directly I get into Johanessburg. If we do not get through we shall all be shot, so what does it matter?

The reformers were right in thinking afterwards that this audacious soldier wasted few anxieties on the fate of those whose names were inside the *trommel* and whom he was coming to rescue.

Sir John Willoughby was thirty-six at the time of the Raid, son of the fourth baronet. Accustomed to success in society, on the hunting-field and on the turf, he owned at the age of twenty-five an eight-thousand-guinea horse called Harvester, which dead-heated first in the Derby. In his leisure moments he had taught the young Winston Churchill the art of war with toy soldiers. His handling of Jameson's troopers, however, suggests that the pupil must soon have outstripped the master. As a junior officer in the Household Cavalry, Johnny Willoughby had been the shortest man among them. Described as 'petit, pale and passionless',[3] he was game for camel-racing, wolf-hunting in the desert ('not at all bad fun') and thought naked natives with long hair 'rum'. In most of his photographs his expression is one of rather haughty vacuity, but in a group of Jameson's officers, each with a large drooping moustache and cap pulled down over his eyes, his face stands out for its absence of British phlegm. Alert, with a small trim moustache, Willoughby looks like a pedigree terrier among a pack of sad bloodhounds.

Commissioned in the 'Blues' in 1880, he wrote home after his first battle: 'I expected I should be in a funk; but I wasn't.' Admirers said he never was. He served in the Egyptian campaign of 1882, on the Nile in 1884–5, and in 1890 was appointed second-in-command to the Chartered Company's forces in Rhodesia. Like Jameson, he fought in the Matabele War. By the year of the Raid he had acquired much military experience of a rather unconventional kind in Africa. Indeed, some of his own previous exploits bore a certain family likeness to Jameson's own plan of 1895.

Once, when the settlers in Rhodesia were having a hard struggle to obtain food and equipment, Willoughby was ordered to open a new supply route, hitherto denied to them, through Portuguese Gazaland. Rhodes evolved the plan, as unorthodox as Jameson's later one, but more effective. The Colonial Office used to refer to it as the 'unofficial war'. Willoughby was to march through the forbidden territory. The Portuguese would fire on him. British protests would follow. The route, to make amends, would be opened by the repentant Portuguese. All went according to plan, or rather better. For when Willoughby was fired on it was only with blank cartridges. Before the march somebody asked Rhodes, 'What will happen if they hit him?' to which Rhodes replied with emphasis: 'They will only hit him in the leg.'[4] In crossing the Portuguese border Willoughby would be deliberately disobeying the High Commissioner, Sir Henry Loch, who had forbidden him to do so. Willoughby applied to Rhodes for advice. Rhodes's solution was, 'Take all . . . ask afterwards.'

Collisions with High Commissioners were to become a familiar pattern of events. On a later occasion Willoughby took it upon himself to threaten Kruger with war if he allowed a band of his Boer trekkers to cross the Limpopo into 'Charterland'. Thereupon the High Commissioner flatly disowned Willoughby. Both Jameson and Willoughby learned the lessons of these curtain-raisers and adapted them to future circumstances.

Young Johnny had ardently admired General Gordon, the man who said, 'This Empire has been made by adventurers and it will have to be maintained by adventurers.' Now he worshipped Jameson. Gladstone he was in the habit of referring to as 'the grand old crocodile'. No doubt, from his cell in Pretoria gaol, Willoughby would soon be devising suitable epithets for Chamberlain. His interests in South Africa were not confined to military adventures. He had large holdings in 'Willoughby's Consolidated Company' which he had founded. Its capital had been increased from £8,000 (less than the sum he spent on Harvester) to £713,000. He also had interests in the Rhodesia Goldfields. Altogether he was a miniature 'Elizabethan adventurer', entirely appropriate to the spirit of the Raid.

Jameson, despite his outrageous action, cannot be dismissed so easily. He had leadership, glamour, a way with him, as his friends said. His appearance, if stocky, was somehow extraordinarily pre-possessing. The firm small chin, short nose, wide apart eyes, broad forehead and challenging set of the head combined to give him sometimes 'an air of good-natured, forcible abruptness', sometimes a look of eager anticipation. One of his officers, Captain Thatcher, likened him to 'a Scottish terrier ready to pounce'.[5] There were times when his expression was anxious and strained, due, thought his friends, to the hardships he had lived through in the old pioneering days. His eyes made a special appeal to Lord Rosebery: 'The eyes of an affectionate dog I used to call them and there can scarcely be higher praise.'[6] George Wyndham said that he had the 'nostrils of a racehorse'.*

Though below the average height, he walked with a slight stoop; he rode slackly or lounged about with his hands in his pockets. In every way this leader of men was highly unconventional. While Chief Magistrate in Salisbury, Rhodesia, he would transact business with his feet up on the table in front of him; behaviour that could

*George Wyndham, a romantic Conservative aristocrat, cousin of Wilfrid Blunt, was afterwards a member of the Committee of Inquiry into the Raid.

perhaps only be paralleled on the front benches at Westminster. Jameson completed the picture of relaxed ease with a tilted chair, perpetual cigarette and stream of pleasant banter. A photograph taken in 1894, the year before the Raid, shows him with three of his officers. Dr Jameson stands out for his charming face and slovenly appearance, despite the care of his valet, Garlick. He wears a crumpled panama hat and is already half slipping off his chair.

Whatever one felt about him or his projects when he was not there, one could not help falling for the man in his presence. This gift of magnetic warmth did not always serve its owner well. He was able to thaw the doubts of the Uitlanders and convince the sceptical among his own troops, persuading them to adopt his plans, when a cool refusal on their part would have saved him from catastrophe. But as everyone agreed, his personality was irresistible.

Jameson, a Scot, was born in 1853. He was the same age as his devoted friend, Cecil Rhodes, and a year younger than Flora Shaw. The youngest of ten brothers, Leander Starr lived for a time as a boy in the Junction Road, London, which lay not far from Holloway, where stood the prison he was later to inhabit. He became a successful surgeon but his health, like that of Rhodes as a young man, was not good. One day his brother Julius sent him a diamond from South Africa. Jameson wore it in his cravat and his thoughts turned more and more to the land where sunshine and diamonds sparkled in harmony. He emigrated to Kimberley where 'the Doctor' soon became one of its most popular citizens. People attached themselves to Jameson with extraordinary fervour, the more extraordinary because he made no effort to feed it. He affected an attitude of tough cynicism towards life, literature and any articulate form of idealism, particularly towards the hero-worship which he himself excited. As a politician he was to remain absolutely devoid of the demagogic or oratorical arts. It was said that he did not even bother to nod to his supporters when he passed them in the House. But when he died *The Times* estimated that his astonishing personal hold over his followers had been equalled only by that of Parnell, the Irish patriot.

His indifference to books stopped short at the works of Sir Walter Scott, of whom Carlyle once said he was not a great man but a very healthy one. Dr Jameson read his Scott every night before going to sleep. Macaulay's essay on Clive also inspired in him adventurous thoughts while he was in Bulawayo before the Raid. He put down the book consumed with longing to ride into the Transvaal at once. 'Clive would have done it,' was his comment. Jameson was later to be the inspiration and hero of Rudyard Kipling's poem, *If*, despite the fact that he lost his head just when 'all about him' – except his leading officers – were 'keeping theirs':

> If you can make one heap of all your winnings
>   And risk it on one turn of pitch-and-toss
> And lose, and start again at your beginnings
>   And never breathe a word about your loss . . .

Jameson was by no means a failure as a doctor, though his activities were criticized during a small-pox epidemic: he was accused and acquitted of falsifying his reports to please big business. He made a good income and his bedside manner must have been fabulous. But 'the Doctor' of Kimberley became bored. At heart (and literally) he was a gambler and he cut free from it all in 1889 to go at Rhodes's behest to Matabeleland. He continued to favour the surgeon's technique, however, long after he had laid aside the knife. There was no situation he felt he could not improve with one deft cut. Like Willoughby he could draw on past military experience of a thoroughly irregular sort. In 1889 Jameson was arrested and imprisoned for gun-running to an African tribe. He contrived and conducted the Matabele War after the settlers – so different from the timid Johannesburgers three years later – had launched him with an imperative 'Go in and finish it!' This war evoked thunderous condemnation from Labouchere, the editor of *Truth*. Wilfrid Blunt called the Matabele War 'slaughter for trade' and believed that as a result of that slaughter there set in the 'gangrene of Colonial rowdyism'[7] that was the Jameson Raid.

It was the Boers' turn to do a little filibustering in 1890 and Dr Jameson shared the satisfaction with others of his race in rushing down to the Floris Drift to halt the Adendorff Trek. A call to Boers in the Transvaal newspapers to join the Trek ended with the words: 'The God of Heaven, who administers all things, can alone put a stop to this trek, but men cannot.' However, Kruger repudiated them and the man who now administered Mashonaland, Leander Starr Jameson, was able to prove the pious filibusters wrong.

The British later made much of this and similar treks, arguing in mitigation of the Raid that the Boers had never accepted the Transvaal frontiers anyway . . .

Two qualities in Jameson's character led him into trouble: overconfidence and impatience. 'Anyone could take the Transvaal with half a dozen revolvers!' he said to a friend before the Raid. It was a distant echo of the six-year-old child who had celebrated his first glass of sherry with the words, 'Now I feel as if I could go and do everything.' With eight maxim guns and three field pieces instead of the half-dozen revolvers, he would surely go and do everything. His maxims were a proud possession: a novelty whose introduction was due to the otherwise unbeatable prowess of the Matabele tribesmen. In a curious way the Matabele War was responsible for Jameson's downfall. The vast size of the country, the horrific reputation of its native warriors, the fact that it was conquered at so cheap a price in white lives, all helped to build up the legend of Jameson as a superman. Though in other ways a man of honest simplicity, he began to believe in himself. He was, said Flora Shaw afterwards, 'a mixture of Imperialist idealism and swelled head'.

In this story not a few of the actors had the same disease, from the small, forgotten Dr Harris to the big, unforgettable Cecil Rhodes. Rhodes, with his passion for the out-size, was not likely to be immune. Partly as a result of easy victories over Lobengula's spears, the British also vastly underrated the fighting power of the Boers. They had forgotten Majuba too quickly. It was true that their opponents had none of the military polish of a Willoughby or a White. Just a rough-and-ready militia of bearded farmers was what they looked like, with their big-brimmed hats of all sizes and shapes, checked or plain civilian trousers or breeches and riding-boots. Bandoliers and Maüser rifles were slung across their ordinary shirts and jackets, most of them sweat-stained and with a mourning band on the arm, for the Boers had large families and someone had nearly always just died. Kruger called the Rand prospectors a rabble. Jameson's professional soldiers returned the compliment. In their foolish contempt and over-confidence, the Boer militia seemed to them no better than a gang of untrained guerrillas.

Impatience was apt to seize Jameson throughout his life, though after the Raid he was chastened into displays of immense perseverance and self-control. His letters contain signs of restlessness and boredom: he sends up a sigh that he is feeling 'simply utterly bored and flat . . .'[8] He would have agreed heartily with Rhodes's advice to a pioneer who had found the going too hard. Let him never forget the 'deadly monotony' of normal existence, said Rhodes, in which his highest hope was to become 'an average country gentleman and a fairly respectable Member of Parliament'. Those who fall in creating a new world, continued Rhodes, 'fall sooner than they would in ordinary lives, but their lives are better and grander'. Rhodes's friend Kipling expressed the same thought in his poem to the pioneers called *Song of the Dead*:

> On the sand-drift – on the veldt-side – in the fern scrub we lay,
> That our sons might follow after by the bones on the way.

In the case of the Raid it was the Boers who followed after and they picked up not bones but code-books on the veldt-side.

Jameson, however, was not the one to dispute Rhodes's views. His utter devotion to Rhodes was perhaps the most profound thing in his character. He was Rhodes's right-hand man. His was the hand to carry out the concepts of the other's brain. 'All ideas are Rhodes's' Jameson once said. And all Rhodes's ideas were right. But that did not mean that the hand could not sometimes act in advance of what it felt sure the brain was thinking. Jameson, on his own account, could not tolerate a pedestrian way of life. He was usually ready to take the short cut, the snap decision, the daring course. And Rhodes had said that it was better and grander so.

# 9

## 'Delay Dangerous'

'Wrong! Is it wrong? Well, may be:
  But I'm going all the same.
Do they think me a Burgher's baby,
  To be scared by a scolding name?
They may argue and prate and order;
  Go, tell them to save their breath:
Then, over the Transvaal border,
  And gallop for life or death!'

The Poet Laureate, Alfred Austin, *Jameson's Ride*, Stanza 1

Weeks of drilling, weeks of waiting had left Jameson and his men 'simply utterly bored and slack'. In their practical uniforms – dark grey or khaki tunics, brown and grey 'smasher' hats with white or blue puggarees, dark blue puttees – they were ready a fortnight ago and still not off. Willoughby had come down from Rhodesia during the second week in December, reporting that a thousand men of the Rhodesia Horse were standing by in the north, for an emergency call. Jameson went about in civilian clothes but fuming like an angry colonel. Some of his men were already beginning to drift home. He feared that Kruger would get wind of his plan. (The Mafeking papers were expressing surprise at the size of the Pitsani force.) As early as 6 November Jameson had become nervous lest the heterogeneous bunch of plotters in Johannesburg should blab. From the club at Kimberley he communicated urgently with Bobby White, in command at Mafeking:

Dear Bobby – I am wiring you that Foley leaves tomorrow to join you at camp – use him and keep him there. Not intentionally but idiotically he has been talking too much . . .

The officers at Mafeking talked too. 'Frankie' Newton, the young and popular Resident Commissioner, had been let into the secret, agreeing to 'go to the races' with Dr Jim.* But about ten days before the Raid, Jameson's officers were talking so wildly that Newton got cold feet and decided to inform the High Commissioner. The latter, for reasons which will appear later, declined to see him, and it was touch and go at one moment whether Newton resigned his post, thus imperilling the whole enterprise. Sir Graham Bower, however, the Imperial Secretary, prevented this débâcle. He pooh-poohed Newton's fears about Jameson, adding that though he also would like to resign it would be dishonourable to desert 'a sick man [the High Commissioner] in the hour of danger' – the danger being not from Jameson's wildness but from Chamberlain's 'piracy'![1] Bower passed Newton on to Rhodes who, after a stormy interview,[2] managed to silence him by firm assurances of Colonial Office support. Rhodes was ably seconded by one of his confederates from old Rhodesian days, Major Goold-Adams, who had taken part in the London negotiations a month earlier and was now Boundary Commissioner for the new Bechuanaland. Thus reassured from several quarters, Newton 'went to the races' – and lost heavily.

Why did Jameson 'bolt'? Though he genuinely feared discovery, the secret was in fact astonishingly well kept. His own temperament, worked on by the behaviour of his confederates, was the real cause. In order to appreciate Jameson's ordeal it is necessary to go further behind the scenes and examine the ciphered telegraphic messages between Pitsani, Johannesburg and Cape Town from 7 to 28 December. During those three weeks a test of patience was imposed upon Jameson which even the most phlegmatic might have failed to pass. The intense irritation that simmered for days, finally boiling up in him, suggests that he did make some effort to restrain himself. Struggling in eddies of hope, disappointment and renewed hope, he was at last whirled away.

As early as the first week in December, Jameson felt he was ready for the starting-gun. A fortnight earlier he had extracted the 'letter of invitation' from the Uitlanders, which gave him all the formal

*Newton originally wanted leave to go to Johannesburg with Jameson to help him, and incidentally to see the races there – a typically light-hearted attitude towards the 'ride'. (Report of the Cape Committee, pp. 137–9 and 177.) Newton had been up at Oxford with Rhodes and was Sir Hercules Robinson's private secretary in 1881 when Rhodes first entered South African politics.

excuse he desired for going in. He also settled the provisional date of the rising, 28 December. He himself planned to cross the border two days in advance so as to perform his rescue work from the very doorstep. Then came the first blow.

## 7 December

A shattering wire arrived from Colonel Frank Rhodes, in charge of military preparations at Johannesburg:

Tell Dr Jameson the polo tournament here [i.e. the rising] postponed for one week or it would clash with race week.

Quite the nicest man among the conspirators was Colonel Rhodes. A typical British cavalry officer, he was making himself an enviable reputation as a soldier in different parts of Africa until his dominating younger brother came along and swept him into his service. Frank's face – a more human, less striking, bonier version of Cecil's – had the same well-cut features but they were sharper and less classical. He looked what he was, an old Etonian; whereas Cecil's dream was to resemble an ancient Roman. There was a current jest that all Frank's remarks began with the words, 'Cecil says . . .' Sir Evelyn Wood (later Lord Cromer) once expressed the view that a man could not live three years in South Africa and remain a gentleman.[3] Frank Rhodes was to live in South Africa for another ten years and to die there, acclaimed by everyone who knew him as a gentleman through and through. Kruger said he was the only man among the conspirators who knew his business. But even he had not the dynamism to touch off a revolution.* Jameson should have been in charge of Johannesburg, Frank Rhodes of Pitsani. The Colonel would have waited patiently on the border until summoned. The Doctor would have used his inflammable personality to set the Golden City alight. Rhodes had got the right men in the wrong places.

## 8 December

Jameson replied to Johannesburg that 'any delay would be most

* A story is told of Dr Jameson coming to consult Frank Rhodes by appointment shortly before the Raid. Dr Jim found only a note awaiting him: 'Dear Jimjams, sorry I can't see you this afternoon, have an appointment to teach Mrs X the bike.' Frank was a lady-killer not a Boer-slayer.

injurious', because of the suspicions which had been aroused; ending his wire with the announcement:

Have everything ready here.

Three days later he repeated these words to Rhodes, adding all too confidently:

. . . the entire journey occupies 2 days.

*12 December*
An anxious telegram sped from Jameson to Cape Town. The Colossus might be able to do something with the Uitlanders. Grave suspicions, said Jameson, were abroad. Even premature action would be better than delay. Then came a heart-rending cry:

Surely in your estimation do you consider that races is of supreme importance compared to immense risks of discovery daily expected?

Let Rhodes, concluded Jameson, inform the 'weak partners' of what to him seemed so obvious –

More delay more danger.

Rhodes forwarded this telegram to the weak partners in Johannesburg, including a cable he had just received from some exceedingly strong partners in London. It contained the same words of warning:

Delay dangerous . . .

What effect would these two messages, both in favour of hurry rather than postponement, have on the Uitlanders?

*18 December*
They responded by thinking up a new reason for delay. The millionaire Alfred Beit was defraying half the costs of the rising. He had just landed at Cape Town. He must come up to Johannesburg immediately, wired the conspirators, and help them sort out their various difficulties. John Hays Hammond telegraphed to Rhodes:

Flotation must be delayed until his [Beit's] arrival.

There was no doubt that Hays Hammond had once been all in favour of revolution. Krugerdom, he had said, was worse than the rule of George III. For an American it could hardly have been put more strongly. Yet here was Hammond asking for delay in the 'flotation'.

*19 December*

What should Rhodes do now? The Uitlanders had plenty of cash for the rising, without personal reassurances from Beit. 'Little Beit' (he was about five feet tall) was in ill-health and more likely to catch the Uitlanders' bug of timidity than infuse them with a robuster spirit. So Beit was advised by Rhodes to send them a tonic in the form of a couple of telegrams:

. . . Our foreign supporters urge immediate flotation.

*20 December*

. . .Immediate flotation is the thing most desired, as we never know what may hinder it if now delayed.

The ultimatum from President Cleveland had just been published, an added reason, surely, against waiting. Every day now the Uitlanders were discovering new obstacles to immediate action or finding old ones more formidable. They wanted to know whether Rhodes would force their cosmopolitan republic into the Empire against the will of the majority? Again, had the High Commissioner promised without fail to come up to Johannesburg the moment the rising started and mediate with Kruger on their behalf? There seemed to be some contradiction here. If they feared the Empire why did they insist on the imperial authority intervening? But Rhodes understood their difficulties and did his best to smooth them away.

*21 December*

At the same time they must be handled firmly. Through Harris, he sharply reminded Frank Rhodes that the rescuer on the border could not wait for ever:

Reply when you can float in your opinion so that I can advise Dr Jameson.

Two days later he sent Jameson's spirits soaring with a glorious piece of news:

*23 December*

Company will be floated next Saturday 28th. 12 o'clock at night.

The message added that Jameson must on no account start before 8 P.M. on the great night; thus making certain that he did not jump the gun.

*24 December*
Jameson replied excitedly:

Will endeavour to delay till Saturday ... Do all you can to hasten it ... Colonel [Frank] Rhodes etc. intolerable.

On the same day another message came to Jameson from Harris, at last indicating a rising temperature in Johannesburg:

You must not move till Saturday night; we are feeling confident it will take place Saturday night. Since Dr Wolff [another American] left [for Johannesburg]. Feeling our subscribers greatly improved.

Harris also warned Frank Rhodes again of Jameson's unalterable decision: he could not allow 'refusal of flotation beyond December'. The Boers were getting to know about it.

That was Christmas Eve. On Christmas Day the Uitlanders' disagreements over the form their future state should take – republic or British colony or what? – came to a head. Everything must be postponed, at least until 6 January. Their leaders must thrash it out personally with Rhodes.

*26 December*
Boxing Day brought poor Jameson an abysmal telegram from his brother Sam in Johannesburg:

Absolutely necessary to postpone flotation ... We will endeavour to meet your wishes as regards December but you must not move until you have received instructions to.

Harris confirmed the decision to postpone with a telegram of his own finishing with the tactless words:

Too awful. Very sorry.

*27 December*
The situation indeed seemed awful. So awful that Jameson felt he would no longer be justified in waiting on the 'pitch-and-toss' of a bunch of hopeless vacillators. Rhodes made matters worse by urging the already frantic Doctor not to be disturbed by rumours. Jameson now began to telegraph in peremptory fashion. He was going to force their hand. A message went from him to Sam saying that men had already gone forward to cut the telephone wires. There was only one thing to do now:

Let Hammond telegraph instantly all right.

He followed this up with another wire to Harris in the same vein:

. . . expect to receive a telegram from you nine tomorrow morning Saturday 28th authorizing movement.

But even this did not now seem strong enough. A few hours later yet another message to Harris burst from him. There was an unmistakably savage note in it. He did not expect, he said, to be able to stop the wire-cutting operations. Things had gone too far. In this case:

. . . we must carry into effect original plans. They [the Uitlanders] will then have two days for flotation. If they do not, we will make our own flotation with help of letter which I will publish . . .

A reply came hurrying back, signed by Hays Hammond, which none but a confirmed 'bolter' could have misunderstood:

Wire just received. Experts reports decidedly adverse. I absolutely condemn further developments at present.

Lionel Phillips mingled his banshee wail with the storm of protestations that flew between the conspirators on 27 December:

If foreign subscribers insist on floating without delay anticipate complete failure.

*28 December*
This was the day long chosen for the rising but now forbidden. The

wires between Cape Town and Pitsani fairly tingled with messages. Jameson vented his fury in bitter complaints to Dr Harris about the Uitlanders:

There will be no flotation if left to themselves . . . All means fear.

The implication of those last words was obvious. The Doctor must take their courage in his hands. As someone put it afterwards, Johannesburg would never be delivered of a revolution without a Caesarian operation. But on behalf of Rhodes, Dr Harris dispatched telegram after telegram to persuade the Doctor to let nature take its course:

It is all right if you will only wait.

There would be immediate opportunities for further discussion: Jameson's old friends, Heany and Goold-Adams, were being sent up by the reformers. Heany would arrive by special train. Jameson must wait for their messages and report back to Rhodes. Then –

You and I must judge regarding flotation.

No doubt fear was causing the delay, but –

. . . we cannot have fiasco.

The two leaders from Johannesburg were now in Cape Town and confirmed the awful fact that the flotation was positively and irrevocably off – at least until the next consultation. So Harris concluded:

Public will not subscribe one penny towards it even with you as director. Ichabod.

To all of which Jameson's uncompromising reply was:

Unless I hear definitely to the contrary shall leave tomorrow evening . . .

Heany or Ichabod, a messenger arriving or the glory departing, it made no odds to Jameson now. He had decided. And that same day a Reuter report came through from Johannesburg to burn away any remaining shreds of doubt. The position in the town, it said, was becoming acute. There were rumours of secret arming in the mines and other warlike preparations. When is a rising not a rising?

Jameson was not going to quibble over definitions. The Reuter report continued:

Women and children leaving Rand . . . [this sounded like an authentic echo of the 'letter of invitation']. Market lifeless, no business, everything politics. *Volksleid* and *God Save Queen* loudly cheered theatre.

At the theatre they were playing *Othello*. 'It is the cause, it is the cause, my soul . . .' Jameson, too, carried a cause in his soul and like the Moor of Venice he intended that nothing should keep him from his deed.

# 10

## Caesarian Operation

'Let lawyers and statesmen addle
Their pates over points of law:
If sound be our sword, and saddle,
And gun-gear, who cares one straw?
When men of our own blood pray us
To ride to their kinsfolk's aid,
Not Heaven itself shall stay us
From the rescue they call a raid.'
*Jameson's Ride*, Stanza 2

Meanwhile the leaders in Johannesburg, having wisely decided not to put all their trust in the telegraph, dispatched two messengers, Captain Harry Holden and Major Maurice Heany, an American, to make absolutely sure, through orders personally delivered, that their rescuer did not start.

Holden rode into Jameson's camp on the Saturday. He had covered the 170 miles from Johannesburg in seventy hours, but the only effect of this great ride was to make Jameson complete his plans for his bolt. Next morning came Major Heany. He had wired Harris from Bloemfontein on 27 December that 'Zebrawood' (Frank Rhodes) wished him to stop 'Zahlbar' (Jameson) and demanding a special train from Kimberley to Mafeking. On the Mafeking mail train, which Heany's 'special' duly picked up at Vryburg, there happened to be a fellow-traveller already involved in the plot – Frank Newton. But the Resident Commissioner must have decided, since his interview with Rhodes, that the least said about Jameson's plans the soonest mended. At any rate no words passed between them. Major Goold-Adams and Inspector Fuller of the Cape Police were also on the train. Heany conversed with Fuller but kept his own counsel as to his mission. He reached Mafeking station in the early hours of Sunday morning. He went straight to the house of a business agent, one Emmanuel Isaacs, knocked him up and bought a pair of riding-boots, a kit-bag and a horse in order to chase Jameson should he have started already. Heany said afterwards that he found the town in a 'queer state'. Things were queerer still when he clattered in his hired cart into Pitsani on Sunday.

Jameson was in his tent. Heany got out his notebook and read aloud the reformers' message. As the messenger went over the all-too-familiar reasons for delay – acute shortage of arms and political disagreements – Jameson 'rather laughed'. He and his lads, he promised, would kick the burghers all round the Transvaal. Then he left the tent and walked up and down outside for twenty minutes.

At last he came back. 'I'm going,' said the Doctor. 'Thought you would,' said Heany, not in the least surprised. When the reformers resolved to send him out to stop Jameson, he warned them that his mission would be a failure. 'What will he do?' asked the agitated reformers. Heany replied: 'He will come in as sure as fate.'

It was the Doctor's turn to question Heany. 'What are you going to do?' asked the Doctor. 'Going with you,' said Heany. 'Thought you would,' said the Doctor.

Jameson and Heany knew each other of old. They had been campaigners together in Rhodesia. It was shockingly bad psychology on the part of the reformers to send a stable companion to stop a runaway horse.

Jameson had made his final preparations when Heany arrived. At nine o'clock on the Sunday morning he sent off two more telegrams – one to the Rhodesia Horse in Bulawayo: let them be ready for a new adventure under their old leader – the other to Dr Wolff in Johannesburg: he must perform the distant wire-cutting and meet Jameson *en route* to decide on the raiders' 'best destination', Johannesburg or Pretoria. Then Jameson sent his very last message. It was addressed to the Chartered Company's offices in Cape Town, for Dr Harris.

### 29 December

Shall leave tonight for the Transvaal.

This was the first sentence and this was the operative one. The rest was a re-hash of Jameson's fears of leakage and his pretended obligations under the 'women and children' letter. It ended with Jameson putting up a universal umbrella over everybody and everything including his own conscience:

We are simply going in to protect everybody while they change the present dishonest government and take vote from the whole country as to form of government required by the whole.

There was something both ludicrous and touching about that last passage, especially the use of the word 'simply'. It was one that always appealed to the Doctor.

This telegram had no effect on events one way or the other. It reached the telegraph office in Cape Town at 10.52 A.M. on Sunday, was picked up from there at 11 A.M. by Harris's clerk, taken to Harris and then rushed by cab to Rhodes, being in Harris's possession during the last hour or two of Sunday morning while the Kimberley line to Pitsani was still open for a return message. When Rhodes at last saw the telegram all lines were closed. But Harris, if he had thought of it, could have wired Jameson again on his own responsibility. He was a man who liked to take responsibility. He missed a great opportunity.

When Harris's clerk collected Jameson's last telegram on the Sunday morning there was another one lying there also undelivered. It was the message of Saturday, 28 December: 'Unless I hear to the contrary shall leave tomorrow evening. . .' This message actually arrived at the Cape Town telegraph office at six o'clock on the Saturday evening, over a day and night before Jameson crossed the border. Why did not Rhodes see it in time to let the raiders 'hear to the contrary' in good round terms that no one could dispute? The answer was that the offices of the Chartered Company, to which Jameson had addressed his telegram, were closed on the Saturday evening, so that Rhodes saw it no earlier than the one dispatched on Sunday morning. Jameson was astonishingly inefficient in forgetting that offices close, or he was deliberately gambling on this fact preventing Rhodes from replying – another touch of 'pitch-and-toss'. For there is little doubt that if a telegram had arrived in Cape Town on Saturday evening addressed to the Prime Minister personally, he would have got it.

Since Heany was going in with Jameson, Holden would not be left out. So this Shakespearean pair joined the column. Sent by the reformers on purpose to utter one last desperate cry of 'back', they both in the end cried 'forward' with the rest of the merry throng. In an official 'Composition of Force' later sent to the War Office, Willoughby blandly described them as 'Officers temporarily attached to Staff'. There was also a Major Crosse on sick leave. He rode in with the column in a cart provided at his own expense and wearing civilian clothes, as a contemporary said, 'to see the fun'. Afterwards he escaped punishment on the grounds that he was only 'a spectator'.

That they were merry is a touch contributed by Wilfrid Blunt. A brother of one of the raiders told Blunt afterwards that the Raid had been 'a regular drunken frolic'.[1] Thirty-six cases of champagne were brought into camp, with leave to get drunk for three days – and then on to the main sport. When the time came to cross the border soldiers were detailed off to cut the nearer communications. The direct lines were duly cut, but the troopers did not know that there was still a small branch line open connecting Zeerust (a township inside the border north of their route) with Pretoria by a roundabout way. According to legend, however, this line was left open because of a more unusual error. Owing to the previous carousal, one drunken trooper performed his task to his own satisfaction by cutting and burying a length of wire fencing. 'It would indeed have been dramatic irony', wrote the editor of the *Cape Times* afterwards, 'if the gallant invaders of the Transvaal had needed Dutch courage.'*

Through this slip President Kruger and General Joubert, intended victims of a surprise attack, actually got the news of Jameson's irruption well before the rest of the world.

> 'There are girls in the gold-reef city,
>     There are mothers and children too!
> And they cry, "Hurry up! for pity!"
>     So what can a brave man do?
> If even we win, they'll blame us:
>     If we fail, they will howl and hiss.
> But there's many a man lives famous
>     For daring a wrong like this!'
>                     *Jameson's Ride*, Stanza 3

A flourish of trumpets summoned Jameson's troops on to the

* The 'legendary' version, besides being agreeably human, finds a place in the text of Dr Jean van der Poel's *The Jameson Raid* and appears to be accepted as fact in Edgar Holt's *The Boer War*. Professor Kruger, however, of Potchefstroom University, favours the less colourful story, as set out above, which he told to me.

square. But his speech to the men on that last Sunday afternoon at Pitsani consisted of more than heroics. He had to prevent a good many reluctant heroes from dropping out at the last moment. Even some of his officers were inclined to hesitate. One of them asked Willoughby if he would lose his commission. As for the men, the majority of them were Rhodesians and unlike the Bechuanaland Border Police (the BBP) they were mostly unseasoned. It was a matter of importance not to lose many of them, since the total number of Jameson's troops, divided between Pitsani and Mafeking (camp of the former BBP), amounted only to some five hundred. This was a very different matter from the seven hundred examples of 'very good horseflesh' which the veterinary surgeon had 'backed himself for' in his telegram to the reformers.

Jameson therefore supplemented his natural persuasiveness by reading aloud to his assembled men the 'women and children' letter. He did not reveal to them the date on which it had been written or the fact that they had been frantically cancelling its supposed message throughout the past ten days. In Jameson's opinion, as in that of many others in this story, the end justified the means. He encouraged his young soldiers by telling them it would be a record march and they would be marching with the tough troopers of the BBP from Malmani (Ottoshoop) onwards. The expedition must be a crusade, disciplined and bloodless. No looting, he ordered. And he assured them that in all likelihood there would be no 'red blood spilt'. He also promised each trooper a special bonus. Did he add one more argument to his already potent reasons for making an invasion, an argument powerful enough in itself to render other kinds of justification almost unnecessary? Sir John Willoughby later informed the Select Committee that he did. The imperial authorities, he said, were backing the Raid.

His troops, drawn up on the square, cheered loudly and burst into the National Anthem. Well might they sing, 'Send her victorious', for they saw themselves not as raiders but as crusaders for Queen and Empire. The column now rode forward, three hundred and fifty-six strong, excluding Jameson's staff. They carried rations for one day, 50 lbs of grain each for the horses and 120 rounds of ammunition. There were no tents or stores. They would find everything they needed on the route. A black horse carried the leader of the expedition, who was still wearing his civilian jacket but now covered by a fawn-coloured dust-coat. '*Post equitem sedet atra Cura*,' wrote Horace – 'Black Care mounts on the horseman's pillion.' But this rider on the black horse was conscious of no 'black care' sitting behind him.

Meanwhile the smaller, more experienced section of the gallant five hundred (the BBP) were making ready at Mafeking to join Jameson's column. Owing to the transfer of Bechuanaland, they had been disbanded. But Chamberlain had given them permission, if they wished, to enlist in the Chartered Company's force under their new commander, Major the Hon Robert White. Many of them, however, did not wish to avail themselves of this opportunity and were awaiting their discharge. Inspector Fuller of the Cape Police had come up to Mafeking to superintend the operation. Would Jameson's officers succeed in persuading any of them to change their minds?

Major White seems to have had a good deal more trouble than Jameson in getting a sizeable contingent to start. One of those who refused to join, James White, was harangued in vain by both Major Coventry and Colonel Raleigh Grey, his commanding officer in the old BBP. They promised him that he would be promoted to full sergeant and would see active service. He still refused; and they did not tell him where the active service would take place. Probably the ex-BBP thought they were choosing a soft option when they volunteered to serve the Chartered Company. 'This they would be delighted to do,' Chamberlain was told by one of his officials, 'as we are strict masters . . .' Now, during this bizarre Saturday evening at Mafeking, it must have struck many of the ex-BBP that the Chartered Company, if not exactly strict, would prove unexpectedly taxing masters in their own way. The trail of rifles, saddles and bandoliers found along the first few miles of the route next day, though attributed to more bouts of Dutch courage, was probably the fall-out from deserters during the night's march.

The news of their destination was broken to the troops by Major the Hon. Charles Coventry in soldierly fashion. 'It is all bosh about fighting Linchwe,' he said. (A rumour had circulated that afternoon that the Company were about to go into battle against the Bechuana chief.) 'We are going straight to Johannesburg. We want you all to come. It will be a short trip, everything has been arranged for.' Then someone put the leading question: were they going under Queen's or Company's orders? Colonel Raleigh Grey gave one of the few completely truthful answers in this tale of mystery and prevarication. 'I cannot say that you are going under the Queen's orders,' he replied, 'but you are going to fight for the supremacy of the British flag in South Africa.' Thanks to the joint eloquence of Major Coventry and Colonel Grey, twelve of those who had previously declined to be taken for a ride by the Chartered Company, changed their minds.

Major White then appealed to Inspector Fuller to bring his personal pressure to bear on the recalcitrant remainder. Fuller refused, threatening instead to report all that he had seen and heard. He did in fact send off one of his officers, Sub-Inspector Browne, on horse-back to follow White's column. Fuller must have been vexed with himself and in no mood to oblige White, for he had received a warning of the projected expedition as early as midday on that Saturday. He did not believe it and took no steps to inform the authorities.

Fuller's warning words to White had no effect either. For at 9.30 P.M. the Resident Magistrate at Mafeking, George Boyes, was surprised to hear the sound of cheering from the camp and then to see troops riding past his gate. A short while later Colonel Grey, whose home was next door, came back to fetch his gauntlets and was heard saying, 'Good-bye, I'm off!' Boyes was sitting on the stoep, after church, with his wife and mother. He got up and went down to the club to see if he could gather some news. Hitherto, it seems, no rumours of Jameson's plan had reached Boyes, despite his key post in Mafeking. He got his news with a vengeance. Major Bobby White had been as good as his word, going straight for Johannesburg and parting from the unco-operative Fuller with a gay, if not entirely accurate sally: 'It's all right, old chap, you can do what you like; the wires are cut.'

# 11

## Into the Transvaal

'So we forded and galloped forward,
  As hard as our beasts could pelt,
First eastward, then trending northward,
  Right over the rolling veldt;
Till we came on the Burghers lying
  In a hollow with hills behind,
And their bullets came hissing, flying,
  Like hail on an Arctic wind.'
*Jameson's Ride*, Stanza 4

The border was crossed at Burman's Drift. It was five o'clock in the morning of Monday, 30 December, when the two columns united at Malmani. So far so good, Jameson's men had covered thirty-nine miles and he confidently expected to do the whole hundred and eighty miles from Pitsani to Johannesburg in three days. The New Year chimes would ring him in.

Inspector Fuller, despite his threats, had done nothing that would seriously impede Jameson's flying start. When Bobby White told him the wires were cut he failed to report it to Boyes, the Resident Magistrate at Mafeking, but waited instead for a further report from Browne, the scout he had sent after the column. It seemed that Fuller's scepticism was deep indeed and he was practising all too faithfully the South African motto, 'Be incredulous'. In the middle of the night the scout galloped in with news which showed that incredulity for once did not pay. The cheering troopers from the Mafeking camp had invaded the Transvaal. At once Fuller sent off a messenger to ride through the night as far as Maribogo, where the wires were intact and word could be got through to Kimberley and so to Cape Town. But Maribogo was fifty miles away and Cape Town would not hear till noon that day. Why did not Fuller report the damage to the telegraph immediately? demanded Boyes. While the two horsemen were flying over the veldt through the hours of darkness, Boyes could have been working on the lines; Cape Town would have heard of the Raid at dawn.

After breakfast at Malmani the whole force set off in good heart on the next lap. But if Fuller dallied, the Boers did not. About the same time as the raiders rode on again, an accurate account of their whereabouts reached Kruger by wire. The raiders who had so successfully cut off Cape Town had left Pretoria in communication with Rustenburg and Rustenburg with Zeerust. Though the line ran a few miles north of their route, it was a fine clear run through to Pretoria, like Kruger's run of luck. There were plenty of Boer horsemen to make the necessary connections between Jameson's men and the telegraph office at Zeerust. Thus Jameson's secret had been kept only until breakfast time on the first day.

There were other respects in which his plans were soon awry. A string of five galvanized sheds, the kind of things normally used by gold-diggers, containing bully beef and biscuits with forage for the animals, had been set up along the route. They were roughly at thirty-mile intervals from Mafeking to Krugersdorp, the last village before Johannesburg. The organizer of this commissariat was Henry Wolff, another of Rhodes's doctor friends. In order to lull any possible suspicions on the part of the Boers, Dr Wolff assumed the title of the 'Rand Produce and Trading Syndicate'. He confided to the Boers that these depots had been set up for the purpose of ironing out the fluctuations in the price of corn and mealies in Johannesburg. Dr Wolff's own employees were thoroughly taken in by this story and many of them looked forward to good profits from the 'Syndicate's' stores. Under the same businesslike disguise Dr Wolff bought up several hundred horses in Johannesburg and stationed them on a Mr Malan's farm as remounts, giving out that they were intended for a new transport service from Mafeking to the Rand – a delightful euphemism for Jameson's ride. (Captain Holden had been instructed to use one of these on his journey from Johannesburg but he preferred to ride straight through on his own horse.)

It was all very ingenious, but when the produce of the 'Trading Syndicate' should have come into use, nothing worked according to plan. Too little time was allowed for the troopers to rest, so that they chose to lie down and sleep rather than tackle the bully beef and biscuits. When the time came on the second day for catching the fresh horses on Malan's farm, to be used not for a coach service but for a raid, there was something of a scene. The deceived burgher, however, expressed his righteous indignation in language that was commendably inferior to the affair: 'Jameson! What do you come bothering me like this for?' But it was Jameson who found himself 'bothered'. His men had not time to round up their remounts, which in any case were a heterogeneous collection of wretched animals, most of them not saddle but coach horses. Dr Wolff seems to have overdone the element of disguise. On they rode with the same tired mounts as before, now stopping every seven hours to off-saddle them, since they were carrying on an average sixteen stone. This further delayed their progress. The horses on Malan's farm, together with the food depots, cost the conspirators £18,000.

Fatigue and hunger were not the raiders' only anxiety. They soon discovered that they had lost the advantage of surprise. After only a few hours' riding, small contingents of armed Boers, 'the most capable mounted warriors since the Mongols' as Winston Churchill called them, were seen to be hanging around their flanks and rear. They passed through a narrow defile, the Lead Mines, only three hours before a strong detachment of the enemy rode up to trap them. General Joubert, making use of the telegraph lines which had been left intact, had been able to send orders to Commandant J. D. L. Botha and to others on the raiders' route to cut them off. And so, on the first evening, when Jameson reached McArthur's Stores hoping for rest and refreshment, he received instead from Botha the first of many discouraging communications. Boers and British, they were both to punctuate his ride with urgent messages. Not one was welcoming; they all said 'Go back!'

At about the same hour in a comfortable suburb of Birmingham, Joseph Chamberlain was putting on his immaculate evening clothes in readiness for the Highbury servants' ball. An express messenger from London suddenly broke the news that Jameson had gone in. Unlike the raiders after their débâcle, he had no time to hum 'After the ball is over',[1] but dashed straight up to London. Cecil Rhodes was also at home, in Groote Schurr. He had known the news since luncheon, but in the evening showed no sign to his friends that anything unusual had occurred.

To Commandant Botha Jameson replied with a typically dogged assertion: 'I intend proceeding with my original plans' and then cited once more the 'women and children' letter. He and his men were coming 'by invitation from the principal residents of the Rand' to secure for them justice and human rights. He said that he intended no harm to the people of the Transvaal and signed his letter, without irony, 'Yours faithfully, L. S. Jameson'.

On the second and third days of his ride, as Jameson steadily drew nearer to his objective, the efforts to push him back were intensified. Two more imperative orders to retire arrived, this time from the British High Commissioner, Sir Hercules Robinson himself. The first was brought by Sergeant James White, who had refused to respond to the blandishments of Colonel Grey and Major Coventry. Dispatched in all haste by Newton from Mafeking, he covered the one hundred and sixty miles there and back in fifty-two hours on one horse, and caught the raiders saddling up ten miles beyond the Elans river. Jameson did not actually seize the messenger and say he was drunk (Rhodes's recipe for dealing with interference from a High Commissioner), but he had no desire to open the sealed packet which the messenger presented. It was passed from one to the other, from Grey to White, from White to Willoughby, Willoughby to Jameson, Jameson back to Willoughby. Finally the Doctor was forced to open it himself. Sure enough, it contained most emphatic 'Go back' orders – not just a general directive to return, but as many individual orders to each officer as there had been time to write. Jameson did not bother to answer Newton's messenger. There were no supplies left on the road back; return was impossible, surrender unthinkable. There was nothing for it but to ride on.

In any case, who was this High Commissioner, to say 'Halt!' and be obeyed? Sir Hercules had once asked Rhodes, when he was conquering 'his North', 'But where will you stop?' To which Rhodes had replied that he would stop where his imagination stopped and that was limitless. This anecdote became one of Rhodes's favourites. Jameson must have heard it often. His own imagination was hardly less unbridled.

There was also the thought that Sir Hercules probably did not mean what he said, and to the successful all is forgiven. Bobby White would have been able to support Jameson here. During the April of 1895, before the Raid, he had visited Cecil Rhodes in Cape Town. The pair fell to talking about the Empire. Rhodes was already involved in secret plans for its expansion. Afterwards White recorded in his diary that part of their conversation which had struck him most forcibly:

> When talking of Uganda he [Rhodes] blamed the officers of our expedition for not seizing and fortifying a point on the Nile and holding on to it. I remarked, 'They may have had orders from our Government as to their line of conduct.' He replied, 'Precisely so. You cannot expect a Prime Minister to write down that you are to seize ports, etc. But when he gives you orders to the contrary *disobey* them!' *Verb. sap.*

It was another case of 'Take all, ask afterwards' – Rhodes's advice to Willoughby in Gazaland. But it was even more apposite. If Bobby White had but known it, the diary was in his *trommel* among Willoughby's baggage, ready to justify Jameson in his hour of decision.

So Jameson disobeyed. Late on the evening of Tuesday, 31 December, they reached Boon's Stores, their next halting-place. Here Jameson had some idea of being met by Dr Wolff. Instead he ran into Kruger's grandson, Lieutenant Eloff. He arrested him and extracted a promise that he would remain at the depot for two hours while the raiders rode on, adding with a laugh that he could call for his rifle at *Pretoria*. This jest was afterwards quoted to prove that the object of Jameson's Raid was to enslave Pretoria not to free Johannesburg.* They were now in hilly country and that night a skirmish took place between the raiders and the encircling commandos. One trooper was wounded. It was not a grave affair and a Boer woman was observed calmly collecting empty cartridge cases during the engagement. Sporadic bursts of rifle-fire continued through the hours of darkness and meant less sleep than ever.

New Year's Day dawned. At van Oudtshoorn's farm, another of their food stores, the biscuits and bully beef were rendered less appetizing than ever by another letter from the world beyond the veldt. This time it was from Sir Jacobus de Wet, the British Agent in Pretoria,

---

*Three months later, young Eloff, whom Lord Selborne described as 'a mere Tony Lumpkin', was involved in a *cause célèbre*. During a drunken brawl at Krugersdorp races he was alleged to have said that 'All Englishmen are bastards and the Queen of England is a – – '. Eloff was tried, acquitted and promoted to Senior Lieutenant of Police at Pretoria. The *Standard & Diggers News* thereupon rechristened Krugersdorp, 'Devilsdorp'.

and represented the High Commissioner's second attempt to turn the raiders back. Surely even Jameson would not dare to treat this order in the same cavalier fashion as he had handled the one carried by Sergeant White? Chamberlain must have had a shrewd suspicion that the High Commissioner's first messenger would not be listened to, for in his telegram of the day before he had advised Robinson to send another message by de Wet.*

Jameson was informed that his crusade had been publicly disowned:

Her Majesty's Government entirely disapprove your conduct in invading Transvaal with armed force; your action has been repudiated. You are ordered to retire at once from the country and will be held personally responsible for the consequences of your unauthorized and most improper proceeding.

Jameson wrote a reply to this stern command on a sheet of blue-lined paper. It was couched in language of extreme naïveté, and the substance stuck to the same old rigmarole of threadbare excuses. He 'must perforce' go on to Johannesburg because his men and mounts could not go back. He has 'molested' no one and assures all Boers he meets on the march of his peaceful intentions. Finally he harks back to 'my promise' and 'my fellow countrymen in their extremity'.

By the third day of their ride, Wednesday, 1 January, it was Jameson's men, rather than his fellow countrymen, who were nearing 'their extremity'. Lack of food and sleep was beginning to tell. True, they had now advanced one hundred and fifty miles into the Transvaal. There was less than thirty miles to go. Jameson had promised to be in Johannesburg by New Year's Day, and it still looked as if he might just do it. The Boers who hovered in growing numbers round his column still appeared unwilling to go in and fight. In fact, they had no artillery to oppose Jameson's much prized maxims. Kruger was keeping back the guns at Pretoria to deal with a surprise attack on the arsenal of which he had been warned.

As things turned out, Kruger's guns were never needed to defend

* The Colonial Office expected de Wet to go in person and they disagreed afterwards as to whether he was justified in merely sending a messenger. One official excused him as being 'an elderly man in feeble health', run off his legs and with a sick wife; another insisted that he should have gone himself in such a crisis even if his wife was on her death-bed! (Colonial Office, 417/177, p. 630.)

Pretoria. The 'surprise attack' on his citadel was in its own way as great a fiasco as the Raid itself. Indeed, it was a key part of the total Rhodes plan, and as such met with the same fate as the rest of it. The Pretoria assault force, disguised as prospectors, beat a hasty retreat as soon as they heard that the Johannesburg revolution was off. But in the end Kruger was fortunate in having to face Jameson's artillery with mere rifles. It helped to impress upon the world the courage of the lightly armed Boers against criminals equipped with the most modern weapons. (In Johannesburg the reformers were proudly exhibiting their three maxims in the Rand Club, while the jubilant populace had mistaken a large iron pipe, travelling through the streets under a tarpaulin, for a cannon. Hays Hammond afterwards said that the pipe was a deliberate ruse to frighten the Boers.)

Unhindered by Boer artillery, Jameson penetrated much further into enemy territory than seemed compatible with eventual defeat. This did him no good. It gave his staff officers more opportunities to make mistakes, the reformers more chances for kaleidoscopic changes of mood, and everyone more scope for misunderstandings and recriminations. Probably Chamberlain himself was one of the few who gained something from the fact that Jameson was so long at large. His firm opposition to the expedition throughout days and nights of rumour, hope, excitement and uncertainty, fixed his impeccable attitude in the minds of friends and enemies alike, in a way that a brief denunciation and swift defeat of the raiders would have made impossible.

It was the Boers' tactics to be content with light skirmishes until they could lure the raiders into a position where their famous guns would be ineffective. Jameson did not suspect this danger, but he did know that his force was in poor trim. The answer seemed to be to press on faster than ever.

Jameson was now riding over the open veldt again, a few miles short of Krugersdorp – on the last lap. Two more messengers met him, this time from the reformers. Rowland and Celliers by name, they were members of the Johannesburg cyclist corps. Though their news was not entirely satisfactory it was better than the 'Sit still' telegrams which the reformers had sent him before he started. So Jameson took heart and put the best possible interpretation on the three notes handed to him by the dispatch riders, an interpretation which the reformers angrily challenged after the Raid had ended in fiasco.

The first note was from Dr Wolff, who had not come out to meet Dr Jameson. It informed him that the best route was through Krugersdorp, a fatal piece of advice. The second note, from Frank Rhodes, reported the reformers' armistice with Kruger; not good news. The third, also from Frank Rhodes, seemed to Jameson much better. It signified the reformers' intention to send out a number of men to meet the gallant fellow. Lionel Phillips added an enthusiastic postscript promising to drink the Doctor's health.

The plight in which Jameson found himself when he received the three messages from Johannesburg seems to have led him to exaggerate the promised escort in his own mind into substantial reinforcements. When quarrels broke out after the Raid between the reformers and the raiders, Willoughby insisted that *three hundred* men had been promised by Frank Rhodes. This was fantastic. There were not three hundred men in Johannesburg equipped to ride out and fight.

Jameson wrote a characteristic reply full of jauntiness, under-statement and warmth:

As you may imagine, we are all well pleased by your letter. We have had some fighting and hope to reach Johannesburg tonight, but of course it will depend on the amount of fighting we have. Of course we shall be glad to have 200 men meet us at Krugersdorp, as it will greatly encourage the men, who are in great heart though a bit tired. Love to Sam, Phillips and the rest.

Two hundred men? The reformers swore they had promised no such thing. All they intended to send was a guard of honour to receive the conquering hero and escort him home.

Two of the notes from Johannesburg and also the Doctor's reply suffered a strange fate. It well illustrated the luck that seemed to brighten Kruger's and darken Jameson's path, once the law had been violated. Jameson tore up the three notes after he had read them and scattered the bits on the veldt. Four months later, despite the deluges of the rainy season, many of the pieces were found by the Boers.

The message from Dr Wolff had disappeared completely, but both the ones from Frank Rhodes, though severely mutilated, could be read with the help of the senders' and receivers' recollections of their contents. That was where the trouble began. Frank Rhodes's second note looked like this, when published by the Transvaal Government:

Dear Dr
The rumour of massa . . . Joburg that started yo . . . relief was not tru. We a . . . right . . . feeling intense. We have armed . . . a lot of men. Shall be very glad . . . to see you . . . not in posses . . . town . . . men to . . . fellow.
Yrs ever, F.R.

The gaps could be filled by general agreement until near the end:

The rumour of massacre in Johannesburg that started you to our relief was not true. We are all right, feeling intense. We have armed a lot of men. Shall be very glad to see you. We are not in possession of the town.

The above was the reconstruction of the first part of the message by Lionel Phillips and Frank Rhodes, to which no one took exception. According to them, the conclusion ran:

We will send out some men to meet you. You are a fine fellow.

But over these lines a violent conflict of opinion broke out. Willoughby, supported by White, Grey and Jameson, had no doubt whatever that the ending of the note was in every way more precise and less ambiguous:

I will bring at least [or about] 300 men to meet you at Krugersdorp. You are a gallant fellow.

An exact number to an exact place; and the possible *double entendre* of 'You are a fine fellow' replaced by the indubitably laudatory 'gallant fellow'. That was the raiders' version to which they stuck. Thus a new apple of discord between raiders and reformers was created by the finding of these tattered fragments 'on the veldt-side', while Kruger used them to incriminate the reformers who in the meantime had delivered themselves into his hands.

Jameson's answer to the ill-fated messages from Johannesburg was dictated to Harry White, signed by the Doctor and then concealed in the bicycle frame belonging to one of the dispatch riders. It was never delivered, for the messengers were intercepted on their return journey by the Boers. Frank Rhodes and his friends were therefore unaware that their rescuer would 'of course' be 'glad' to have two hundred men meet him at Krugersdorp. What would have happened if the note had got through and the reformers had grasped the precarious state of Jameson's fortunes? Frank Rhodes might have persuaded the rest of the Committee to let him send out a small reinforcement; or the less valorous members might have persuaded Frank Rhodes to let Jameson know the truth about their intentions before it was too late. This in turn might have saved the raiders from making for Krugersdorp, their fatal error. But among all the possibilities one thing is certain: if the reformers had received Jameson's note there would have been no agreement on what to do about it.

How was it that Jameson's note, hidden in the frame of a bicycle, ever came to light? This was another of those strange strokes of fate. The cyclists Rowland and Celliers, when intercepted, abandoned their machines with the note still in one of them. There they remained for many months. The machines were damaged but the note was preserved until in the course of overhauling the bicycles it was found. In some ways it was just as well for Jameson, for it proved that he had really expected a large number of men to meet him at Krugersdorp.

# 12

# 'Ichabod'

'Right sweet is the marksman's rattle,
    And sweeter the cannon's roar,
But 'tis betterly bad to battle,
    Beleaguered, and one to four,
I can tell you it wasn't a trifle
    To swarm over Krugersdorp glen,
As they plied us with round and rifle,
    And ploughed us, again – and again.'
                            *Jameson's Ride*, Stanza 5

The Boers, on New Year's Day, prepared a perfect ambush for the raiders. It lay in a steep valley three miles from Krugersdorp, with a stream at the bottom, a drift across it, and old mine workings and farm buildings on either side. Manning the further ridge and using all this ready-made cover, they needed no more than rifle fire and their natural genius to make the road into Krugersdorp impassable.

Willoughby had been against attacking Krugersdorp; Jameson insisted. After all, he argued, their friends in Johannesburg had particularly picked that route and directed them to follow it. They were sending out a contingent to join forces with them there. So they rode on towards Krugersdorp, reaching Hind's Stores, the last of the 'Trading Syndicate's' depots, where they found little in the way of food to detain them. They took time only for a short rest and again pushed forward. Even so they were falling more and more behind their schedule for latterly they had had to cut their way through wire fencing on either side of the route.

So far there had been only light skirmishing. The raiders were aware that their enemies had been gradually closing in round them, as their numbers steadily increased. But neither side had yet tried to come to grips. When Harry White's advance guard surprised two hundred Boers, seven miles west of Krugersdorp, the enemy had withdrawn rapidly. Willoughby still hoped that they would get through to Johannesburg with 'no red blood spilt'. He dispatched a message to the Boer Commandant, Cronje, announcing that his intentions were not hostile but that his 'friendly force' would shell the town unless it were allowed through unopposed.* The Boers made no reply. Their answer was to come in the form of rifle fire from their prepared position at the ruined Queen's Mine in the valley.

The road to Krugersdorp led Jameson to the top of a 400-foot incline. From there he looked across at an enemy standing for the first time foursquare against him. It was clear that the Boers had changed their tactics at last. There was to be an end of long-distance pushing and squeezing from flanks and rear. The way forward was firmly barred. But the sight of Boers did not cause Jameson to change his mind about Krugersdorp. The moment had come to challenge their 'marksman's rattle' with the British 'cannon's roar'. The time was four o'clock in the afternoon of New Year's Day.

Willoughby brought out the guns and pounded away at the impregnable positions before him. Not a Boer was killed. Then followed an attempt to storm the ridge. But the marksmen lying in ambush were deadly. In the course of the charge Willoughby lost sixty of his men, killed, wounded and captured. It was now five o'clock. No hope remained of the British ever forcing that drift to be opened, like those over the River Vaal. They must find a way round Krugersdorp to the south, ride all night and slip into Johannesburg at dawn the next day before the Boers could catch them. The much-vaunted guns were at least of some use: they helped to cover the retreat.

But the god Mars whom Willoughby loved now left him. Luck failed; though the carelessness of his own actions at this point was such as to invite disaster. His own angle on the series of dismal events which followed swiftly one after the other is supplied in his account sent from Pretoria gaol to the War Office. Willoughby was able to spin a real tale of woe. The raiders' position, as New Year's Day drew to an end, would be disastrous unless they could quickly find some way round Krugersdorp. What they needed was a guide, and sure enough a guide was there to show them a road leading

---

* Jameson's comrades afterwards praised the Doctor's humanitarian scruples which prevented him from winning an easy victory by blowing up Krugersdorp. (Captain Thatcher, *Illustrated London News*, February 1896.)

'direct to Johannesburg', by-passing Krugersdorp. This guide had apparently been picked up from nowhere and next morning vanished into nothingness. It was said afterwards that he was a Boer agent whom Willoughby in his straits had blindly trusted. Willoughby, however, advanced to the War Office a different explanation for his failure. He had been deceived, so he constantly and bitterly averred, not by the Boers but by his own faithless allies inside Johannesburg. Why, oh why, had they never come out to deliver their deliverer?

Hardly had the raiders started along the guide's chosen road than they heard gun-fire from the direction of Krugersdorp. It was the Boers celebrating the arrival of their long-delayed artillery. They, not Jameson, had at last got telling reinforcements. But Willoughby at once took it to be his comrades from Johannesburg. Dumping his wagons and baggage on the road, he began marching back to meet them. Again he had not gone far before his march was interrupted: not by a strong force of Bettington's Horse, but by the Boers to right, to left and in front. Back he turned for the third time to save his dumped transport, back into the arms of the ubiquitous enemy. For the guide had found him a road leading direct to Commandant Cronje. Save for the protection of their guns it would have been the end already.

Now that the chances of a swift night march had been thus frittered away, the last hope of reaching Johannesburg had gone too. Or, as Willoughby put it, less unkindly to himself: 'Precious moments had been lost in the attempt to effect a junction with our supposed friends.' There was nothing for it but to bivouac for the night, exhausted and hungry as usual, with only muddy water to drink, and now also kept awake by bursts of firing, the scream of a wounded horse or mule and their own miserable thoughts. Two troopers were killed; they were buried with less pomp than the dead at Corunna. Next day a visitor to the battlefield 'was shocked to see the feet of one of these poor fellows sticking out from the heap of earth which his comrades had shovelled over him'. Unable to wait for dawn, Jameson sent off a bugler in the early hours with another message for Johannesburg. But even now he could not bring himself to face the grim truth. 'The Doctor is all right,' ran this exercise in meiosis, 'but he says now he would like some men sent out to meet him.'

'Then we made for the gold-reef city,
    Retreating, but not in rout.
They had called to us "Quick! For pity!"
    And He said, "They will sally out.
They will hear us and come. Who doubts it?"
    But how if they don't, what then?
"Well, worry no more about it,
    But fight to the death, like men."'
                                    *Jameson's Ride*, Stanza 6

The man whom the Poet Laureate had thus referred to with bated breath as a semi-divine 'He', received for answer from the reformers nothing but a slap in the face. It was delivered in the form of a proclamation from the High Commissioner forbidding British subjects to aid the raiders, and a message from the reformers confirming their obedience to this command. The message reached Jameson at eight o'clock in the morning of 2 January. He had now become what he had striven at all costs, even at the cost of forgery, to avoid: an outlaw.

For one brief moment, indeed, it had seemed that Bettington's Horse might deliver the deliverer after all. Frank Rhodes interpreted the Doctor's request for some men to 'meet' him as a natural wish on the raiders' part to enter Johannesburg in style, with a guard of honour. He therefore assembled Bettington's Horse, one hundred strong, in the early hours of 2 January and sent them clattering out of the town. But when the sleepy reformers heard what was being done in their name, they protested violently. Suppose Kruger took this for – insurrection? No escort for an outlaw! Within a short time Bettington's Horse, having made their 'little promenade', were clattering back again into Johannesburg. Jameson's last hope of reinforcements had gone.

Jameson's battered force had been on the road again since 5 A.M., still trying to work round to their elusive goal. The road as usual turned out to be misleading, thanks to another of Willoughby's 'guides'. A running fight proceeded as the raiders were gradually shepherded southwards at right angles to Johannesburg, until at length the moment came for the Boers to let them swing round towards the town, for a last stand at Doornkop. The guide had led them to a steep *kopje* held by Boers, now with *Staats Artillerie*, and entirely dominating the road. There was no way round. In this cul-de-sac the raiders did not give in without a fight. Five of the maxims were fired until they jammed, and the 12-pounder had only half an hour's ammunition left before the white flag went up. Sir John Willoughby described the end:

Surrounded on all sides by the Boers, men and horses wearied out, outnumbered by at least six to one, our friends having failed to keep their promises to meet us, and my force reduced numerically by one-fourth, I no longer considered that I was justified in sacrificing any more of the lives of the men under me.

He had sacrificed seventeen killed, thirty-five missing and fifty-five wounded, among the officers being Raleigh Grey, Coventry and Cazalet. On the margin of the soldier's apologia appears a withering epilogue added by one of the intended beneficiaries of all this heroism:

*Marginal Comment by a Member of the Reform Committee*
Wonderfully considerate! Seeing how they deliberately risked the lives of thousands in Johannesburg when they started.

The Poet Laureate, however, persisted in seeing everything from noble start to tragic finish, in a light that Willoughby would thoroughly approve when he read the seventh stanza of the famous ballad:

> 'Not a soul had supped or slumbered
>    Since the Borderland stream was cleft;
> But we fought, ever more outnumbered,
>    Till we had not a cartridge left.
> We're not very soft or tender,
>    Or given to weep for woe,
> But it breaks one to have to render
>    One's sword to the strongest foe.'
>                    *Jameson's Ride*, Stanza 7

Jameson, in the presence of three Boer commandants, Cronje, Malan and Potgieter, and an interpreter, 'rendered his sword' at Doornkop where he had made the last stand. According to Cronje he was trembling 'like a reed',[1] but he had spirit left to sweep off his hat as he pronounced the words of surrender in English: 'I accept your terms.' He stood among broken men, some wounded, some weeping for woe as the poet said.

Crowds flocked out from Johannesburg now that it was too late. They found Jameson exhausted in body, but still strong in heart. He and his men had fasted for a night and a day. The Boers gave them food, tended their wounded and buried their dead. By the morning of 3 January Jameson and his officers were all shut up in Pretoria gaol. Less than three weeks later Kruger handed them over to the British Government on the Natal border to be shipped back to England and the Bow Street police court. Incongruously their ship was named *Victoria*.

*The Westminster Gazette* published a fitting commentary on this ignominious end to the great conspiracy. It was a cartoon entitled 'Retreat from Johannesburg' showing Rhodes on horseback in a cocked hat with hunched shoulders and all the signs of Napoleonic defeat. Behind him, unattainable, lay no golden cupolas but the unlovely gear and chimneys of a mining-camp.

Edmund Garrett, ardent editor of the *Cape Times* and co-author of *The Story of an African Crisis*, showed himself a true son of his age when he professed to find peculiar bathos, symbolic of the whole Raid, in one 'grotesque fact' attendant on the surrender. 'The white flag', wrote Garrett, 'used on this occasion was not, as a matter of fact, a torn shirt plucked from a weary trooper, but was the white apron of an old Hottentot "tanta" who was standing somewhere at hand on the farm when it was borrowed from her to be waved as an emblem of peace.' So low had the white man sunk . . .

But perhaps the best parody of the Raid was furnished unconsciously by a popular broadsheet romance entitled '*Pals*': *The Heroine of Krugersdorp*. It is Christmas week, Johannesburg. The town is in a state of insane excitement. Pals, a little artiste, has been left behind in the Empire Theatre whence all but she have fled, some by cart, some by train, the men who try to board the trains being shot dead on the spot. One of the reformers, Mr Joel, attempts to escape in an egg-box but is discovered by a station porter on the platform and sent to prison. The news of the Doctor's surrender reaches Pals. She is determined to go to Krugersdorp and nurse the wounded. But on the way to the hospital Pals has a sickening encounter. A Boer stops her and asks, 'What colour is the English flag?' 'Don't you know?' exclaims Pals, 'it is red, white and blue.' 'Oh no,' retorts the callous Boer. 'I have seen it twice: at Majuba and Doornkop. It is a dirty white rag.' In South Africa after the Raid many versions circulated of this story about the British flag. It was always a favourite.

The picture of Rhodes, when he heard the news of Jameson's capture, is sufficiently macabre. No one who saw it ever forgot the dreadful collapsed face in the Cape cart that carried him home from Government House; or the high falsetto voice rising to meet the moment of truth with a ghastly screech: 'Well, it is a little history being made; that is all.'

# 13

# The Kaiser's Telegram

'I suppose we were wrong, were madmen,
    Still I think at the Judgement Day,
When God sifts the good from the bad men,
    There'll be something more to say.
We were wrong, but we aren't half sorry,
    And, as one of the baffled band,
I would rather have had that foray
    Than the crushings of all the Rand.'

*Jameson's Ride*, Stanza 8

The news of Jameson's defeat plunged the nation into gloom. In a letter to a friend written on 2 January the Prince of Wales spoke for the country: 'The accounts from the Transvaal have been an unpleasant New Year's card! Matters look grave and our position is quite unfortunate.' The twenty-one-year-old Winston Churchill was shocked to see the Conservative Government acting so 'timidly' in the crisis: he felt that Dr Jameson's brave officers, many of them personal friends of his family, were rightly out to 'avenge Majuba'. Mrs Moberly Bell, wife of the manager of *The Times*, recorded in her diary that her husband had gone to the office on Tuesday, before he knew of the Raid, 'very depressed'; when he heard that Jameson had gone in he returned home very happy. That was two days before: how black would be his gloom now? In far off Rhodesia the Volunteers had been waiting since Christmas Day for the word to march. They had no idea where the Doctor intended to lead them, but they were all agog to follow him somewhere. The news of his defeat caused them to curse the reformers and this ominous beginning of the year 1896.

When the people of Britain woke up on 3 January one thought occupied every mind: the colossal folly, fiasco or misfortune, according to whichever way you looked at it, of Jameson's ride. But when they went to bed that night another event had occurred which swept the shock of the Raid clean out of their systems. On the very heels of Jameson's New Year 'card' came another card from the German

Emperor so exceedingly unpleasant that, like the bitterest medicine, it acted as a tonic. This was the notorious 'Kaiser's telegram' sent to President Kruger on 3 January 1896:

*Berlin.*
I express to you my sincere congratulations that without calling on the aid of friendly Powers you and your people, by your own energy against the armed bands which have broken into your country as disturbers of the peace, have succeeded in re-establishing peace, and defending the independence of the country against attacks from without.

*William I. R.*

With modesty and piety Kruger rendered thanks:

I express to your Majesty my deepest gratitude for Your Majesty's congratulations. With God's help we hope to continue to do everything possible for the existence of the Republic.

In little more than fifty words the Kaiser managed to do what no British statesman could have hoped to achieve after ten times the effort. He rallied the whole nation. What was more, he created an uproar in which Jameson was either deified or forgotten. Two phrases of the telegram in particular brought to England's mortified pride the caustic cure of anger. First came the implication that Kruger might have appealed over the head of Britain, the suzerain state, to outside 'friendly Powers'. Second, suzerainty itself was challenged in the brazen assertion of Transvaal 'independence'.

With a cry of 'Hands off Africa!' an abashed jingoism found its voice again. The Tory *Saturday Review* boomed in sonorous Latin that Germany must be blotted out, while the Liberal papers joined in expressing the shock felt by the whole nation. Lord Derby had once called the Kaiser 'an energetic young savage'. Now he had run amok. Abusive letters descended upon the Kaiser, forming a violent postscript to the tactfully upbraiding message he at once received from Queen Victoria:

My Dear William
. . . I must now also touch upon a subject which causes me much pain and astonishment. It is the Telegram . . . which is considered very unfriendly towards this country, not that you intended it as such I am sure – but I grieve to say it has made a most unfortunate impression here.

The action of Dr Jameson was, of course, very wrong and unwarranted, but . . . I think it would have been far better to have said nothing. . . .*

To this kindest of rebukes the Kaiser at once returned an apology both barbed and crawling:

Most beloved Grandmamma
Never was the Telegram intended as a step against England or your Government. [I thought the raiders were] a mixed mob of gold-diggers . . . the scum of all nations, never suspecting that there were real Englishmen or Officers among them . . . I was standing up for law, order and obedience to a Sovereign whom I revere and adore.

Kruger's comment on these emotional exchanges, made to the German Consul, was tart: 'The old woman just sneezed and you ran away.' But despite William's filial climb-down, the effect of his telegram remained. Throughout the tortuous sequel to the Raid it was this telegram and the exaggerated fears it generated which helped to drive so many statesmen, otherwise bitter enemies, into drawing together for the defence of the realm. In the course of their collaboration they were led to suppress another set of telegrams as notorious as the Kaiser's own.

Cecil Rhodes himself has perhaps summed up most vividly the dual effect of the whole episode. In a conversation with the Emperor three years after the Raid he said: 'You see, I was a naughty boy, and you tried to whip me. Now my people were quite ready to whip me for being a naughty boy, but directly *you* did it, they said, "No, if this is anybody's business, it is *ours*." The result was that Your Majesty got yourself very much disliked by the English people, and I never got whipped at all!'

On 4 January 1896, after the publication of the telegram, Chamberlain began a letter to the Prime Minister with the irony of one who claimed to understand crowd psychology:

My dear Salisbury,
I think what is called an 'Act of Vigour' is required to soothe the wounded

---

* *Punch* printed a parody of this epistle on 18 January:

'Mein lieber Willy: Dies ist aber uber alle Berge. . . .Was bedeudet eigentlich deine Depesche an den alten KRUGER der für Dich doesn't care twopence? . . .
So lange! Don't be foolish any more. Deine Dich liebende
                                                                Grandmamma'

vanity of the nation. It does not matter which of our numerous foes we defy, but we ought to defy someone . . .

The letter ended with an interesting postscript: 'Telegrams this morning say Johannesburg *grateful* to the Boers for their moderation. 500 prisoners 70 dead and some 20 wounded.' Two days later he sent Kruger a vivid warning: 'The President would find that the little finger of Germany is thicker than England's loins.'

Part of Chamberlain's 'Act of Vigour' consisted in the strengthening of British naval and military defences. This seemed to give force to a widespread view, gradually taking shape, that the menace of German aggression was at the bottom of the Raid. To many people, Jameson had simply gone in before the Germans: it was an amply justified act of preventive warfare. When Rhodes said in England that he longed to go down to Trafalgar Square and proclaim from a soap-box the true motive of the Raid, his friends assumed he would shout: 'To keep Germany out!'

People suddenly noticed significant omens. A German warship, for instance, was kept sweltering for months off the pestilential coast of Delagoa Bay. Why? As if to give colour to these intuitions, a cartoon appeared in the German press on 24 January of Kruger dressed like a farmer standing on guard before a flock of sheep, having whipped off a lion. Beneath ran the caption: 'Heil Kruger!'

Even Jan Hendrik Hofmeyr, leader of the Dutch 'Bond' in the Cape Parliament, was almost brought back into the fold by the Kaiser's telegram. Deeply shocked by the Raid he had declared, 'I am no longer pulled both ways (towards the Dutch and English); Jameson has decided me.' But when the news of the Kaiser's intervention reached him he wrote to the *Cape Argus*: 'The first German shot fired against England would be likely to be followed by . . . the acquisition by England of all German colonies . . . which would not be an unmixed evil for the Cape.'[1]

This feeling, however, did not prevent Hofmeyr, nicknamed 'The Mole', from cabling Chamberlain to demand a full inquiry into the circumstances of the Raid. On 7 January Chamberlain cabled back his assent. Little did the Colonial Secretary realize what an important step he had taken. He did not suspect one tenth of the compromising material with which the Committee of Inquiry, himself among them, would have to deal. The High Commissioner knew more of what lay in store for the representatives of imperial authority. Nevertheless, when Hofmeyr informed him of the demand for an inquiry, Sir Hercules Robinson replied: 'Chamberlain will deny everything. He has lots of pluck. He will call on those darned fellows to prove it.'[2]

Amidst the general clamour and closing of the ranks against the supposed designs of the German Emperor, Blunt's was a dissentient voice. With delight he noted in his diary on 9 January: 'We have now managed in the last six months to quarrel violently with China, Turkey, Belgium, Ashanti, France, Venezuela, America and Germany. This is a record performance, and if it does not break up the British Empire nothing will.'

The reaction of France to the Raid may be taken as typical of European opinion. A ceremonial sword was presented to President Kruger. It was adorned with a Boer throttling the imperial lion. This, despite the fact that the lion, in the person of Joseph Chamberlain, had emphatically repudiated Jameson; while the incriminating documents inside Bobby White's box had not yet been published. Well might Chamberlain say in the House of Commons four years later, that certain sections of opinion both at home and abroad had very early made up their minds about imperial collusion and no amount of inquiries would change them. This, of course, did not necessarily mean that they were altogether wrong.

To Chamberlain himself the news of Jameson's capture brought release from the worst tribulation he ever knew as a minister. Throughout the agonizing period of waiting his family were separated from him. He was in London, his wife in Birmingham. His officials at the Colonial Office had nothing to report but rumours from abroad and rudeness at home. What would happen if Jameson got through and made Britain a free gift of the Rand? Exultant jingoism would certainly have no use for the game-keeper who had refused to turn poacher. Even if the Cabinet stuck to him, as indeed they must, what policy could he now recommend towards Jameson? No longer Jameson the filibuster, but Jameson the empire-builder. It is hard to forgive failure. It is harder not to forgive success.

Yet how could he condone an act he had so roundly denounced? Resignation. It was not surprising that his three-day ordeal of waiting for news reached a climax with one of his shattering headaches, a malady to which he was subject. '*Post Chamberlain*', wrote *Punch* with penetration, '*sedet atra cura*,' and offered these words to the Colonial Secretary as a new motto. But the family motto which he himself had chosen as a young man proved more appropriate in the end: '*Je tiens ferme.*' To him, lying in a darkened room of the lonely house at Prince's Gate, the Permanent Secretary, Sir Robert Meade, brought the news that Jameson had failed.

By midnight Chamberlain was sufficiently recovered from his attack to write to his wife. The letter contained a dig at his enemies, the jingo newspapers. Such a reaction was irresistible to so robust a fighter; but Chamberlain expressed it in phraseology well calculated to provoke the Olympians. 'They (the jingoes) have been waiting to jump on me,' he wrote. 'I think I have great cause to congratulate myself that I stood firm and separated myself from what was a disgraceful exhibition of filibustering. My messengers met Jameson and he refused to turn back – so this is the end.'[3]

Chamberlain could now listen with comparative equanimity to the angry backwash of argument over the Raid. That tumult, he was sure, would gradually recede, leaving him in serene command. The jingoes, for instance, were still chanting bravely. Let them. Among them was Alfred Austin, the new Poet Laureate, who had been chosen because William Morris refused and the Queen would not have Swinburne; or, as Lord Salisbury said, 'for the best possible reason, because he wanted it'.[4] Austin made his debut in *The Times* with the set of verses pointedly entitled *Jameson's Ride*, which provide such a matchless running commentary on the raiders' exploits. Curiously enough, on the very day that *The Times* published this ballad, 11 January 1896, *Punch* issued a ceremonious request to 'Alfred, monarch of minor poets' for 'an appropriate song, impromptu and to be sung immediately'. Alfred, miraculously, had already obliged.

Wilfrid Blunt charitably called *Jameson's Ride* 'spirited doggerel'. He had a soft spot for Austin, that 'absurd little cock-sparrow of a man'. But towards Jameson, Blunt was ruthless. His diary for 5 January runs: 'There is excellent news. Those blackguards of the Chartered Company in South Africa, under Doctor Jameson, have made a filibustering raid on the Transvaal and have been annihilated by the Boers, Jameson a prisoner. I devoutly hope he may be hanged.' Even Arthur Balfour, Leader of the House of Commons, shocked his sister by saying that though Jameson's character was the only attractive feature in the whole matter, 'he ought to be hung' all the same.[5]

Thus in England the turmoil of conflicting emotions could only find issue in words: words frothy, judicial or passionate. In South Africa the chosen people were able to take the path of action.

# 14

## *Prisoners in Pretoria*

Kruger had no need to be sorry that he did not hang Jameson. He gained far more from his policy of magnanimity than ever he could have won by Old Testament retribution. In fact, the more merciful Kruger showed himself towards his enemies, the more he seemed to divide them against each other. It was a case of forgive and conquer. After Jameson's capture, the atmosphere in Johannesburg was a mixture of 'Armageddon and a psychopathic ward'.[1] Within a few weeks recriminations were flying about between almost all those concerned in the affair – raiders, reform leaders, the Johannesburg rank and file, the British and Afrikanders in Cape Town, Sir Hercules Robinson and Joseph Chamberlain. Rancour crept into all their exchanges, while Kruger stood above the din, Bible in hand, dispensing Christian charity.

In the circumstances of the surrender itself occurred one of the few mistakes made by the Boers. Willoughby obtained written terms of conditional surrender guaranteeing the raiders' lives from Commandant Cronje on the battlefield. But shortly afterwards Commandant Malan arrived on the scene with the news that General Joubert had already insisted on unconditional surrender. He reprimanded Cronje for speaking out of turn. The Boers held that Jameson was compelled to accept the revised terms, thus making himself and his men candidates for Kruger's mercy and incidentally pawns in Kruger's game against Johannesburg and London. Willoughby, however, seems to have retained in his possession the paper stating Cronje's original terms until it was taken away from him in Pretoria gaol. Each party accused the other of deception. The raiders continued to regard themselves as legally in no danger, conveying this view to Chamberlain.

Chamberlain, acting on that assumption, bombarded Sir Hercules Robinson with telegrams on behalf of the reformers and their claims. But the High Commissioner thought otherwise.

On 9 January Kruger caused to be displayed in Johannesburg a proclamation. It commanded the population to surrender all weapons by six o'clock on the following evening. With the exception of the ringleaders, those who obeyed would be pardoned. This ultimatum was impressively printed in Dutch and English and ended with the solemn words, 'God Save Land & People – *Land en Volk*'. In every way it contrasted strikingly with the reformers' earlier amateurish and untidy notices inviting volunteers to join the defence forces.

Robinson insisted that by accepting Kruger's ultimatum the reformers would be saving the lives of the hostages and saving the country (and himself) a lot of useless trouble. Sir Hercules was certainly unfit to battle with Kruger in an effort to salvage something from the wreckage – Chamberlain's immediate instinct. Robinson disliked and distrusted Chamberlain. He distrusted those dynamic qualities which made him jump ahead into new activity almost before the previous policy had been carried out. Already on 4 January he was telegraphing to Robinson deploring the fact that Kruger's victory might harden him against concessions to the Uitlanders:

If this is the attitude they (the Boers) adopt, they will in my opinion make a great mistake ... I have done everything in my power to undo and to minimize the evil caused by late unwarrantable raid ... and it is not likely that such action will ever be repeated; but the state of things of which complaint has been made cannot continue for ever. ...

Rarely can a High Commissioner have felt a ministerial approach to be so premature. To Robinson's dislike of Chamberlain and disagreement with his judgment must be added the fact that he was a sick man. Seventy years old and disabled with dropsy, he had set out from Cape Town on 4 January to effect a settlement between the reformers, Kruger and Chamberlain, any one of whom might prove irreconcilable. He arrived at Pretoria Station accompanied by his nurse. With difficulty he descended on to the platform and was conveyed to a house a hundred yards from where Jameson and his men lay in gaol. Never once did he visit the prisoners. Not only because of his infirmities but because it was Kruger's wish. The Boers' discussions with Robinson were conducted literally *de haut en bas*. Kruger and his Executive Council sat over a prostrate High Commissioner stretched out beneath them on a sofa. Nor was this a British lion *couchant*, but a poor old man who felt he had no ace up his sleeve, and not even the Almighty on his side to put one there. Hofmeyr had refused to accompany him on his mission from the Cape, a fact that greatly weakened Robinson's hand; while his own Secretary, Sir Graham Bower, was all in favour of making peace with Kruger as quickly as possible. Chamberlain, meanwhile, was offending Kruger further by tactless demands for redress of Uitlander grievances. How could the High Commissioner demand redress for men accused of high treason? He must have felt that Kruger and Chamberlain both had imperious personalities, but while Chamberlain was three thousand miles away, Kruger was there. How dismally Chamberlain's cabled admonitions sounded in the old man's ears. 'It will be your duty to use firm language. . . .' The only firm language poor Robinson felt justified in using was towards his own master. When the Colonial Secretary several times suggested strengthening his position with troops and ships at the Cape, he bluntly told the Minister to mind his own business:

Prospect now very hopeful if no injudicious steps are taken. Please leave matter in my hands.

So Chamberlain was thwarted and Robinson's 'hopeful prospect' duly unfolded, though the High Commissioner, as a matter of fact, had some difficulty in persuading the Uitlanders to throw themselves on Kruger's mercy. Sir Jacobus de Wet, the British Agent in Pretoria, made the first attempt to get Robinson's order carried out. He had no success. In response to his urgent request that the assembled Uitlanders should give up their arms, there were loud shouts of 'Who to?' 'Never!' It was only after the popular Sir Sydney Shippard, urgently summoned, had declared himself to be fervently on their side – 'I, whose heart and soul is with you' – that with mingled cheers and groans they obeyed.

Obviously if anyone was running a risk in thus surrendering, it was the signatories of the 'women and children' letter – Frank Rhodes, George Farrar, Lionel Phillips and John Hays Hammond. They were the special objects of the Boers' hatred: 'a hole drilled through them' was what the burghers were believed to desire. Someone suggested that they should assume disguises and bolt. Frank Rhodes stuck out his legs in characteristic fashion saying he would stay; Farrar agreed, tugging at his moustache. All four remained to stand their trial.

There was an ugly moment during the surrender of arms when Kruger, expecting a torrent instead of a trickle of rifles, ordered a commando to attack Johannesburg. Robinson pacified him, saw the surrender completed and then, lest Chamberlain should be tempted to propose further 'injudicious steps', he hastily bent his own towards Cape Town. His departure narrowly anticipated another telegram from the exasperated Colonial Secretary:

Do not on any account leave Pretoria or make preparations for departure pending further instructions from me which you will receive tomorrow.

But the High Commissioner's preparations were already completed and he had gone.

While the High Commissioner grumbled and the Uitlanders began to feel they had been left in the lurch, Chamberlain's popularity at home once more soared upwards. Booed at the beginning of January, he was adulated at the end. There was a general feeling that he had handled a most perilous situation with masterful coolness. On 21 January he made a confident speech referring to 'sensational occurrences' which pass away leaving not a trace behind. His speech went on to defend Britain's colonial policy:

I have heard it said that we never have had a colonial policy, that we have simply blundered into all the best places in the earth. I admit that we have made mistakes . . . but after all is said this remains – that we alone among the nations of the earth have been able to establish and to maintain Colonies . . . in all parts of the world. This may be a comforting assurance when we think of occasional mistakes. . . .

The moral which the orator drew was not the need to avoid such 'mistakes' in future, but to increase imperial activity: 'Let us cultivate the loyalty of our children throughout the Empire.' He became 'England's Darling', a title borrowed from Alfred Austin's recent poem on King Alfred the Great. The people had liked his defiant attitude to the Kaiser's telegram and now they revelled in the tone of his voice during public speeches when he mentioned 'foreign nations'.

\* \* \*

The disagreements of Chamberlain and Robinson were paralleled by strained relations between the raiders and reformers. As prisoners of the Boers, the raiders had marched off gallantly enough into Pretoria gaol singing, 'After the ball is over . . .' But their mood soon changed. The officers believed the Uitlanders had left them in the lurch. On the cell wall at Pretoria one of them wrote out the couplet begun by Essex and completed by Elizabeth I in the Tower of London:

> – I fain would climb, but I fear to fall;
> – If thy heart fail thee, climb not at all.

It was the Uitlanders who had wished to climb but whose hearts had failed, landing their allies where they now found themselves. At the Cape also people showed where their sympathies lay. A petition was signed by thousands for presentation to the High Commissioner on his return from Pretoria. The petitioners declared that they 'had rather the Uitlanders went voteless for ever than that a hair of Jameson's head should be touched'.

The Uitlanders had their own grudges, some stored up, some fresh. When the news of Jameson's invasion first came through they had cursed Chamberlain, the Government and Rhodes for the 'damnable and unscrupulous use made of our grievances to further Rhodes's schemes. . . . It is a cruel and wicked policy to split us all up again, to divide us by race hatred and to make South Africa a hell of fighting devils.'[2] But as soon as Chamberlain's proclamation repudiating Jameson was heard by the leaders, incongruously the Colonial Secretary was cursed again. Later, with yet another switch, they felt Jameson's defeat was a good thing because it prevented bloodshed. 'Had he got here,' said the secretary of the Reform Committee, 'there would have been the devil to pay.' Then, to their intense indignation, despite Jameson's capture and their own surrender to Kruger's ultimatum, the devil was still to pay, and almost entirely by themselves, though Beit and Rhodes raised the hard cash. Their own naïveté had furnished Kruger with the names of the sixty-four ringleaders. But Major Robert White's gratuitous statement while in prison that the copy of the 'women and children' letter of invitation found in his dispatch case was genuine, saddled its signatories with additional guilt and punishment. So they cursed Bobby White too.

It is not easy to assess Kruger's own attitude. Of course, there were times when human nature asserted itself. Who could resist occasionally playing off the demands of some of the more excitable Boers for condign punishment against the Uitlanders' pleas for redress? At one moment Kruger would assure the High Commissioner that his Boers were straining at the leash, and it would be more than his position was worth to make concessions; at another that they were, as always, under perfect control.

The verdict of Sir Graham Bower, however, was that 'Kruger behaved throughout like a chivalrous gentleman',[3] his only serious error being the arrest of the sixty-four. Bower added that 'John Bull was generous and ashamed and was prepared to do things handsomely, short of cancelling Article IV of the London Convention'. (This was the Article by which England retained, however tenuously, her suzerainty over the Transvaal.) But imprisoning these leaders was trying John Bull almost as hard as if Kruger had challenged the Convention. However generous he was feeling, John Bull could not afford to see so much solid wealth treated with the ignominy reserved for common felons. The reform leaders, said Bower, 'represented forty million sterling'. Moreover, 'they were hospitable, cultivated, popular men . . . the most popular men in Johannesburg'.[4] It was a sign of Kruger's untutored ignorance that he treated such expensive material so roughly.

There was no doubt, also, that Kruger succumbed to deplorable theatricality, particularly over the reformers' trial and sentences. After more than three and a half exceptionally disagreeable months in prison, the four signatories of the letter and Fitzpatrick (replacing Leonard) were brought before Judge Gregorowski. They were led into the dock, a black box, by warders dressed in black like undertakers. Gregorowski was built up locally into a minor Judge Jeffreys. It was widely believed that he had been imported from the Free State because he was particularly anxious to try 'those reformers; he would give them what for'. Rumour had it that he several times attempted to borrow a black cap from colleagues, and after he passed sentence of death on the leaders his face kept breaking into smiles. Dr Leyds, the Transvaal State Secretary and another Mephistophelian type in the eyes of the reformers, was believed to be smiling too, until a month later an anonymous letter decorated with a skull and crossbones wiped the smile from his face and made him take to his bed.*

Worst of all, there was a scare that the leaders were to be lynched. Commandant Henning Pretorius, encouraged by a Boer newspaper, brought to Pretoria part of the gallows from Slachter's Nek, where in 1831 five Boers were hanged by the British for rebellion. Though Pretorius later said he intended it for the National Museum, the reformers felt sure its original destination had been the public square. When the 'Museum' explanation reached the Colonial Office, Fred Graham minuted that the gallows would not be an attraction in 'a Boer show', to which Edward Fairfield, the agreeably facetious African expert, retorted, 'unless they have a Chamber of Horrors'.[5]

After advising all women to leave the court, Gregorowski passed sentence of death upon the leaders. 'Good God!' exclaimed Rhodes when he heard the news. 'Surely Kruger wouldn't dare to do a thing like that.' It was commuted after a painful interval of twenty-four hours. This was the first of a series of 'cat-and-mouse' acts, felt to be directed by Kruger against the prisoners' morale. His genuinely humane instincts deteriorated every so often into what came to be called 'magnanimity by inches'.

The rest of the reformers were sentenced to two years' imprisonment and a fine of £2,000 each, together with banishment for three years after release. Barney Barnato, the colourful cockney mining magnate whose young nephew, Solly Joel, was among the prisoners, met the judge after the trial at the Pretoria Club and denounced him. 'You are no gentleman, Mr Barnato!' shouted the judge in Afrikaans. 'You are no judge, Mr Gregorowski!' Barney shouted back in English.

On 20 May, after a tragedy in the gaol, Kruger took another step along the path of mercy. (Fred Grey, father of six children, had borrowed a razor, sat in the closet with it for half an hour and then committed suicide. The press carried piteous appeals for better

---

* On 3 June *The Cape Times* portrayed Kruger as a top-hatted bearded patriarch, with an enormous *New Testament* in front of him, saying 'Isn't there a text somewhere about forgiving one's enemies?' Behind him the horned figure of Dr Leyds, wearing a German decoration, answers: 'No, No, President! Don't turn to the New Testament – Stick to the Old! No mawkish texts about forgiveness there!'

treatment from the other prisoners – 'old, delicate, unhinged as some of us are'.) The leaders were sentenced to fifteen years' imprisonment, but eight prisoners were released at once on payment of their fines and the remainder given sentences of up to one year, provided fines were paid and, of course, humble petitions renewed.

Kruger, however, now received more petitions than he bargained for. Among other personal visits, he received one from Barnato, clad all in black and threatening to close his mines within a fortnight. So more mercy was shown. All except the leaders were offered immediate release, on payment of fines and acceptance of a three-year ban on politics. Protests on behalf of the leaders thereupon swelled to monster proportions, including a deputation of fifty mayors and torrents of telegrams, cables and letters.

Kruger sought advice elsewhere. Opening 'the Book', he discovered it was time for yet another advance in clemency. Their sentences were remitted once again. On payment of the enormous sums of £25,000 each, they were at last released on 11 June. But there was to be no more opportunity of political leadership for the signatories of the 'women and children' letter. They were offered a choice of a fifteen-year ban on politics or banishment. All except Frank Rhodes were thankful to choose the ban. He chose exile. His bearing throughout the trial, said Sir James Rose Innes, observer for the British Government, had been 'very manly'. He was escorted over the border that evening. Farrar came out cursing Jameson as a 'cad'.

Only two of the reformers obstinately refused to avail themselves of Kruger's softer moods. They were Aubrey Wools Sampson and Walter D. ('Karri') Davis. Rather than humble their pride, as they put it, before the hated Boer, and beg or pay for mercy, they stayed in 'tronk' for another whole year until Kruger made a gift of their unconditional release to 'Ou Ma' on the occasion of her Diamond Jubilee. Upon discharge, Wools Sampson wrote to Rhodes for a job, adding in a postscript, 'Nothing shady of course'. Karri Davis became one of the most popular men in Johannesburg. Their joint defiance was considered the highest manifestation of Uitlander solidarity. (The Colonial Office, however, privately dubbed the heroic pair 'two headstrong young men' with 'patriotism in excess of their country's demands'.)

The lowest behaviour was attributed to Dr Wolff, who organized the 'Trading Syndicate', and to Charles Leonard, who drafted the 'women and children' letter. Both these professional men escaped extradition and fled ignominiously from the Cape, the former under a false name and the latter under false pretences. Wolff was sharp enough to slip through the round-up of leaders in Johannesburg and reach Cape Town. Leonard was lucky enough to be in Cape Town already, where, after the Raid, he developed symptoms of 'nervous prostration' like poor Beit,* but complicated in Leonard's case by 'congestion of the brain'. This served him with an excuse for not returning at once to face the music in Pretoria. The excuse he later found for travelling to England when he was fit, instead of to the Transvaal, was that duty called him to put the reformers' case to the Committee of Inquiry. He made little impression, however, on the Committee and the prisoners of Pretoria never forgave their rather too plausible Chairman.†

Taken all round, it was not so much Kruger's behaviour as the appalling conditions in Pretoria gaol which were responsible for most of the prisoners' sufferings. It has been urged in extenuation that this gaol could not properly accommodate the large number of gentlemen prisoners suddenly thrust into it. But it is clear that the prison conditions were no more fit for the normal prison population of black and white offenders than for the inrush of 'gentlemen'.

The cells were at all times filthy and ill-ventilated, crawling with vermin. The prisoners were not denied food; as Edmund Garrett put it, 'they were to eat, and to be eaten'. They slept on the floor and washed in the yard from a trickle of water that ran away down an open gutter. A few feet away from this leaky channel stood the urinals, three closets and six buckets between the two hundred and fifty prisoners, black and white. Sometimes they were emptied only once in four days. In a temperature of 105 degrees in the shade, restless and miserable, the Americans played marbles, the English

---

* See p. 224 below.

† Sir Thomas Upington tried to get Leonard extradited from Spain and Portugal on his way home, behaviour which Fairfield characterized as that of an 'ill-conditioned fellow'; though he admitted that 'there *was* something very mean about (Leonard's) running away'. (C.O. 417/181,8401.)

walked round the compound. Yet it is clear that what the reformers went through was an example of Boer backwardness rather than vindictiveness. Writing in 1899 Fitzpatrick remarked that these conditions 'prevail still in Pretoria gaol',[6] long after the last 'gentleman' had been released. Kruger had no Elizabeth Fry among his burghers. Small wonder, since he did not believe in women doing public work. Their natures, he said, were already far too haughty.

The reformers felt that Kruger's demonstrations with his Bible were pharisaical. Oom Paul was an adept at throwing the lions to the Christians. He was inclined to show clemency only in response to mammoth petitions. When Chamberlain intervened on their behalf, as he constantly did, Kruger deliberately postponed his acts of mercy. After they were released it was intimated that a pilgrimage of thanks to the President would be appropriate. Those who agreed were treated at the interview to another of Kruger's parables: 'You must know that I sometimes have to punish my dogs, and I find there are dogs of two kinds. Some of them who are good come back and lick my boots. Others get away at a distance and snarl at me. I see that some are still snarling. I am glad that you are not like them.' Fortunately not all of the pilgrims understood his remarks, and Kruger had the grace to waive a translation.

Some hard thoughts among the Uitlanders were natural. But at other moments the reformers recognized the essential generosity of the Boers' behaviour. If all aggressors fared no worse than Jameson and his comrades fared at the hands of the burghers, the history of the world would be a happier one. Even in his 'magnanimity by inches' Kruger was falling short of a standard at which many statesmen would not have aimed. By the year 1897 there was not a single reformer left in prison. No doubt his treasury was enriched by thousands of pounds' worth of fines imposed on the prisoners. But why not? They were not John Balls or Jack Cades, these revolutionaries: their great wealth was responsible for much of the trouble. Kruger even granted one concession of the kind Chamberlain constantly urged, and Robinson considered it would be 'ineffectual and impolitic' to mention. On 10 January, while the last of the reform leaders were being rounded up, Kruger promised municipal government to Johannesburg, embellishing his proclamations with the usual theatrical touches:

I ask you earnestly, with your hand on your heart, to answer me this question: Dare I, and should I, after all that has happened, propose such a thing to the Volksraad? . . . Inhabitants of Johannesburg, make it possible for the Government to appear before the Volksraad with the motto, 'Forget and Forgive'.

About the same time, the imprisoned raiders had tried to get a message out to their friends. It cost them a bribe of £25, the same sum that *Jameson's Ride* cost *The Times*, and the note was smuggled out inside a matchbox. In its small way it was yet another tribute to Kruger, for the message amounted to an admission that they were 'all right'. Even when the days dragged into weary weeks, most of the prisoners were still all right, enlivened by visits from their wives with roasted poultry smuggled in their bustles. Mark Twain, permitted to break a lecture tour to visit them, coined a happy phrase to describe their incarceration – 'A rest cure for tired businessmen' – and raised the spirits of his fellow-countryman, Hays Hammond, with the following dialogue:

*Hammond:* How did you ever find your way into this Godforsaken hole?
*Mark Twain:* Getting into gaol is easy. I thought the difficulties arose when it came to getting out.

Thanked by Chamberlain, praised however grudgingly by the reformers, felicitated by the outside world, Kruger's star rode high at the beginning of 1896. So did Chamberlain's. His name was the one most on foreign lips, his future the one to be watched. *Punch*, on 18 January, celebrated the magnitude of his triumph in verses entitled *The Pilot that Weathered the Storm*:

> When wonder and doubt in the hearts of us reigned,
>     When a semi-piratical flag was unfurled,
> He the honour and faith of our country maintained,
>     And set us all right in the sight of the world.

But inside *de trommel van Bobby White* lay startling new facts which were to throw doubt on the strength of Chamberlain's position. A hint of what lay in store had already been given in one of the acrimonious telegrams sent to the Colonial Secretary by Sir Hercules Robinson. There was a rumour, he said, that the Transvaal Government had 'written evidence of a long-standing and wide-

spread conspiracy' to seize the country and forcibly incorporate it
with that of the British South Africa Company.

Chamberlain replied with a curt reference to this 'supposed plot'
and renewed exhortations to Sir Hercules to press the Uitlanders'
claims. But the ground was about to open beneath him. Gone were
the first breathless days of the invasion when a newspaper headline
could sum up the whole thing as 'One Man's Madness'. It was soon
to be proved 'a wide-spread conspiracy'. The next question would
be, how wide?

# 15

## *Trial of the Raiders*

On the day of defeat Bobby White's *trommel* had accidentally
tumbled off Willoughby's cart somewhere outside Krugersdorp. The
Boers picked it up. From that moment it was only a question of time
before the next storm broke. There was a loud detonation on 29
April. Kruger published a first instalment of White's documents. A
month later the evidence piled up further. A full report of the
reformers' trial and all White's papers, gathered together in the
Transvaal Green book, burst upon the world. Not only Jameson but
Rhodes also stood exposed and condemned. The British Government were under a powerful blast of suspicion. Then there was a lull
until 17 July when the Cape Parliament published its own report on
the Raid in a Blue book. It made the pattern of conspiracy clearer
still so far as Rhodes and his associates were concerned, despite the
fact that many of them, including the master-mind himself, contrived to be absent and so avoided giving evidence. (Rhodes was in
'his North', putting down the Matabele rebellion with a riding-
crop.) But for a moment the tide of suspicion lapping round
Chamberlain crept no higher. In the Cape Blue book no references
were made to imperial collusion.

The last stages in the process of enlightenment were approaching:
the trial of Dr Jameson and his officers and the British Government's Committee of Inquiry. Jameson's trial would be the first
opportunity for revelations to be made – or suppressed – on British
soil. How would the Government handle this curtain-raiser to its
grand Inquiry? Jameson might keep dark the cables and forget the
speeches delivered on the parade ground. But if he chose to recollect
his words, the Government would have to make him eat them. How
much better if nothing were said of the awkward fact that most of the
raiders believed they were soldiers of the Queen.

The trial opened on 20 July, just three days after the Cape Blue book
was published. Immense concern for the fate of Jameson and his

officers was felt throughout the country, especially in the highest reaches of society. Before the trial many people hoped that a favourable verdict might somehow be obtained. While on bail, Willoughby visited his old friends the Randolph Churchills. Lady Randolph, astutely deciding that the Raid must be treated as a nine days' wonder rather than a far-reaching catastrophe, invited 'honest John' Morley to meet Johnny Willoughby at luncheon. They arrived before their hostess was ready and proceeded to show how far the emotions aroused by the Raid had invaded private relationships. Morley refused to shake hands but made 'a stiff little bow' while Willoughby 'stared unconcernedly without acknowledging it'.[1]

Jameson's counsel were the best in the land, Sir Edward Clarke and Edward Carson.

But Clarke found himself forcibly prevented from defending his clients in the only way which might have saved them from prison. Having been shown certain secret cables sent between Jameson, Rhodes and Harris, he was forbidden by Jameson's solicitor, Bouchier Hawksley (who was also Rhodes's), to use them in a manner that might compromise the British Government. Hawksley was as loth to give as Clarke to receive these instructions. Their clients were adamant.

Thus without once referring to the hidden cables Clarke had to do his best for Jameson. And a very good best it was. Flora Shaw, who felt almost as badly about the trial as Clarke himself, described his defence as 'very clever'. But it could be based on nothing more substantial than ingenious interpretations of the law, which the judge rightly rejected, and glowing tributes to the virtues of his clients. (They were 'men of honour and repute, loyalty and high character'.) Miss Shaw was extremely indignant about the judge's line, accusing him to her friends of having 'enjoyed' convicting the prisoners.[2] Even her chief support, C. M. Bell of *The Times*, helped to put her on edge, for instead of concentrating on the trial he was being 'odiously tiresome', absorbed in his own family affairs.

Throughout the trial the newspapers were full of reports of the Matabele rising in Rhodesia; reports written from Bulawayo or a 'Fort near the Matopos'. Somehow these addresses sounded nearer to the centre of reality than the Law Courts, and the reports helped to increase public sympathy with Jameson. Unlike the white settlers of Johannesburg, the half-starved black peoples, their cattle ravaged by *rinderpest*, were only too ready to make their rising – as soon as the formidable Doctor was off the scene. As one journalist put it bitterly, Jameson should have been out there restoring law and order, instead of eating his heart out in Holloway prison. That journalist spoke for a large proportion of the British public.

Dr Jim was given a trial-at-bar before a special jury. The Lord Chief Justice, Lord Russell of Killowen, sat with Mr Baron Pollock and Mr Justice Hawkins of the Queen's Bench. The Attorney-General, Sir Richard Webster, appeared for the Crown, together with the Solicitor-General, Sir R. B. Finlay, and four junior counsel. It was a portentous affair, the special procedure underlining its unusual nature. Even the indictment, which contained twelve counts, was unusual. The defendants were charged under the Foreign Enlistment Act of 1870 with preparing 'a military expedition' against 'a friendly state'. There had been only one other similar case, in 1887, when the punishment was a fine of £500 and one month's imprisonment. Why all this rare and formidable paraphernalia for Dr Jim?

The answer was generally assumed to be simple – in order that he should not get off. But despite the Government's precautions it seemed at one moment that even a special jury might be difficult. They tried to evade a straight verdict of 'guilty' by taking into account the 'great provocation' of Kruger's régime. This was in the same vein as Sir Edward Clarke's winding-up speech in which he dwelt movingly on the 'purity' of Jameson's motives. But the Lord Chief Justice was having none of this. Directing a cannonade against the twelfth man who obstinately stuck to his guns, Russell at last wrung from a reluctant jury the verdict which the Government desired. Jameson and Willoughby were then sentenced to fifteen months' imprisonment, Bobby White to seven, Harry White, Grey and Coventry to five. All the sentences were to be served without hard labour but the judge inadvertently gave the last three 'with hard labour'. This was quickly corrected. Their friends crowded round the prisoners congratulating them, shaking hands and showing every sign of emotion.

It was nearly eight o'clock in the evening of 29 July before the prisoners left the Law Courts, by a back entrance to avoid a demonstration. They were spotted nonetheless and the affectionate crowds gave them the heartiest possible send-off, first to Wormwood Scrubs and then, through government intervention, to Holloway, that magnificent pile which Lord Beaconsfield is once said to have mistaken for a feudal castle crowning London's northern heights. The exuberant scenes were reported in all the papers and were doubtless read by Kruger and his Boers with enormous resentment. *The Times* urged that bygones should be bygones: 'These men have done wrong . . . but they undoubtedly erred from excess of zeal for what they thought the interests of the Empire in South Africa and of their fellow-subjects in Johannesburg.' The article ended with a blunt attack on the promised Inquiry: 'Nothing much of importance remains to be discovered and only new discoveries would justify further stirring up of the muddy waters which are now, happily, subsiding.'

There were many who shared *The Times*'s view; W. T. Stead, for instance, strongly deprecated the House of Commons's 'childish persistence in demanding an Inquiry'. It was like taking a maxim gun to pieces to see how it worked just when a Zulu impi was charging down upon the square. Unfortunately, however, contrary to *The Times*'s opinion, there was much of importance still to be discovered.

Dr Jameson's behaviour before and during the trial throws light on the man. Before it opened he wrote to his brother Sam a jaunty letter breathing an unrepentant spirit of mischief:

Graham Bower [the Imperial Secretary] has been here an hour. He and High Commissioner as pro-Boer as ever; but there is one comfort, that they are in a mortal funk, and I had the pleasure of increasing the same by assuring him of the publication of the cables during the next few days.

Was Jameson in two minds up to the last moment about whether to drag in the Government or not? Or was it that he could not resist pulling the legs of those whom he intended to shield? It was probably the latter, for we now know that Chamberlain had paid the Doctor a secret visit in prison, no doubt to warn him against giving the show away by making a verbal 'bolt' during his trial. The evidence for this secret (and very compromising) meeting comes from Queen Victoria, no less. She recorded in her journal for 4 March 1896 that Mr Chamberlain came to see her after tea and talked 'very interestingly' about the Transvaal. 'He had seen Dr Jameson,' she innocently continued, 'but without anyone knowing.'*

This impish spirit, however, quickly evaporated when the trial began. People noticed that he gazed abstractedly at the ceiling, occasionally brushing his hand across his face as if to rub out unpleasant thoughts. No attempt was made to countermand Clarke's original instructions not to reveal anything startling. Indeed, by the end of the seven days' trial the other side of the Doctor's contradictory character, his melancholy and self-criticism, had got complete control. When Clarke attempted to appeal against the sentences Jameson insisted on accepting his fate. Morally disturbed both by the thought of his record and the crowd's reaction to it, he was determined, in his own words, to 'get square' in some sphere more significant than a court of law. When Rhodes heard the sentences he said: 'A tribute to the rectitude of my countrymen who have jumped the whole world!'

Not surprisingly Jameson moped in prison. His conscience continued to stab rather than to prick him. Why did society and the London crowd persist in making him a popular hero? As he brooded in his room at Holloway, unwilling to see visitors or have any contact with the outside world, remorse and severe attacks of gallstones (for which he was operated on in November) effectively dispelled for ever his former ebullient personality.

W. T. Stead tried to cheer the prisoners' relatives by painting Holloway as a home from home, and their sentences as an agreeable rest-cure. Stead himself, when imprisoned there for exposing the white slave traffic by staging the abduction of a child, had found it so. The raiders, all 'first-class misdemeanants', did not wear prison clothes or the broad arrow; their cells were furnished 'to taste' and they had plenty of books, writing materials and letters; two visitors a

---

* The astute Dr Jean van der Poel suspected that Chamberlain might have interviewed Jameson secretly, but she had no evidence. I found the evidence accidentally while researching my biography of Queen Victoria (*Victoria R.I.*, 1964).

week; and none of that brown bread and gruel tasting like the contents of the editorial paste-pot.

Jameson found no sweetness in adversity. Unlike Stead, he had no wife and 'bairns' to 'romp with during visits'. Strange rumours got about regarding his prison pursuits: he was writing his memoirs according to one; how improbable a hobby for the uncommunicative Jameson can readily be seen. According to another, he had taken up Buddhism but had to do without spiritual advice as no Buddhist prison chaplain was available. At the end of four months his health was so bad that he was granted a Queen's pardon and sent home. For the rest of his life he preferred not to discuss the Raid to which he had given his name.

Sir John Willoughby, while serving his term, became a prey not to remorse but to self-pity. He decided to send a protest letter to the War Office in the hope that his own commission and that of his fellow-officers might be saved. On 1 September, at the end of four weeks' imprisonment, it was ready. (The Committee of Inquiry were to hear its contents eight months later with considerable disquiet.)

*H.M. Prison, Holloway, September 1st 1896*
To General Sir Redvers Buller, VC, GBE, etc
Sir,
I have the honour to state that I took part in the preparation of the military expedition and went into the Transvaal in pursuance of orders received from the Administrator of Mashonaland [Dr Jameson] and in the honest and *bona fide* belief that the steps were taken with the knowledge and assent of the Imperial authorities. I was informed by Dr Jameson that this was the fact. . . .

Not only did Willoughby dispatch this poisoned dart himself but he also persuaded Jameson to send a covering letter to his colonel. Jameson's letter disclosed the fact that he himself had based his invasion of the Transvaal on 'the telegrams now in the possession of Mr Hawksley',[3] which in turn had been shown to Willoughby and the other officers. It looked as if the raiders, who had remained so loyal throughout the trial, crumbled under the atmosphere of Holloway. Sir Graham Bower's comment on Jameson's part in the affair was acid:

I am quite unable to understand his letter to the Colonel of the Blues. My belief is that when he consults his friends he will regret an act which is so unlike his previous record.[4]

The answer was that the solicitor Hawksley, not Jameson, or even Willoughby, was the moving spirit behind the whole of this curious episode. Hawksley drafted the letters, and Hawksley, as will emerge in due course, had been working hard ever since the Raid to shift responsibility from the Chartered Company to the Government, where he felt it belonged. The Willoughby–Jameson letters would be useful tools for the job, though minor ones compared with his own secret weapons – 'the telegrams now in the possession of Mr Hawksley'.

For a fortnight Willoughby sat back and awaited hopefully the result. At first it seemed that he might succeed. Sir Redvers Buller regarded sympathetically the two letters and decided to reopen the case of the officers' commissions on the spot, that is in Holloway gaol. His plan was promptly quashed by higher authority. On 15 September 1896, a splendidly censorious reply from the War Office, inspired by Chamberlain, put poor Willoughby in his place:

I am to observe that you disregarded the order of the High Commissioner to retire immediately from Transvaal territory. I am to add that to an officer of your standing and experience it should have been evident that an authority given by the Administrator of Mashonaland to organize and take part in an attack on a friendly state was *ultra vires* and invalid, and in such a case it was your duty to verify that authority by direct application either to the High Commissioner [Robinson] or to the Secretary of State [Chamberlain].

The Secretary of State's comment when he heard of Willoughby's letter had bristled with angry dashes and exclamation marks:

. . . He says it was not his fault – he was only obeying orders! He lies – and the only orders he received were to come back, which he disregarded. Such is a Stock Exchange hero![5]

The Stock Exchange hero perforce served eight out of his ten months' imprisonment and when freed walked straight from the cell in Holloway to the Court of Inquiry at Westminster.

# PART II
# Backstage

# 16

# 'The People's Joe'

The time has now come to go right behind the scenes; to look not so much at the façade of public events as at the hidden things going on in the background. But it is necessary first to know something more of the character and career of the most dominant yet inscrutable figure in this story. What kind of man was Lord Salisbury's Colonial Secretary, Joseph Chamberlain?

The Colonial Secretaryship was his first and last great office of state. Appointed in 1895 he resigned in 1903 over the issue of imperial preference and retired from politics, a sick man, in 1906. Once already, while Gladstone was forming his Liberal Ministry in 1886, Chamberlain had asked for the Colonial Office. 'Oh! A Secretary of State!' blurted out the Grand Old Man, taken aback and making it clear to the brilliant leader of his radical wing that he considered him unfit for really high office. After refusing the Admiralty Chamberlain reluctantly accepted the Local Government Board, a position scarcely less humble than the Board of Trade which he had held in Gladstone's previous government. A few weeks later he resigned. The split over Irish Home Rule had begun.

Gladstone soon found to his cost that he had vastly underrated Chamberlain's powers. When the latter trained all his immense debating skill against the first Home Rule Bill, Gladstone commented plaintively: 'He never spoke like that for us.' Charles Stewart Parnell, the Irish leader, laid the death of the bill at Chamberlain's feet. 'There goes the man who killed Home Rule,' he said one day as Chamberlain went through the lobby. For nine long years following this act of sincere but misguided destruction Chamberlain inhabited a political limbo. He called himself a Liberal but now he was a Liberal Unionist, cut off from the Liberal Party by his belief in the indissoluble union of Great Britain and Ireland. His anomalous position lasted beyond the six years of Salisbury's first Ministry. He was neither Liberal, Conservative nor good red radical. By temperament he was not a strong party-man, a source of weakness in a country increasingly involved in the party system. His early years in Parliament did nothing to remedy this defect. He saw the Grand Old Man mocked and both parties degraded by the case of Charles Bradlaugh, the atheist MP; while Randolph Churchill showed him how to ridicule a leader when he christened Sir Stafford Northcote the Grand Old Woman.

When Salisbury's Ministry fell in 1892 Chamberlain sat below the gangway though still on the Liberal side of the House. The next stage came in 1895 when the Tories returned to power. At last Salisbury and Chamberlain felt able, the one to offer, the other to accept, a Conservative Secretaryship of State. How was it that this man who, by the age of close on sixty, had never yet held one of the highest Cabinet posts and who was still considered by many Tories to be 'not one of us', managed to seize one of the Conservative plums? How is it that a man whose completed ministerial record looks on paper so modest (five years at the Board of Trade, a few weeks at the Local Government Board and eight years in the Colonial Office), leaves a name that will never be forgotten?

To answer these questions it is necessary to go back to 1854, the year when Joseph Chamberlain, aged eighteen, left his parents' home at Highbury, London, to work in his uncle Nettlefold's screw business in Birmingham. He carried with him a school mathematics prize entitled *Eldorado or Adventures in the Path of Empire*. Young Joe was remembered afterwards as a slim, fresh-faced boy who bustled round the shabby old factory giving it an entirely new look. After twenty years he had transformed Nettlefold & Chamberlain's into an immensely successful and wealthy firm.

While still under forty he was able to sell out his share, retire from business for ever and devote himself to his absorbing interest, politics. The screw factory was the first of Chamberlain's 'undeveloped estates' (to use an expression he applied later to the colonies) to be reorganized and vastly extended by his thrusting energies. The municipality of Birmingham was the next 'estate' to be so dealt with and the British Empire was the last.

What did the screw business contribute to the politician? A respect for businessmen and methods. Understanding of working-men's needs, particularly education. A certain ruthlessness in dealing with competitors. 'You could put the screw on if you liked,' said one journalist, apostrophizing Joe after his death.[1] 'Hard as his own nails,' was another pleasantry. But when a political opponent held up one of Joe's screws at Sheffield during his first parliamentary fight, accusing him of turning the screw on his workers, a crowd of Smethwick trade unionists rushed to his defence. Chamberlain's honesty was never questioned by those who had intimate dealings with him. No man could make a fortune in his own town, become its first citizen and retain its devotion throughout a life of extreme political controversy without establishing a reputation for probity in the eyes of those who knew him best. When assessing all kinds of hypotheses based on allegations of turpitude, this must be remembered.

Chamberlain's business training helped to form the style of his speeches. By temperament he was extraordinarily reserved but at the same time emotional. He had a spontaneous love of acting, mimicry and entertaining sometimes found in reserved characters. The uninhibited portrayal of fictitious feelings serves them as a safety-valve. The whole Chamberlain clan shared this talent for self-expression in charades and shyness everywhere else. But Joe's theatrical sense never invaded his oratory. Every sentence was a business-like expression of his thoughts. With all their pith, force, irony and epigram, they were based on life not on literature. His illustrations were homely, plain and unfailingly apposite. He was an industrialist and his speeches anticipated the age of functional art.

One more item of Chamberlain's political equipment must be put down to his business training. He thought in terms of projects rather than of policies. In the end, no doubt, his projects turned into policies, but they were not born in his business-like brain with that kind of abstract consistency. Hence the imputation of opportunism. With Gladstone it was totally different. He saw the Irish question as 'something alive'.[2] To Chamberlain it was simply a problem to be solved. He did not see that you could solve a problem but not a people. In the same way he thought of the future of Johannesburg in terms of a sound business project. The thing that was 'alive' in the Boer nation eluded and thwarted him.

Chamberlain's political training took place inside his native city. His mission was to reorganize completely the municipal life of Birmingham along socialistic lines. He swept away the old people, powers and practices, giving Birmingham new gas, water and sewage works, housing, and an entirely reconstructed civic centre – all commercially profitable. Before Chamberlain's reforms there was a hill of solid sewage just outside the town.[3] Of three councillors who once went to inspect the middens, all three caught the fever and one died of it. Having been Mayor of Birmingham three years running, he entered Parliament in 1876, sitting as a Liberal member for the 'new model' city which owed as much to him as Athens to Pericles. His departure to higher regions was marked by the erection of a soaring fountain behind the Town Hall. Like Jacob, he had worked for seven years, and his grateful fellow-townsmen felt that a memorial rising from a basin of clear water was the most appropriate commemoration of one whose public services had been the dazzling apotheosis of parish pump politics. It was afterwards observed that the 'bloodthirsty utilitarians' of Brummagem drew off the water, littered with paper and orange peel, into a special channel and used it to wash out the fish market.[4] Chamberlain was himself a confirmed utilitarian. He believed that human life, adorned above ground like his own fountain with flowery pinnacles, must seek the greatest happiness of the greatest number through all sorts of channels, some of them menial and perhaps even ignoble.

Two questions must now be asked. In what respects did Joseph Chamberlain differ from the other businessmen who had sat on the Birmingham Council before him? When Birmingham sent him to Westminster, what gifts did he carry with him from his municipal training?

On the Council, Chamberlain found himself one of an already conspicuous minority, the Nonconformists. Under his leadership they became the dominant element in the city. The old universities were barred to them, which meant that they were excluded from the governing class. In Birmingham most of these intelligent men chose a life in industry. In culture and education he and his family stood out from the mass of their fellow-townsmen as aristocrats. Small businessmen in those days often had not even a secondary education. Before Joseph Chamberlain came along the city fathers settled their municipal affairs in the bar of 'The Woodman' before the Council met – a befuddled gathering of backwoodsmen. A local poet commemorated Chamberlain's cleansing of these Augean stables:

> Who raised our Midland town from low estate,
> Swept from her Councils men of low degree . . .
> Who rooted out this scurvy, scullion crew,
> Gave dignity and pride to public life?

The answer was Brummagem Joe.

Chamberlain and his brothers and sisters read aloud the works of Matthew Arnold and Browning in their family circles, discussed the effects of evolutionary theories on religion, and sent their daughters in the wagonette or governess cart to the new, progressive Girls' High School at Edgbaston. When Chamberlain became a Member of Parliament and rubbed shoulders with the flower of Oxford and Cambridge, he was no doubt found to be neither a scholar nor a gentleman. The remarkable fact about him was not his supposed inferiority, so tediously reiterated, but his immense superiority over most members of his own class. The gossip that his principal private secretary, Harry Wilson, supplied his chief with the classical allusions for his speeches was not true. That he could only quote from Dickens was a myth.

As Joe's radicalism weakened, his weakness in the classics became endearing rather than contemptible to his new Tory friends. Lord Salisbury, on being told that Joe had once won a Latin prize, 'waved away the discreditable story'.[5] Nevertheless, he had to accept jokes to the end of his life about his Midlands background. In 'Saki's' *The Westminster Alice* (1902) Salisbury and Chamberlain were depicted as the King and Queen of Hearts. 'The King is only made of pasteboard, you know, with sharp edges,' says the Cheshire Cat to Alice, 'and the Queen' – here the Cat sinks its voice to a whisper – 'the Queen comes from another pack, made of Brummagem ware, without polish, but absolutely indestructible. . . .'

Chamberlain's appearance, which at first astonished and always intrigued Parliament, was utterly remote from the common idea of a Brummagem screw-manufacturer. Radicals were supposed to be bearded. Chamberlain was clean-shaven with pale skin, sharp features, an adventurous nose,[6] long lean head and sleek black hair. Working-class champions should wear cloth caps, mufflers and no waistcoats. 'The People's Joe' was flawlessly attired in silk hat and morning coat. Literary gentlemen with short sight, like Rudyard Kipling and Emile Zola, wore plain spectacles or pince-nez.

Chamberlain preferred a monocle. Fraternal delegates stuck metal buttons in their lapels. Chamberlain chose an orchid. With his quick, springy step, he always managed to look twenty years younger than his age. While sailing to Spain with his friend Jesse Collings he found there was only one bed on the steamer and a small sofa. The captain said to Collings: 'You can have the bed and the youngster can knock it out on the sofa.' The youngster was then forty-three.

Having forced himself into Gladstone's 1880 Cabinet, he devised an 'Unauthorized Programme' for the 1885 General Election, sweeping it before the country's mesmerized gaze on a stream of oratory like molten steel. It caused the Queen, most of his colleagues and all the Opposition to vibrate with horror. This was the period of his great radical tirades. With calculated ferocity he threw acid in the face of the establishment. There was more than a hint of republicanism in his early speeches. At the John Bright Jubilee in Birmingham he observed that the representatives of royalty were absent. Encouraged by the prolonged applause which greeted this remark he went on to say that 'nobody missed them' – a sally that was received in Birmingham with ecstasy but at Windsor with execration.

Class hatred was used to slash the landed nobility. Of his future leader he said, 'Lord Salisbury constitutes himself the spokesman of a class – of the class to which he himself belongs – "who toil not neither do they spin."' The Duke of Argyll took up the cudgels on behalf of Lord Salisbury and was quick to turn the class weapon against its wielder. What could members of the manufacturing class understand of the immense industry and capital put into the management of land? Their horizons were bounded by mills and 'chimney stalks'. Undeterred, Chamberlain pursued his vendetta against the House of Lords, a 'miserable minority of individuals' no better than 'ancient monuments' – 'a club of Tory landlords, which in its gilded chamber has disposed of the welfare of the people with almost exclusive regard to the interests of a class'.

In 1884 he whipped up the agricultural labourers against the Tories who wished to deny them the vote: 'If you were turbulent they would say that you were unfit for liberty; and as you are orderly and peaceable they dare to say that you do not want it.' And at the beginning of the next year he made a great speech in Ipswich.

Almost every sentence was loudly cheered. 'We are told that this country is the paradise of the rich; it should be our task to see that it does not become the purgatory of the poor.' To facilitate this task, Chamberlain had already sponsored the Liberal 'caucus', a machine to canalize the voting power of the enfranchised masses and to translate words into action.

For the 'old race' of yeomen he demanded reform, his proposals being ironically dubbed 'three acres and a cow'. Jesse Collings introduced the 'three acres and a cow' amendment which defeated Salisbury's caretaker Government in 1886. Whereupon Chaplin, a conservative, remarked: 'The hand is the hand of Jesse but the voice is the voice of Joseph.' His philosophy of 'Ransom' shook the stately homes of the establishment from Chatsworth to Hatfield, from Inveraray to Blenheim. Chamberlain menacingly invited the wealthy to pay danegeld: 'Property must ransom the evil it has done!' No other word sounded so grim to the 'haves' or so glorious to the 'have-nots' as that word 'Ransom'. Ten years later old Paul Kruger applied it to the case of the British South Africa Company and the Jameson Raid. Property was made to pay a heavy ransom for the evil it had done.*

The 'Unauthorized Programme' won the election for the Liberals in the villages but not in the towns. 'Next time we must have an urban cow,' said radical Henry Labouchere to radical Joseph Chamberlain, during the last few months of their friendship. But there was no next time and the urban cow did not get into Joseph's ark. Like all the rest of his radical livestock it was swept away in the flood of the Home Rule controversy.

By the year 1895 Chamberlain was entering upon the twentieth year of his parliamentary career. A change had taken place both in him and in the country. Partly owing to his efforts, the classes which he represented, the Nonconformists and the commercial middle-class, were no longer underdogs. Thus he himself was no longer the underdogs' champion. His emotions, indeed, had never been deeply engaged by the idea of minorities as such. In a sense he preferred the oppressed majorities who were potentially strong, the sturdy

* Sir Graham Bower said that Rhodes preached the philosophy of 'Ransom' and practised it in his will. (*Apologia.*)

artisans, skilled labourers, industrious practitioners of self-help. When the need to crusade against the feudal tyrannies of church and landlords seemed to him to have slackened, he turned with unconscious relief to his true bent, the organization and multiplication of constructive enterprises.

It was here, however, that a certain narrowness in his outlook became apparent. Like most politicians he wore blinkers and his pair was made in Birmingham. He was English to the core, Midlands to the core, middle-class to the core. Anything of value that Birmingham could teach him he learnt with avidity and passed on to others. Anything that Birmingham could comprehend, he penetrated more profoundly still. But where Birmingham was blind he deliberately shut his eyes. What was good enough for Birmingham was good enough for Dublin and Johannesburg, Charles Stewart Parnell and Johannes Paulus Kruger.

Local self-government, municipal pride and prowess; these were splendid things which, increased a hundredfold, were to become the red corpuscles in the great imperial bloodstream. But nationalism was another matter. As a good Brummagem man, he left out the small nations, jumping in imagination straight from the memorial fountain in Chamberlain Square to the red maps and the Seven Seas and the Queen-Empress. Chamberlain could no more sympathize with Irish or Boer aspirations than he would have tolerated a threat from one of his local wards to break away from the rest of Birmingham and set up on its own.

He had never been a Liberal, if liberalism meant the freedom of a people to be itself even when that 'self' seemed an ugly anachronism and a brake on mankind's evolutionary advance. Gladstone once said 'with a laugh' that radicals had no adequate conception of public liberty.[7] Chamberlain was at first a radical, then a Tory. The transition was easy, *via* the elements of authoritarianism in both. Moreover, he had been brought up to admire the gun-boat diplomacy of Lord Palmerston. As a young man about town he was said to have been torn between conservatism for foreign policy and liberalism for home affairs. Since the town in which he walked about, to and fro between lodgings and factory, was the Birmingham of stinking courts, back-to-back houses and far more pubs than stand-pipes, he chose the Liberals and social reform. But even on the

City Council, in order to put through his huge schemes he formed an alliance with the Tories. His personal relations with them during the 1870s were happy. If Parliament had been peopled by the same Tories who worked with him in the town hall, Chamberlain would have made them an acceptable and outstanding Prime Minister. But Toryism at Westminster was still ruled from Oxford and Cambridge, *Debrett* and Burke's *Peerage*.

It remains to depict the inner man with whom Kruger, Rhodes, Jameson, Salisbury and the rest would have to deal. From the founts of his inexhaustible energies, mental and physical, sprang all his qualities both good and bad. A man in a hurry to get things done does not waste time over circumlocutions. Joseph Chamberlain was an admirable man to work with, of engaging frankness, no pose, intensely loyal to his friends, courageous, never failing in fibre or backbone. But he could be ruthless, impatient, imperious, indiscreet, brash. His tongue was provocative and bitter, his sarcasm (a weapon to be used sparingly in politics) kept ever at the ready. The Irish believed that he reserved a special instrument for their discomfiture: his monocle. It was all very well to be quizzed by one's social superiors; but the Irish, feeling themselves to be nature's aristocrats, despised the shop-keeping taint they sensed in Chamberlain.[8] Afterwards, when young Austen Chamberlain showed the House how a monocle could be worn without annoying the Irish, it was clear that it had been the eye behind his father's monocle which froze.

Chamberlain needed the company of women but he would be their master as well as their slave. Between the deaths of his first two wives and his third marriage, he fell in love with the remarkable Beatrice Potter who afterwards became Mrs Sidney Webb. Of her it was said that she had beauty, charm and 'the attraction a rather learned woman has when she allows a touch of the feminine to peep through, even in the delicacy of her shoes'.[9] But shoes, however entrancing, which seemed to peep out from a pair of trousers, were not the ones for Joseph Chamberlain. Nor in the end was the girl who drove hatless in Regent's Park with hair blowing. A few years later he married Mary Endicott, the charming twenty-four-year-old daughter of an American judge. Lord Salisbury used to call her 'the

Puritan maid'. She smoothed Chamberlain's way to Windsor and into all the drawing-rooms of Mayfair.* Chamberlain's Unitarian faith did not survive the appalling misery of his second wife's death. He confided his sufferings to John Morley in letters poignant with agnostic despair, but to few others, and his reputed coldness and reserve was largely due to this inner wound. In later life he held his beliefs in suspense 'lest he should lose his integrity' and dissociated himself from church-going 'from a sense of honesty'.† For the same reason he declined a state burial in Westminster Abbey.

Thruster he was, opportunist and autocrat.‡ But his standards forbade him to stoop deliberately to actions mean or dishonourable. Those who knew him and were not prejudiced by party spleen or the extraordinary acrobats of his political career, recognized this fact.

---

* Mrs Chamberlain (then Mrs Carnegie) told the author in 1956 of a characteristic encounter with Mrs Gladstone at Buckingham Palace, where Joseph Chamberlain had taken his young bride to be presented to the Queen. 'What are you doing here?' was Mrs Gladstone's greeting. 'I have come to be presented,' replied Mrs Chamberlain. Whereupon Mrs Gladstone, dressed in deepest black with black feathers in her hat and carrying a huge bouquet of snowdrops like a white muff, extended her flowers to Mrs Chamberlain, breathing rapturously, 'From Hawarden. . . .'

On another occasion Mrs Chamberlain met Mrs Gladstone coming out of the little buffet behind the ladies' gallery. She bowed to Mrs Chamberlain and whispered with reverent joy, 'I believe *he* is going to speak.' She felt there was only one *he* for all of them.

† Words used to the author by Alderman Byng Kenrick.

‡ His friend Sir Charles Dilke, MP, gave him the nickname of 'Joe King'. While staying with Chamberlain at Highbury, Birmingham, he wrote to his future wife Mrs Pattison: 'Breakfast with Austen at 8.30. (J. King does not get up till much later.) . . . After lunch I play tennis with the King in person. . . .'

# 17

# Looking up the Files

History has never agreed upon Chamberlain's part in the Raid. Three radically different verdicts present themselves for assessment. Not Guilty. Guilty. Partially involved. The first verdict is typified by Article VI of the Select Committee's conclusions:

Neither the Secretary of State for the Colonies nor any of the officials of the Colonial Office received any information which made them or should have made them or any of them aware of the plot during its development.

A powerful plea of Guilty is advanced among modern historians by Dr Jean van der Poel in her arresting book *The Jameson Raid*:

... The worst consequences of the Raid might have been avoided if there had been a frank avowal of the part played in it by the Imperial authorities, and if the responsible minister [Chamberlain] and his party had then suffered the ordinary constitutional penalties.[1]

A verdict of partial complicity is less readily illustrated by a single quotation. But it is implied by historians such as R. H. Wilde (*Archives Year Book for South African History*, 1956): 'It is not easy to avoid implying that Chamberlain and his staff knew and intended more than they actually did.' Two incidents, moreover, will convey something of the story's 'frightful tangle' (Flora Shaw's expression) from which clear-cut verdicts of Guilty or Not Guilty might well not emerge.

When Flora Shaw was about to appear before the Committee of Inquiry Chamberlain wrote to his private secretary, Harry Wilson, instructing him to ask her a question:

... I should myself like to know beforehand what her answer would be if I asked her, whether she had ever, in the course of any conversation with me, mentioned what is now known as Jameson's plan viz. the placing of troops on the border in order to be able to assist an insurrection. I do *not* believe that she ever said a word on the subject but I should like to know what her recollection is.[2]

The remarkable thing about this letter is Chamberlain's evident preparedness to hear that he *had* been told by Miss Shaw about Jameson's plan, despite his own belief to the contrary. There was surely something very tangled up in the Colonial Secretary's mind if he could put a question like this.

About a month later, Flora Shaw questioned Chamberlain. On this occasion the impression of 'double think' is even more striking:

*Flora Shaw:* I put you on your honour to answer me. Did you know about the Raid beforehand or not?

*Chamberlain:* You put me on my honour. Very well. The fact is I can hardly say what I knew and what I did not. I did not want to know too much. Of course I knew of the precautions, the preparations, if you like, in view of the expected trouble in Johannesburg, but I never could have imagined that Jameson would take the bit between his teeth.[3]

These two exchanges seem to constitute a warning against any attempt to impose an artificial sharpness on the blurred margins of human self-knowledge, motive and will.

In order to tell the story of the Raid from inside, it is necessary first of all to go back to the month of August 1895 when a person with an air of self-importance mounted the steps of the Colonial Office for an interview with Joseph Chamberlain.

Dr Rutherfoord Harris has been described by many of his contemporaries but rarely in flattering terms. He was a man of some attainment: Member of Parliament for Kimberley, Government Whip, Secretary of the Chartered Company of South Africa and Rhodes's confidential agent in London from July to November 1895. He had once escaped from the mob at a Barnato election meeting by jumping out of a window. He had small, pale eyes, a moustache with exuberant waxed tips, and no crown to his head. He was 'slim', unscrupulous, untruthful, a gambler and a heavy drinker; he looked like a bounder. Sir James Rose Innes called him 'Rhodes's Man Friday', Percy Fitzpatrick said he was 'Rhodes's evil genius'. 'The mischief-maker of the whole affair' was how Flora Shaw summed him up. (Her acerbity was not surprising: Harris afterwards asserted that she, being a woman, must have revealed the Rhodes plan to Chamberlain just because she was told it was a secret.) Edmund

Garrett picked out Harris's inherent weakness as a negotiator: 'a sanguine and persuasive diplomat', Harris always thought he had carried people along with him further than he had; tolerable as Whip in the Rhodes Government, he was quite unsuited for negotiations with the Colonial Office. Like Dr Jameson, Dr Harris had a record of medical practice in Kimberley followed by some rather sharp practice of a political kind in Matabeleland. Unlike Dr Jameson, Harris had not succeeded as a doctor and was only too glad to exchange a bedside for a political manner. He was a glutton for work and always ready to take responsibility. In the Rhodesia of the early settlers he found plenty of both. In London he was faced with responsibilities of a subtlety and seriousness for which he had no aptitude.

The official reason for his visit to the Colonial Office was straightforward enough: to arrange for the promised transfer of Bechuanaland. But Harris had been directed by Rhodes to order arms while in England for the Uitlander rising. No doubt he paid a visit for this purpose to the famous arms factories of Chamberlain's native Birmingham. On the Chartered Company's account, a total of 4,000 rifles, three maxims and 200,000 to 300,000 rounds of ammunition were bought by Harris and shipped to the Cape, labelled 'for Rhodesia'. The Cape Premier then arranged for them to be smuggled (Harris, in the presence of the Committee of Inquiry, preferred to use the word 'diverted') into Johannesburg, with the secret assistance of the De Beers and Chartered Company's organizations.

The general manager of the De Beers diamond firm, an American, sent the arms to Kimberley, where they were kept in a De Beers store. When the time was ripe they were smuggled into Johannesburg by Captain Holden of the Chartered Company, the same who was later sent by the reformers' Committee to halt Jameson's ride. Holden fared better as a smuggler than as an emissary of law and order. He successfully conveyed the arms to Johannesburg in oil tanks provided with false bottoms and taps which would drip slightly if a customs official tried them.

When Chamberlain first went into the Bechuanaland files he found much to arouse his interest. The previous Liberal Cabinet, in which

Lord Ripon was Colonial Secretary, had not only taken decisions for
the transfer of this vast territory away from direct imperial control; it
had also discussed plans for dealing with possible trouble in
Johannesburg. A year before Chamberlain took office Sir Henry
Loch, then High Commissioner for the Cape, had been involved in a
more aggressive form of imperialism than Loch himself cared to
admit when questioned on the subject in Parliament. (In May 1896,
a few months after the Raid, *Le Temps* was responsible for a
statement, reprinted by *The Times*, to the effect that Loch had
intended to invade the Transvaal.)

After the Pretoria incident, when Kruger had been swathed in the
Union Jack, Loch was besieged by excited deputations from the
Uitlanders begging for his assistance in their struggle for their
rights. He asked them an unwise question. How many rifles had
they in Pretoria? Was it because he wished to know how long they
could hold out unassisted if they revolted against Kruger? Or simply
to show them how few they had and therefore how foolish it was to
talk big, Loch's own public explanation? The Johannesburgers told
Loch they had 7,000 rifles and asked for help.

Loch was sore tempted. He told his Imperial Secretary, Sir
Graham Bower, that he would make the Transvaal a British colony
'by raising a hand'. Bower protested violently; Loch in turn took
offence and accused his Secretary of being 'no Englishman but a
Bondsman at heart'. It was a bitter play on the name of the Dutch
party in the Cape Colony. So outraged was Bower that he promptly
offered his resignation. In the end calmer counsels prevailed. Loch,
however, 'continued in correspondence with the Johannesburgers,
and at the same time kept pressing Lord Ripon so hard for a huge
increase of troops' that the Colonial Office began to fear, as they
were to put it afterwards, that he might 'do a bit of "Jameson"
himself on his own account'. Loch's plan, however, differed basically
from the Jameson–Rhodes plot, in that the military force was to take
orders from the Crown not the Company.

The full details of Loch's 'coquetting' (Bower's word) with the
Uitlanders were probably not known to Chamberlain when he
assumed office in July 1895. But of the salient facts he was well
aware. Sir Henry Loch had stationed imperial forces at Mafeking
and proposed strengthening the South African garrison to the tune

of 5,000 men in case of a rising, which incidentally he promised Lionel Phillips to 'assist'. This 'Loch plan' undoubtedly influenced Chamberlain deeply and through him the whole course of this story. He must have seen Lord Loch, as he became on retirement, and discussed the Transvaal and Bechuanaland with him. In considering personal influences it should also be noted that Lord Loch hated his supplanter, Sir Hercules Robinson, 'with a deadly hatred'.[4]

Loch's plan was part of a definite thrust towards imperial expansion. He regarded a revolution in Johannesburg as inevitable and was confident the result would be re-annexation of the Transvaal. This in turn would be the prelude to the federation of South Africa under the British flag. All independent elements he wished to discourage: colonial parliaments, Rhodes, the 'continental' financiers. All influences making for direct imperial rule he wished to see reinforced, particularly the Crown's troops. His Permanent Under-Secretary, Meade, advised him against stirring up 'premature ebullition' in the Transvaal by such action.[5] Ripon seized the first chance to get rid of him. When his term came to an end early in 1895 he was not reappointed. A very different High Commissioner reigned in his stead.

Sir Hercules Robinson, the new High Commissioner, suited Lord Ripon's own non-aggressive type of imperialism admirably. Experienced and cautious, he was trusted by the Boers and intimate with Rhodes. Indeed, his enemies, Chamberlain among them, opposed Robinson's appointment on the ground that he was too much of a 'Rhodes man'. But in the end his friendship with Rhodes won him the position. The Queen, hesitant, was told that Rhodes wanted Bechuanaland and Rhodes wanted Robinson. As he was certainly going to have the one he had better have the other as well. Loch would never willingly hand over power to a colonial parliament. Robinson it must be.

# 18

# *The Matrix*

Before closing the back files, Chamberlain may well have asked himself why the Liberal Government maintained their decision to hand over Bechuanaland to Rhodes at a time when they knew trouble was brewing in the Transvaal. And did the Liberal Government carry on with something like the Loch plan after its author had been removed? Edward Blake, MP, a member of the Committee of Inquiry, told the House in 1900 what he considered to be the lesson of the Raid:

... the necessity for this country, if she will engage in enterprises in all corners of the earth, at least resolving to keep the care of her own responsibilities ... instead of handing them over to persons no matter how great or to chartered companies no matter how wealthy.

The attitude of the Liberal Party at this date towards imperial possessions was ambivalent. Frequently beset by scruples, often ready to shift the burden, few Liberals nevertheless were entirely unresponsive to the glories of empire, particularly as an instrument for international peace. Of the leaders, Rosebery was frankly imperialist; but even Sir William Harcourt, the Liberal statesman and Rosebery's anti-imperialist rival, could congratulate Queen Victoria on the 'larger dominions' she would leave to her successors. His reaction to '*fin de siècle* imperialism', a mingling of rejection and cynical acceptance, is illustrated by a conversation with Wilfrid Blunt. Towards the end of 1893 Harcourt was lamenting the slaughter of the Matabele War: 'But why do you do it?' asked Blunt. 'Oh,' said Harcourt, parodying his socialist epigram:* 'We are all burglars now.'

It needed a Lenin, twenty years later, to utter an uncompromising and thoroughgoing denunciation of imperialism:

Finance capital strives to seize as much land as possible, fearing to be left

* 'We are all socialists now.'

behind in the insensate scramble for the last available morsels of unapportioned territory, or for the last partition of those which have already been parcelled out.[1]

Lenin called Chamberlain and Rhodes 'the most cynical exponents of imperialist policy'.\* But the Liberals, too, must be counted as 'exponents' in their own more moderate way; they, too, were watching Germany anxiously, 'fearing to be left behind' or to lose their paramount position in those territories which had already been 'partparcelled out' to England's advantage. The fundamentally equivocal attitude of all Liberals towards the idea of empire made it easy for determined men like Rhodes to seize the initiative when the time came.

Was it possible that the Liberal Cabinet, having substituted Robinson for Loch – a 'safe' for a 'dangerous' High Commissioner – decided that some sort of Loch plan was after all necessary, provided it was carried out by a reliable person? At any rate, Robinson told Chamberlain after the Raid that Lord Ripon had instructed him to proceed to Pretoria in the event of a rising and arbitrate between Kruger and the Uitlanders, *promising him a large imperial force of 10,000 men.*

There is no record of this promise in the Colonial Office files and twenty-seven years later Sydney Buxton, who was Ripon's Under-Secretary in 1895, denied that such a promise had ever been made. Francis Younghusband, *The Times* special correspondent in South Africa in 1895, corrected the story in 1922, stating that Lord Kimberley (the Liberal Foreign Secretary) and not Lord Ripon had ordered Robinson to intervene with force. Whereupon Buxton riposted: 'Kimberley was a man who talked incessantly. He was *not* Secretary of State for the Colonies and had no right to butt in. . . . It is hard that Lord Ripon's name should be besmirched by Lord Kimberley.'[2]

What is the truth? It is possible that Sir Hercules Robinson invented the whole episode in order to strengthen the position of himself and Chamberlain after the Raid by involving the Liberals.

---

\* The very summer that Chamberlain became Colonial Secretary Lenin went abroad and began to study European monopoly capitalism, later incorporating the results in his *Imperialism* quoted above.

This, however, would have been a dangerous game and one that Chamberlain, relying on the solidarity of the leading Liberals in the House of Commons, would have hesitated to play. It is perhaps worth noting that several contemporary journalists believed Ripon went very far in plans for intervention. Edmund Garrett remembered a conversation at the Colonial Office about the High Commissioner 'going up' and added that he might have rushed away and telegraphed to his paper there and then: 'Lord Ripon is in it up to his neck';[3] W. T. Stead, in his *History of the Mystery*, written during the autumn after the Raid, referred to a 'bargain' which Ripon had made with the Uitlanders. None of this proves, of course, the truth of Robinson's statement. But it does show that there was much speculation, whether ill or well-informed, about the record of the Liberal Government.* Chamberlain must have felt that he had a shrewd idea of how far the Liberals had intended to go towards intervention. The policy which he himself was soon to adopt for dealing with the expected rising would have seemed to him a justifiable though somewhat delicate development of his predecessors' plans.

There was one other matter which had caused a certain amount of nervousness among Chamberlain's Liberal predecessors. They were aware of a potential German menace in South Africa. In January 1895 Kruger suddenly rubbed it in. The occasion was the Kaiser's birthday. Kruger proposed a toast to the German Emperor. He likened his young Republic to a growing child whose restrictive infant clothes (all bearing the label *Made in England*) will burst. With jocular plaintiveness he continued:

When we asked Her Majesty's Government for bigger clothes, they said: 'Eh, eh? What is this?' and could not see that we were growing up. . . .

---

* Lord Ripon's biographer has nothing to say on this specific question, but he emphasizes Ripon's desire for a strong policy against Germany in South Africa which led him and Kimberley to persuade the Cabinet to dispatch a powerful British squadron to the formal opening of the Delagoa Bay railway. As regards the Transvaal, his policy was eventual federation under Britain, but allowing the Boers to retain their republic if necessary. (L. Wolf, *Life of Ripon*, Vol. II, pp. 222–35.)

Already the Republic had begun to free its limbs but more freedom, he hinted, was on the way:

I feel certain that when the time comes for the Republic to wear still larger clothes you Germans will have done much to bring it about. . . . I wish also to give Germany all the support a little child can give to a grown-up man.

It only needed a moment's thought for Englishmen to reverse that last sentence and to see the grown-up man supporting the little child against its harsh stepmother. At any rate this was how one Englishman in South Africa interpreted Kruger's toast. Cecil Rhodes began seriously to plot against the Transvaal forthwith. By the summer of 1895 he succeeded where Loch had failed. He screwed up a number of leading Rand capitalists into joining the Uitlanders' National Union. With their accession to the cause a revolution was on the cards at last.

Rhodes now had his eyes on the rejected Loch plan. Two points particularly interested him: the police on the Transvaal frontier and the High Commissioner to negotiate with Kruger after the rising. But Rhodes retouched Loch's plan to make the overthrow of Kruger more certain. The police on the border were to be his own. The High Commissioner was also to be his own man, a puppet mediator who would 'go up' as soon as trouble started and arrange a settlement. An inkling of Rhodes's proprietary attitude towards the High Commissioner is given in one of the secret cables sent on 24 November 1895 to Dr Harris, while the plot was being hatched:

. . . A. Beit to stay with me here and go up with us and the Governor. . . .

Note the 'us and the Governor'. It sounded a lop-sided triumvirate, as it were Caesar, Antony and Lepidus, of whom Lepidus, the Governor, was being treated with appropriate condescension:

> This is a slight unmeritable man,
> Meet to be sent on errands.

The rising in Johannesburg would be preceded by a midnight attack on Kruger's arsenal at Pretoria, which would serve the dual purpose of disarming the Boers and arming the rebels. As Henry Labouchere, MP, put it during the Inquiry, it would be 'carts all round to cart off the whole of the ammunition' while the Boers slept.

Since the hundred or so men of the *Staats Artillerie* who guarded the Fort (a collection of gimcrack buildings) were nearly all in bed by 9 P.M., this should not prove too difficult. In the happy event of a bloodless victory, the frontier police would not have to go in at all. If there were a struggle they would go in at the High Commissioner's request to protect lives and property. But – and here came a most significant modification of Loch's plan – if the Uitlanders appeared to be getting the worst of it, Rhodes would use his border force to tip the scales. As he put it to Sir Graham Bower who would 'go up' with the High Commissioner:

If trouble arises I am not going to sit still; you fellows can act if you like, but you are infernally slow. I am not going to see my countrymen shot down. If you do not act I will.[4]

And it went without saying that if by any chance no spontaneous rising occurred at all, Rhodes would instigate one from the outside.

Instructed in the outlines of the Rhodes plan, Alfred Beit went to Johannesburg in the autumn of 1895 to sound the Uitlanders' leaders on the possibilities of an armed rising. He succeeded in getting them to meet Rhodes himself at Groote Schurr, outside Cape Town. Five conspirators gathered on the Prime Minister's pleasant veranda, with its basket chairs, gate-legged table and superb views of the wooded slopes beneath Table Mountain. The five were Cecil and Frank Rhodes, Charles Leonard, John Hays Hammond and Lionel Phillips.

Phillips had hitherto favoured 'constitutional' action. He had tried by means of 'substantial funds'[5] and places in the great mining companies to get a more liberal type of Boer into the *Raad* (Parliament) who would then overthrow Kruger from within. He does not seem to have been very successful. Cecil Rhodes cynically observed to the Committee of Inquiry that one or two of these 'liberal' Boers, once they reached the *Raad*, forgot their mission to oust the President and 'were worse than the ones they turned out'. 'It is very amusing,' Rhodes added. Phillips also had the misfortune to say in a letter to Beit that most people in Johannesburg 'did not care a fig' about the vote. He said it in June 1894, long before things had come to a head; nevertheless it was, and is, constantly quoted against him and his friends, to prove that the revolution had no popular support.

Charley Leonard talked big and liked the sound of his own eloquence. He was not the man for a tight corner. But on this important occasion all the conspirators seemed to be as one and the die was cast. Johannesburg adopted the Rhodes plan.

It will be seen, however, from the list of 'ifs' and 'ans' in the Rhodes plan as outlined above, that the intentions of the Uitlanders were by no means cut-and-dried nor completely harmonious. Leonard, for instance, understood that Johannesburg was to remain part of an independent Republic after the rising, while Rhodes was determined that it should end up under the British flag. In Rhodes's own mind, what actually happened in the way of fighting or fraternization would depend on the circumstances. The border force was 'to be used probably in certain eventualities'. With policies so flexible – sometimes almost indistinguishable from the Loch plan, sometimes approximating far more closely to the Jameson Raid itself – Rhodes would have no difficulty in imparting appropriate versions of his secret to his heterogeneous accomplices. One of the London directors of the Chartered Company, Earl Grey, for instance, was allowed to form a very different impression of the Rhodes plan from that which Rhodes conveyed to his inner circle on the Rand. Which, if any, of these divergent projects did he adumbrate, through various intermediaries, to Chamberlain and his officials?

# 19

# Uncongenial Officials

The Colonial Office files were undoubtedly interesting. Chamberlain found a climate of opinion definitely hostile to aggressive imperialism and only tepidly sympathetic to his own dynamic approach. Edward Fairfield, the expert on South African affairs, was a Liberal, a Little Englander, a humorous, popular, civilized official with Irish blood in his veins who delighted in writing provocative minutes and drawing unprintable caricatures. Born in Tralee in 1848, he was educated at Harrow and Rugby and offered a professorship of modern history in Bombay. He refused it for a post in the Colonial Office, where he was given legal training and called to the bar. His literary interests continued to show themselves in occasional articles for the *Pall Mall Gazette* in the old days when Flora Shaw, Alfred Milner and Edmund Garrett were all being trained by W.T. Stead. He was the uncle of Dame Rebecca West.

He took a philosophical view of imperialism in the Colonial Office. It had come to stay; but when imperialism came in at the door, morality flew out of the window. He believed, wrote Stead after his death, that the inevitable consequence of sending 'our people to live in places of such very different moral meridians to our own would tend to level down our moral standards'.[1] It is hard to imagine a lieutenant whom Chamberlain would have been less likely to choose from scratch. Fairfield in turn had no use for Chamberlain's ally Flora Shaw.

Sir Robert Meade, a man of sixty and Fairfield's chief, had something in common with his African expert. His family also came from Ireland, his father being the third Earl of Clanwilliam. He, too, was distrustful of Chamberlain's spread-eagle policy for the Empire. At home he was an old-fashioned free trade Manchester Liberal. At no point did the background or ideals of Meade seem to touch those of his new Minister.

But if the Colonial Office was not exactly in love with Chamberlain's 'new imperialism', there was a regular visitor to its inmost recesses who was. That visitor was Flora Shaw, the same who in 1892 had found Johannesburg so uncongenial a city. She was quite at home among Chamberlain's officials. As colonial expert on *The Times*, her habit was to call in once or twice a week for an exchange of news and views. Such a position for a woman in those days was remarkable. But then, Flora Shaw was a remarkable woman.

There was a story that while a young girl she climbed her favourite apple tree to read a new book. A revolution took place amid the branches. 'I went up the tree a Royalist and a Tory,' said she afterwards; 'I came down the tree a passionate Democrat.' And the book? It was Carlyle's *French Revolution*.

Flora Louisa Shaw, daughter of a soldier and a French mother, was granddaughter of a distinguished Irish politician and lawyer, Sir Frederick Shaw. Starting as a writer in the 'eighties with £100 in her pocket, she was introduced by her friend George Meredith to W.T. Stead as 'the finest flower of modern womanhood' endowed with 'the reasoning capacity of a man'. She worked with Stead on the *Pall Mall Gazette*, where he said she was a 'docile and diligent' pupil.

In 1889 we hear of Miss Shaw going to Egypt with General Younghusband and his wife, the General being father of Francis Younghusband who was later to play a prominent part in the Raid story.

In his book, *Blastus, the King's Chamberlain*,* a political romance about Chamberlain and his circle written in September 1895, Stead gives an intriguing glimpse of 'Miss Florizel' at a Highbury dinner-party. Thin, eager, 'not without vindictiveness', she was in some respects a counterpart of 'Joseph Blastus' in whom she believed as ardently as she believed in Cecil Rhodes. Like Joseph, she was famous for her grasp of finance and for her lucid power of sizing up the strength and weakness of financiers; and if she had been a man, like him she would have been a Cabinet Minister. When 'Mrs Blastus' rose to leave the gentlemen over their port and cigars Miss Florizel followed her with reluctance. In her own eyes, said Stead, the compliment most treasured by Miss Florizel was that she thought like a man. In this last detail, however, Stead misjudged

* A character from the Acts of the Apostles.

Flora Shaw. Though she could not help realizing that she was much cleverer than most of the men she met, she had no wish to be thought a blue-stocking. What men saw in her as a woman mattered a great deal and she always prized her femininity above her brains.

After being what Stead called 'a regular Pall Maller' for some years, Flora Shaw determined to get on to *The Times*. She was invited to do a trial article for the managing director, C. F. Moberly Bell. With characteristic aplomb she chose to write on his own special subject, Egyptian finance. She joined *The Times* in 1890, eventually becoming its first woman special correspondent. Her work was favourably noticed by John Walter, the owner, who did not realize, however, that this new acquisition was a woman:

*John Walter:* Excellent letter in *The Times* on South Africa . . . The man who wrote that not only knows what he is writing about but how to write it.
*Moberly Bell:* It's by Miss Shaw.
*J.W.:* By Mister – by Mrs – by *what*?
*M.B.:* By *Miss* Shaw, the same lady who wrote the article on Egyptian Finance which struck you so much.
*J.W.:* Miss, did you say, Miss? Miss What?
*M.B.:* Miss Shaw, who writes our colonial articles.
*J.W.:* Hm Hm. Well, Hm Hm. I don't know who wrote it but it was excellent. *Miss* Shaw – Hm . . . I read it twice, it just showed me things as he – as the person who wrote it – saw them and saw them as an intelligent – Hm Hm – person.[2]

Miss Shaw was soon 'Flora' to the Bell family, dining regularly at their house and even retiring to bed there on the frequent occasions when her health was giving her trouble. She and Moberly Bell were both vigorous imperialists. Not only did she represent the majesty of the 'Thunderer' when she visited the Colonial Office, she also enjoyed the friendship of Cecil Rhodes. Dr Jameson she had heard speak at the Imperial Institute, meeting him personally afterwards. To her, Rhodes was one of the immortals.

Thus equipped with talents and enthusiasm, she was not likely to regard Chamberlain's imperial hopes with the rather jaundiced eyes of his own staff. Indeed, her zeal for the 'new imperialism' was later on to prove almost excessive. Altogether the Flora of this story, as her name suggests, was something of a goddess. Brilliantly clever, tall and graceful, she needed all a goddess's uninhibited wiles to extricate herself and *The Times* from the morass into which she plunged it. At the time of the Raid, Flora Shaw was forty-five years old and still unmarried. Her enthusiasm was boundless, her energy tireless. She is still remembered sitting on the floor of *The Times* library, too engrossed to waste time in lifting books from the bottom shelves on to a table or herself into a chair. On all sides she was praised for her dual heritage of beauty and brains. She was 'as much at home in a Blue book', said Sir Hercules Robinson, 'as in a drawing-room'. Her interviews were 'a benediction'.

There is a story of her interviewing two Boers in 1890, Joubert and Mills. The latter became extraordinarily voluble, always referring to Miss Shaw as 'that dear little girl'; while Joubert, though more judicial in his praise, was equally flattering. Her questions, he said, were the sharpest that had ever been put to him. He summed her up: 'She is intelligent, she understands politics.'

Only one skill was perhaps lacking in this greatly gifted creature. The power to bring a lump into one's throat. She never made her readers 'cry or swear'. She did not desire to. For she could unleash their emotions only by letting herself go first, and that she never intended to do. After the Jameson Raid, when so many people had let themselves go disastrously, it was Flora Shaw's capacity for cool, tight self-control that saved her and her confederates.

In the High Commissioner's office at the Cape, Chamberlain's personality and point of view found no more favour than it did in the Colonial Office – a fact that afterwards contributed something to the disaster. Sir Hercules Robinson was a man of seventy-one. Behind him stretched an honourable career of public service in Australia, New Zealand and above all in South Africa, lightened by an interest in sport and business. On one occasion Robinson was riding back to Bloemfontein from the Rand. He stopped on a ridge and said to his Secretary, Graham Bower, who had been with him in Australia: 'If you were in Australia, Bower, what would you think of this formation? Would you not prospect for gold?' Five years later that ridge had become the Transvaal's goldfields.

Appointed to the Cape in 1881, his mission had been to reconcile the British and the Boers. He found himself presiding over the annexation of Bechuanaland (threatened by Boer raids) in 1885 and over a treaty with Lobengula in 1888 by which Cecil Rhodes beat the Boers in the race for 'the North'. By the next year Robinson had had enough of South Africa. What with Boers raiding into territories marked out as British spheres of influence, and Rhodes pursuing a forward policy little better than large-scale raiding, he was glad to have done with raids and raiders for good. By 1889 there seemed to be once more a hope of peaceful relations between the two white races. Provided, of course, that there was the minimum of interference from home.

In his farewell speech at the Cape, Robinson ostentatiously attacked 'direct-imperial rule'. Then he sailed home to spend six peaceful years on the boards of various companies. But the new Mecca of South African business enterprise began to bedevil Anglo-Boer relations once more. Who but Sir Hercules Robinson should be sent back as peacemaker? Reluctantly the old man accepted the Liberal Government's pressing invitation. His task was not rendered sweeter by the fact that many members of the House of Commons violently opposed his reappointment. Among them was Joseph Chamberlain. He had not forgiven the man who attacked imperial rule. Nevertheless, by the end of May 1895, Robinson was back at his old post. Less than two months later the Liberal Government was defeated, Lord Ripon left the Colonial Office and Chamberlain himself became Colonial Secretary and Robinson's chief.

Robinson heard the news of Chamberlain's promotion with dismay. When he received a friendly telegram from the new Colonial Secretary he at first refused to acknowledge it. Chamberlain, said he, was 'dangerous as an enemy, untrustworthy as a friend, but fatal as a colleague'.[3] Sir Graham Bower expostulated with his chief. An attitude of passive resistance was out of the question for a High Commissioner. Robinson must make up his mind to co-operate with Chamberlain or resign. The High Commissioner declined to do either. Resignation was financially impossible: he had just given up his directorships and could not get them back. Co-operation was equally dangerous. 'He would sit still.' Sir Hercules had an added reason for wishing to sit still. He was already a semi-invalid. Before arriving to take up his duties at the Cape he had a heart attack on board ship. The doctor called it indigestion as Sir Hercules was 'very nervous about himself'. The High Commissioner's health, which steadily deteriorated during the critical months that followed, was to make no small difference to the course of events.

It seems that Chamberlain was not altogether trusted among Cape politicians either. Bower had reason to believe that one of them, John Xavier Merriman, poisoned Robinson's mind against him. After the news of the appointment, Merriman came into Bower's office in a state of alarm saying: 'I know Chamberlain and you do not. Mark my words, he will have this country in a blaze before a year is out.' According to Bower, Merriman repeated this opinion to the High Commissioner. It was not an auspicious beginning to the new Colonial Secretary's career.

Sir Graham Bower, though he showed a vigour and decision lacking in his chief, found Chamberlain equally uncongenial. Retired from the Royal Navy to become a civil servant, by 1895 Bower had accumulated a remarkable record of disinterested service, particularly to Sir Hercules Robinson, with whom he had worked for about fifteen years. Above all he had been Robinson's right-hand man when the Transvaal was handed back to the Boers in the early 1880s. He was later to describe himself as a Conservative, an imperialist (though he often attacked imperialism), a pro-Boer and a free trader. This unusual mixture shows that he was a man with a mind of his own but not a rigorously logical one.

However, it was undoubtedly his special brand of independent imperialism coupled with friendliness towards the Boers which made him such a loyal servant of Robinson, with whom he saw eye to eye on these matters. Robinson gave him a handsome testimonial in 1889 when there was a move to have him 'kicked upstairs' for being too popular with Jan Hendrik Hofmeyr and his compatriots. Bower, said his chief, had 'during three inter-regnums been practically High Commissioner and done admirably'.[4]

Four years later he surrendered a chance of promotion at the request of Rhodes who wanted to keep someone so experienced in the intricacies of Anglo-Boer relations. In spring 1895 Bower gave up another opportunity for promotion (as Governor of Newfoundland) at the urgent plea of the aged Robinson, now returning to the Cape. Bower treasured two glowing tributes paid to him that May by the Colonial Office. Sydney Buxton wrote that he had acted 'very patriotically';[5] while Lord Ripon praised his 'handsome conduct'.[6]

During his long residence in the Cape Colony, Bower seems to have imbibed all the standards, good and bad, of the settlers among whom he worked. Calling himself a friend of both British and Boers, of Rhodes and Kruger – 'both were rich men and both were simpleminded and simple-living men'[7] – he felt that co-operation between them, had it been possible, would have served Africa better than dictation by people thousands of miles away. Ten years after the Raid, when both Rhodes and Kruger were dead, Bower was still pleading that South Africa should be left alone: 'I have never known imperial interference end in anything but discredit and disaster.'

But as long as the Empire played the rôle of policeman, Bower could tolerate, even welcome British paramountcy in South Africa. 'John Bull rightly understood', he said, 'is the best Afrikaner of us all.' In Bower's eyes, however, neither John Bull nor Africa were rightly understood by the Colonial Office, which was universally distrusted and was 'controlled by missionaries, philanthropists and Jews'. Money did not count in South Africa, wrote Bower. 'Birth, provided your blood be pure white, does not count at all.' In any case, the Boers were the same race as ourselves: 'identical with the Lowland Scotch'.* The Boers had 'backbone, pride and determination' and lacked any affinity with such a one as, for instance, Barney Barnato. Bower was indeed unashamedly anti-Semitic. He disliked international Jewry, especially the 'House of Rothschild', but 'despaired of' ever making London understand the feelings which existed in the United States, Australia and South Africa against the Jews.† Yet the ignorant folk at home were wont to use 'alien officials' in the Colonies, 'suspected of having coloured or Jewish blood in their veins'. Colour was to him synonymous with barbarism. The African mine-workers Bower regularly referred to as 'black savages', 'raw savages'. No wonder he included among the seven devils of

---

* Chamberlain had defended the Pretoria Convention of 1881 with much the same arguments: the Boers 'had the best characteristics of the English race . . . Is it against such a nation that we are to be called upon to exercise the dread arbitrament of arms?'

† Alfred Milner was one of the first to point out that the influence of Jewry in Johannesburg was grossly exaggerated. 'If you go into a crowded room', he said, 'and find two Jews there you come away saying the place was full of Jews.' (H.W. Nevinson, *Changes & Chances*, p. 319.)

imperialism not only Sir C. Warren, Mr Stead, Mr Arnold-Forster, Sir E. Ashmead-Bartlett, the Empire League and Mr J. Chamberlain, but also the Rev. J. Mackenzie and the Aborigines Protection Society.

But whatever may have been the gaps in Bower's ideals of commonwealth, he was ready to make the heaviest sacrifices for those in which he believed. '*L'Empire c'est la paix,*' he liked to quote; and to keep the peace for the British Empire and the world, he would be willing to play the part of scapegoat, alive and dead, for fifty years.

His slightly 'quarter-deck' manner concealed a kindly nature and his human foibles were entirely innocent ones. He had a taste for discovering and preserving politicians' secrets. Bower once told an interviewer that there had been a time when he did not know how to hold his tongue. But with much practice and perseverance he had schooled himself into a state of absolute reliability. He could even offer politicians advice on how to keep silent. They should smoke steadily so as to avoid opening their lips until they could 'see their way clear through the reefs'. The sad thing was that Bower, though he knew so well how dangerous it was to reveal a secret, never discovered that it was even more dangerous to become the repository of one. His catastrophe was not to talk but to listen too much.

# 20

# Rhodes v. Chamberlain

There was no lack of personality among the many politicians, civil servants, soldiers and businessmen who would now be scarcely remembered but for their connection with the Jameson Raid. As for Rhodes himself, he was the almost fabulous principal behind the elaborate network of agents and associates.

Born in 1853, Cecil John Rhodes was Chamberlain's junior by as much as seventeen years. But other differences between the two men struck the eye more forcibly. Chamberlain would rise to greet his guests, impassive of face, quiet and suave in manner but tense with controlled energy. If his face resembled any well-known hero of the past, it was Pitt, 'the Great Commoner'. The uncouth, shambling figure of the colonial Prime Minister also had its historical image: Rhodes liked to believe his massive head and strong features reminded old classical friends at Oxford of the Roman Emperor Titus. Perhaps his curiously loose garments also had some faint flavour of the imperial toga, for he did not wear them; they hung on him. When he first entered Parliament he shocked the Cape Dutch as much by his slovenliness as Chamberlain, five years earlier, had amazed Westminster by his elegance. Rhodes consistently refused to wear a top hat and conventional black suit. He said he could 'legislate as well in Oxford tweeds as in sable clothing'. And in 1895 he looked more like a digger than a don and less like a Prime Minister than either.

As a youth in South Africa he had seemed to the Boers 'damnably like an Englishman': tall, slim, fair, with blue eyes so transparent that they almost seemed watery, wavy hair and classical features. By now, however, his complexion was often grey with the heart disease that had recently given him sharp warnings of the littleness of life. His cheeks were loose and flabby; his clipped moustache seemed to depress the mouth at the corners; his chin was deeply cleft. There were heavy bags under his very prominent eyes. But his smile, said a female admirer, was 'like sun on a granite hill'. He had rather a limp hand-shake, perhaps because he extended only two fingers, keeping the other two in his palm.

At forty-two there was still something of the child about him (Chamberlain could never be imagined as a baby), but a child now gifted with unprecedented strength of character and personality. Chamberlain had a singularly clear, resonant voice; Rhodes's speech was squeaky and staccato. Rhodes appeared to be often in a daze, only half awake from some inner dream; while it seemed unlikely that Chamberlain ever slept at all. The contrasts between the two did not end here. Rhodes was born into a different class from Chamberlain. Son of a country parson, he made his fortune in the diamond mines of Kimberley and then sent himself, still a youth, to the Mecca from which Chamberlain's Nonconformist religion excluded him, Oxford.

As a young digger Rhodes carried a Greek lexicon with his other kit: as a millionaire he ordered all the classical authors mentioned in Gibbon's *Decline and Fall* to be translated for him and placed in his library. One further gift which Rhodes may first have picked up from his historical reading was sympathy with what Jan Hofmeyr called 'true Nationalism'. Unlike Chamberlain, Rhodes understood nationalists and appreciated that their fiery hearts could not be put out with water from the parish pump of local self-government.

But a subtle change, likely to make Rhodes's imperialism as ruthless as Chamberlain's, had been coming over him during the preceding four years. In 1891 he broke his collar bone. This accident was followed by serious influenza and then the heart trouble. He seemed to lose the hard-won mastery over his naturally hot temper, becoming despotic towards his foes and unmanageable even by his friends. Truculent impatience impaired his former talent for careful statesmanship, though it was ennobled in his dying words, 'So little done, so much to do.'

So much to do . . . Like most great men he felt the need of a host of agents to work out the details of his huge schemes. As with many great men his choice of agents was often startling. Mrs O'Shea laboured for Gladstone, Captain O'Shea for Chamberlain, Dr Rutheerford Harris for Rhodes. Rhodes's reckless plans for invading the Transvaal and seizing Johannesburg may have been partly due to his incipient break-up: at any rate, the Raid finally removed from his side all the moderate Afrikaner patriots who might otherwise have continued with him to build a bridge between British imperialism and Boer nationalism.

That Rhodes and Chamberlain had a deep devotion to the British Empire is the best known fact about both of them. More interesting is the manner in which the South African picture of empire differed from the Birmingham one. Chamberlain believed profoundly in the many-sided genius of the British race, but on the whole he cared more about the development of the 'estates' Britain already possessed than the acquisition of new ones. It was obvious to him that Britain's mature industries needed blood transfusions from new markets overseas. If this occasionally involved the contradictory process of blood-lettings in war, it was no worse than a temporary halt in the way forward. 'Think Imperially' was Chamberlain's motto. Rhodes preferred to dream imperially and think practically. He reserved his accurate thought-processes for the making of money. His imperial dreams were grandiose, some no better than nightmares and discarded as he gradually woke up to the facts of the real world. At one time he even dreamed of Britain recovering the lost American colonies.

Always he saw the English-speaking race dominating the world and, under God, imposing a *Pax Britannica* on the warring nations. Though both Rhodes and Chamberlain were afflicted with religious doubts, Rhodes dealt with his in the more buoyant fashion. He concluded that, there being a fifty per cent chance of God existing, he would give Him the benefit of the doubt. 'If there be a God,' said Rhodes, 'I think that what He would like me to do is to paint as much of the map of Africa British as possible and to do what I can elsewhere to promote the unity and extend the influence of the English-speaking race.' After the Jameson Raid the moral influence of his race was for a long while sadly diminished.

By the time of the Raid, the tribute Rhodes drew from his vast financial empire was over a million pounds a year. He controlled De Beers (diamonds) at Kimberley, the Consolidated Goldfields at Johannesburg and the Chartered Company of Rhodesia. Like Chamberlain, he created his own fortune, arriving in South Africa with the slenderest means at the same age as Chamberlain started up in Birmingham, eighteen. His first ten years were spent as a pioneer on the veldt, enjoying the camaraderie and rivalries of diamond digging in the early days. It was not long before he had accumulated enough to afford Oxford, where in 1870 he heard Ruskin deliver his tremendous Inaugural Lecture on art: 'This is what England must either do or perish: she must found colonies as fast and far as she is able, formed of her most energetic and worthiest men . . .' It was one of those miraculous occasions in history when genius meets genius, to teach and to learn. The famous Ruskinian phrases fell on ears well-tuned to the message and within a short time Rhodes was able to prove, in the master's words, his own surpassing energy and to test his worth.

A quarter of a century passed between the Ruskin lecture and the Jameson Raid. During the years that culminated in the conquest of Rhodesia, a number of names crop up which reappear in the Raid story: Rochfort Maguire, a director of 'Chartereds', Harris, Goold-Adams, Shippard, Willoughby and above all Jameson. None of them emerges from the Matabele adventure without the taint of questionable behaviour. If this is remembered it helps to explain the Raid itself. To many people the whole fantastic episode seemed and still seems incredible. How could a brilliant doctor be so mad? How could British officers be so reckless? Read the story of Lobengula's fall and you see in it a rehearsal for the fall of Rhodes. Many of the same individuals and much the same spirit which destroyed the poor old savage later brought down his conqueror.

Rochfort Maguire, while concession-hunting, gave Lobengula information as inaccurate as that which he was afterwards to give Fairfield. Harris was an inferior doctor and an inferior negotiator with a passion for shooting, whether in Matabeleland or Scotland. Willoughby twice paid more attention to the bidding of Rhodes than to the forbidding of a High Commissioner. Goold-Adams was the officer used by the Administrator of Bechuanaland, Shippard, to kidnap a rival syndicate on Rhodes's behalf. Later, Goold-Adams arrested Lobengula's envoys to the High Commissioner; doubtless without his knowledge they were then murdered by his men; a later peace-offering of golden sovereigns was stolen. He also carried out the scheme by which the BBP took over some of Jameson's frontier duties at the taxpayers' expense, thus freeing the

Mashonaland Police for Rhodes's war in Rhodesia, an early example of imperial collaboration with the swashbucklers.

The truth is that the Jameson Raid was no bolt from a clear sky. Minor incidents, some of them on the Boers' side, were continually occurring during those irresponsible days of the pioneers' picnic. The colonial skies were full of ugly signs and omens and Jameson's ride though more spectacular was not different in kind from the rest. A perusal of the newspapers of the time brings out this point. The Raid took people's breath away. But the long whistle they emitted was in part admiration. They hoped it would sound like horror. Jameson himself was profoundly repentant. But even he said quite frankly that had he succeeded he would have been forgiven. That was a true estimate of the spirit of his own time, and perhaps of any other.

Hitherto Chamberlain's relationship with Rhodes had not been a happy one. He once told his son Austen about their first meeting.[1] It took place in Lord Rothschild's house. But the port was powerless to mellow Rhodes. In his unpolished way he suddenly bearded Chamberlain, the man he knew to be opposing the grant of his Charter: 'I am told you do not like me,' challenged Rhodes. Chamberlain replied with a tart rebuke and a dig at Rhodes's fame which cannot have been strictly true:

. . . why should I? I only know three things about you. The first is that you are reported to have said that every man has his price. It is not true, and I do not like the man who says it. The second is that you have talked of 'eliminating the Imperial factor' in South Africa. The third is that you gave £10,000 to Parnell, and that is not exactly a claim on my gratitude.*

By the time Dr Harris was making his way to the Colonial Office, however, in August 1895, much of this had changed. Parnell was dead and with him had disappeared the prospect of Home Rule in the near future. Moreover, the views of Chamberlain and Rhodes on

---

* Rhodes also secretly gave £5,000 to Liberal Party funds in 1892, in order to get an Egyptian policy he approved. (*Spectator*, August and October 1901, and J. A. Spender, *Life of Campbell-Bannerman*, Vol. 1, p. 204.) On 12 May 1899 Rosebery noted that Rhodes spoke of a seat in Parliament, inquiring if £50,000 for the Liberal election fund would be sufficient.

the 'Imperial factor' had drawn closer together. Rhodes had lost his former impartiality between Briton and Boer and now dreamed of an Africa claimed for the British race; while the Colonial Secretary had come to believe that the 'Imperial factor' must in some sense be eliminated if the Empire was to develop as rapidly as possible.

On 1 August 1895 (the very day of Harris's first interview) Chamberlain wrote to Lord Salisbury about the Treasury 'factor' in disparaging terms: 'The Treasury is of course very Gladstonian . . .'* In his speech to the House after the Raid, he argued in favour of using chartered companies; new territories would never be opened up at all if everything depended on the Colonial Office. Even Sir Graham Bower agreed with Chamberlain on this point. The Company, he wrote, was more likely 'to make two blades of grass grow where only one grew before'.² Sir William Harcourt was to put the opposite point of view when, after the Raid, he condemned the method of empire-building through chartered companies. Such attempts to get power without responsibility ended by getting responsibility without power.

As to the first cause of Chamberlain's dislike for Rhodes – his remark that 'every man has his price' – Rhodes was about to offer Chamberlain an inducement to transfer the Protectorate guaranteed to appeal to any businessman turned statesman: a large financial gain to the country. Indeed, the Colonial Office as a whole were swayed by Rhodes's generosity. As Bower wrote to Fairfield while negotiations were in progress: 'The privilege of paying £40,000 a year of John Bull's money' should be relinquished, by handing over the Protectorate.³ Chamberlain hoped that he and Rhodes would reach agreement 'as sensible men of business . . .'. Ominous phrase. There is no doubt that, like his son Neville after him, Chamberlain failed to see the danger in a given policy through looking at it too much as a business deal.†

Though Rhodes intended to get his own way, he was not lacking

---

* Cyprus, he went on, was starved and snubbed, but if he could get a little money he might make it a paying proposition. (Chamberlain to Salisbury, *Salisbury Papers*, Christ Church, Oxford.)

† The first time Harcourt met Rhodes (at Tring in 1891) he was dazzled by his offer to 'run Uganda for us for £24,000 a year'. Rhodes might be a great jingo, but then he was 'a cheap jingo'. (Sir Edward Hamilton's *Diary*, 31 October 1891.)

in a kind of inhuman humility. For him the cause was always greater than the man who worked for it. On one occasion a fellow-Commonwealth Prime Minister died suddenly while Rhodes was in the midst of trade negotiations with him. 'Oh well, he's in Heaven now, so we shan't get any free trade between the Colonies yet,' said Rhodes. 'It's a pity he did not do it at once.' Rhodes went on to speculate on the dead man's successor, defending his callous haste by remarking: 'Only goes to show how soon you'll be forgotten, and *all* of us, the instant we're dead the crowd closes over us. It doesn't matter what we've done, we're forgotten.' He was to express the same thought to Chamberlain at the Colonial Office, as part of an impassioned plea to quash the inquiry into the Raid. 'In twenty years you will be gone, snuffed out, but the country will remain.' Chamberlain rebuffed Rhodes at the time, but when the next general election came round an echo of those words found its way into one of his own orations. 'I might die tomorrow and still there would remain this great Empire.' Harcourt, who showed no taste for self-dramatization or the grandeurs and miseries of great men, parodied the 'immortal sentence' with another from the fable of the ox and the frog: 'When I burst the ox will still remain.'

Rhodes was a genius not subject to normal human feelings: childless, wifeless, he was ready to jeopardize his brother's military career for the sake of the cause (in fact he ruined it) and a few months later to sacrifice his own partial vindication for the transcendent cause of England's peace and honour. He liked to have about him big and simple things; barbaric, if you like, admitted Rhodes. What a contrast to Brummagem Joe, with his urban background, conventional yet spacious bourgeois comforts, and his deep-rooted need for the family circle and especially the women who created it.

The difference between the two houses in which Rhodes and Chamberlain chose to live adds something to this study in contrasts.* Both men had built or reconstructed their homes according to their heart's desire and Chamberlain was as devoted to Highbury

* After this was written I came upon Desmond MacCarthy's enchanting comparison between Groote Schurr and Kruger's 'unlovely little bungalow near Pretoria'. (*Portraits*, pp. 204–8.)

as Rhodes to Groote Schurr. Highbury, in Birmingham, stands above its neat lawns and shrubberies, flanked by the ghosts of sixteen vanished green-houses, filled with orchids and stretching to the end of the long terraced walk. The huge red brick villa is a triumph of fertile Victorian fancy. Floral and geometrical designs are everywhere; windows are mullioned, sash or dormer. Inside are elaborately moulded ceilings, an abundant variety of ornamental woods including much satin wood, stained glass and coloured tiles. Round the hall runs a carved gallery off which the bedrooms radiate: it is decorated with a frieze of sunflowers and horse-chestnut leaves. Vast, romantic pictures by Alma Tadema used to adorn the gallery and the house was full of William Morris tapestries and lustre ware. Ruskin would have been perfectly happy at Highbury: Rhodes never.

Rhodes's house was the 'Great Barn' of old Dutch colonial days. He kept the rooms extraordinarily bare, at least for Victorian taste. The living-rooms were panelled in teak, hung with tapestry or a few pictures and contained books and one or two occasional tables holding vases of flowers. The furniture was solid and plain, often of antique design. In the white-washed hall the great beams of the old barn were fully exposed. Its centre was occupied by a massive oblong table, generally heaped with curios left by dealers for the millionaire's inspection. Only the large marble bathroom went in for sybaritic splendour in keeping, perhaps, with its owner's fancied resemblance to the ancient Romans.

This man without a private life, who had renounced self not through religion or morality but because he had found 'an extension of self into the national life for which he lives' (as Flora Shaw wrote of Rhodes) – this man Rhodes would prove a formidable colleague, whether one agreed with him or not.

On a smaller scale, there was one quirk in the character of the Colossus of which Chamberlain may not have known, but which affected this story for ill. Like so many of the great, Rhodes hated letters – whether writing them or reading them. (Parnell used to say, 'Never write to me; always wire to me.') The bluntness of his style and the uncouthness of his script compare significantly with Chamberlain's meticulous calligraphy and courteous phrases. Rhodes ignored punctuation, most of his loops were blotted, and there were numerous other blotches on his pages. But to us of a later age there is something free and galloping about Rhodes's handwriting that is more attractive than the finicky preciseness of Victorian script.

The first letters exchanged between Chamberlain and Rhodes point the contrast in a telling manner. That from Rhodes on 9 July 1895 which introduced himself and his cause to the new Colonial Secretary is more like the 'Stand and deliver!' of a literary highwayman than the opening notes in a diplomatic duet.

Dear Mr Chamberlain,
    I am glad you have taken the Colonial Office because even if you differ with me . . . I know full well you will always come to a decision . . .
    I hope to hear on Saturday that I can bring in Bill to annex British Bechuanaland to Cape. You will find if you look at correspondence that Protectorate is promised to Charter, it is merely question when you will hand over.

Chamberlain's reply on 31 July falls like holy oil on a pagan's forehead.

Dear Mr Rhodes,
    I . . . do not doubt that we shall be able to co-operate cordially for the mutual interests of the Colony and the United Kingdom. As far as I understand your main lines of policy I believe I am in general agreement with you, and if we ever differ on points of detail I hope that as sensible men of business we shall be able to give and take, and so come to an understanding . . .

Instead of letters Rhodes used the telegraph or human intermediaries who were instructed with extreme brevity, leaving a broad path open for misunderstandings. To the architect of his house, Herbert Baker, he would only say, 'You must do this. You must think. Remember, you must think, think. You must use your brains.' To an agent charged with a huge land purchase he rapped out, 'I don't ask your advice. I want you to buy it. Buy it!' Now there was Rutherfoord Harris, preparing to act as intermediary between himself and Chamberlain. He, too, had been told to think, to use his brains. Harris explained to the Committee of Inquiry something of his chief's methods. Rhodes did not instruct him step by step. He simply allowed the agent one long deep look into his master's mind and then left him to fill in the details. And what Harris read in the master-mind was an urgent command: 'I want you to get it. The Protectorate. All of it. Get it!'

# 21

# The 'Guarded Allusion'

The activities of Dr Rutherfoord Harris at the Colonial Office are centred around one question: did he succeed in adding Joseph Chamberlain to the list of Rhodes's confederates? Much hangs on the interpretation of the first meeting between them. It has been argued that the Colonial Secretary's behaviour during this opening chapter of the drama 'quite disposes of charges afterwards elaborated against Chamberlain and of slanders still whispered'.[1] On the other hand, emphasis has been laid on 'a conflict of evidence' and 'a strange refusal' by Chamberlain to receive confidential information from Dr Harris.[2] Does this suggest that he already suspected something of Rhodes's plans before the interview and learnt more of them during it?

The first interview between Chamberlain and Harris, on 1 August 1985, was not well attended by witnesses.* There were no officials in the room nor was Chamberlain's Under-Secretary, Lord Selborne, present; but, as sponsor of Dr Harris, there was Earl Grey, a director of the Chartered Company and warm admirer of Rhodes. Lord Grey belonged to a family famous in English history. His long face surmounted by a high, bald dome, his finely cut nose and kindly expression seemed to radiate serenity and charm. Yet Grey's part in the drama was a curious one and it was probably due only to an unspoken gentlemen's agreement between the Government and Opposition that his activities were not probed. Had they been, the results would have proved unpleasant to himself and painful to his friend Chamberlain.

Edward Fairfield was not present at the first three interviews between Harris and Chamberlain. As African expert, he expected to be kept better informed than he was, and he complained to Bouchier

---

* See E. Drus, *Bulletin of the Institute of Historical Research*, Vol. xxv (1952), pp. 43 and 47. This corrects the account given by J.L. Garvin, *Life of Chamberlain*, p. 37, and repeated by J. van der Poel, *The Jameson Raid*, p. 27.

Hawksley, Rhodes's solicitor and a personal friend, that Harris did not come to his room to give him a résumé of the interview, after spending 'a long time' at the Colonial Office with Chamberlain 'in August'.[3] So Hawksley obligingly got hold of Harris, and Fairfield was then put in the picture – during a rather confidential meeting *à trois*. It is now difficult to decide how much Chamberlain and Fairfield talked over their respective interviews; but a short passage from a private *Memorandum* addressed to Sir Hercules Robinson by Chamberlain on 12 June 1896 confirms the impression that the contact between Fairfield and Chamberlain was not close.

A few days later [i.e. after the interview with Harris on 1 August] *I heard from Lord Selborne that* Dr Harris had seen Mr Fairfield and talked very wildly to him about an impending revolution at Johannesburg . . . [4] [Author's italics.]

Chamberlain, Harris and Grey sat down together. Harris first tried to play his hand without reference to affairs in Johannesburg. He hoped that the lure of railway development in Bechuanaland, plus the weight of previous Liberal promises, would be enough to persuade Chamberlain to hand over the Protectorate promptly. Would the Colonial Secretary act in time for Rhodes to begin the rail extension northwards from Mafeking before the October rains? Chamberlain was torn. Chief Khama and his friends, supported by Liberal public opinion, objected. He himself, before he knew how far the previous Government had committed him, thought it would have been better to maintain imperial control over 'this great South African reserve'. But communications were Chamberlain's passion, and here was Rhodes wanting to build a new railway. 'Cape to Cairo' was a slogan that rang as sweetly in Chamberlain's ears as in those of Rhodes or the romantic Edwin Arnold of the *Telegraph* who invented it. The legitimate urge to extend, from his base at the Colonial Office, those thin black lines of communication over the pink spaces of the African map, as a general moves his flags, was irresistible. Rhodes had chosen his bait well.

Harris, the go-between, played his big fish during nine-tenths of the fateful interview on the long line of railway talk. This included the question of transferring the Bechuanaland Border Police to the Chartered Company to guard the new enterprise while it was under construction. Chamberlain conveyed to Harris that he was enthusiastic about the whole rail project. So far the interview had gone better than Chamberlain, who took an immediate dislike to the go-between, expected. He intended to bring it to an end by offering Rhodes a preliminary strip of land just wide enough for the railway. The rest of the transfer would probably have to wait for a period of up to two years. He insisted on carrying the African chiefs along with him in any future changes.

This suggested compromise was by no means the fulfilment of Harris's mission, as outlined by Rhodes at Groote Schurr – 'The Protectorate! Get it! The whole of it! Now!' The time had come for Rhodes's right-hand man to think, to use his brains in the manner which the master was so fond of urging upon his subordinates. If necessary he was at liberty to add one more reason, the most potent of all, for immediate transfer of the whole Protectorate. Harris must play his trump card: *the grave situation in Johannesburg*.

Harris sketched in the main features of the trouble in the Transvaal. Then, dropping his voice and as if about to admit the Colonial Secretary into some secret brotherhood, he began: 'I could tell you something in confidence . . .' But the word 'confidence', the altered tone of voice and the conspiratorial air alerted Chamberlain. He stopped Harris at once. 'I do not want to hear any confidential information,' he snapped. 'I am here in an official capacity. I can only hear information of which I can make official use.' The High Commissioner, he added, would of course keep him informed of anything he ought to know.

The Whip from Cape Town had failed to whip in Chamberlain. Lord Grey thereupon ushered his discomfited colleague from the room. Chamberlain had distrusted the man from the first and was glad to see him go. But Grey himself returned to the charge, hoping that a more informal interview might have better results. He was no more successful than Harris. Chamberlain again declined to receive confidential information which he would be obliged to use officially 'even if it were to the injury of those who tendered it'. In the *Memorandum* for Robinson already quoted, Chamberlain made his attitude quite clear: 'My feeling at that time was that it was unnecessary and undesirable that I should receive from a private friend details of the proceedings of the revolutionary party in

Johannesburg which I could not afterwards act upon without a breach of confidence.'

This account of the interview of 1 August derives from Chamberlain himself: partly from a letter to Grey, partly from his *Memorandum* to Robinson, partly from his evidence before the Tribunal. It tallies with Lord Selborne's recollections and permits a quite natural explanation of Chamberlain's 'strange refusal' to listen to Harris's confidences. Namely, that he and Selborne both assumed the interrupted revelations concerned Johannesburg *internally*.

Information about conditions inside that city was constantly reaching the Colonial Office. Chamberlain had no need to grab at every shady item of news that was thrust upon him. Moreover, he sympathized with the Uitlanders' resolve to 'secure for themselves the common rights of free men', as Grey put it later. Without in any way failing in his watchful duty as representative of the paramount power in South Africa, Chamberlain felt no obligation to bend over backwards in order to discover means of frustrating a reform movement he deemed righteous.

Here, then, is the evidence from Chamberlain's side. It is unfortunate for him that it conflicts with that of both Harris and Grey. The crucial evidence of Dr Harris is confined to one or two sentences which he addressed to the Tribunal in the course of a long cross-examination. Though so brief it is none the less deadly. Chamberlain, as a member of the Tribunal, sat opposite Harris listening, much as he had sat opposite him in the Colonial Office a year and nine months before. But on the latter occasion the distrust he had felt for Harris from the first rapidly turned into exasperation or, as some have said, into intense alarm.

According to Dr Harris, he was able to get in a reference not only to unrest at Johannesburg but also to the consequent desirability of a colonial police force on the Transvaal border, before Chamberlain stopped him. The need for this force was to be his clinching argument for immediate transfer of the Protectorate. Harris, however, realized the delicacy of the topic on which he was now embarking. He had never met the redoubtable Minister before and, according to his own account, he felt a novice at the game. He therefore referred only 'guardedly' to the rôle of the police. Even so

Chamberlain 'at once demurred to the turn the conversation had taken' and Harris made his embarrassed exit. Though he had further interviews with Chamberlain at the Colonial Office he never again alluded to the subject of the border police and their watch on Johannesburg.

A certain mystery still shrouds the now famous 'guarded allusion' of Dr Rutherfoord Harris. Sir William Harcourt, with his habitual flair for the significant in history, at once sensed it. 'It is a remarkable phrase which will probably attract a great deal of attention,' he said to Dr Harris at the Inquiry. It has indeed done so. What exactly were the 'guarded' words which Harris claimed to have used? He revealed them to the Tribunal at his second appearance before them:

> . . . We shall be here [i.e. on the Transvaal border] and if a rising takes place at Johannesburg, of course we shall not stand by and see them tightly pressed.[5]

The 'guarded allusion' was thus a brief reference to Rhodes's modification of the Loch plan: a border force *removed from imperial control* and not only intended to keep law and order at the High Commissioner's bidding but also *to assist the revolutionaries in their struggle against Kruger*.

Chamberlain denied that he ever heard this 'guarded allusion', or if he did, he did not comprehend it. At the beginning of August, he stressed, he was a novice in his job; Bechuanaland was, to adapt a phrase later made famous by his son Neville, a far-off country of which he knew nothing. In response to this explanation, Dr Harris was good enough to tell the Tribunal: 'I accept Mr Chamberlain's statement that he did not hear me make the allusion.' This cynical and partial retraction, like so many others made during the hearings of the Committee, added to the unpleasant atmosphere but could not damage the Colonial Secretary's indomitable will to survive.

The picture of Chamberlain and Harris, two astute old parliamentary hands, both presenting themselves to the Committee as innocents abroad, is not without its black humour. While Chamberlain protested that he did not even know where Gaberones was on the map, Harris excused his cryptic utterances on the ground that he had never been to any such interview before and therefore, as a novice, did not care to say too much. Yet he had attended the Protectorate negotiations under Lord Ripon, had met the Under-Secretary Sydney Buxton, and in his own words had been to the Colonial Office 'over and over again . . . ever since 1892 off and on'.

Did Harris succeed in making his 'guarded allusion'? It seems probable that Chamberlain was right and that Harris was interrupted before the crucial words were out. As Chamberlain put it to the Tribunal, the allusion, as recollected by Harris, was not 'guarded' at all; and if it had in fact been made in those words, Chamberlain could not have failed to recognize it for what it was. But even if the evidence of the Colonial Secretary is accepted against that of Rhodes's agent, the former is not yet out of the wood. For the evidence of Lord Grey differed from that of Chamberlain on a point remarkably similar to that of Harris.

Grey's account of his interview with Chamberlain was not given before the Committee of Inquiry – he was never summoned to appear – but in a private letter to the Minister. Due attention must be paid to this letter for it is no longer a case of weighing the words of the questionable Dr Harris but of the upright Lord Grey. Grey believed that Chamberlain received the gist of his confidential information before he interrupted. This, of course, was the second attempt made on behalf of Rhodes on 1 August 1895 to let Chamberlain into the plot, and this time Grey believed it was successful. He wrote to Chamberlain on 10 December 1896, when comparing notes, in preparation for the Inquiry:

. . . If I am called before the Committee and asked whether I informed you in any way of the impending Revolution at Joh$^g$, I shall be obliged, either to refuse to answer, or to say that I told you privately that the long expected and inevitable rising . . . would shortly take place, and that being so it was desirable that an armed force sh$^d$ be stationed on the Transvaal border for use if required. Altho' you declined to receive this information, which you said you wd be obliged to use officially, if it were pressed upon you, the subsequent acts of the Govt showed that you agreed with our view that it was desirable to give the BSA Co. an opportunity of placing a force upon the frontier.

For so much that Dr Harris' cables show I must take my full share of blame, and if allowing Rhodes to be informed of this involved an abuse of confidence, I think you know that it was done . . . with [the] singleminded intention of helping on a patriotic cause . . .[6]

Lord Selborne has left some *Notes* on these interviews between his chief and Harris and Grey respectively, according to which Chamberlain interrupted Grey *before* he could give the confidential information:

... As soon as ever the S. of S. [Secretary of State] saw what subject the director [Grey] was going to enlarge upon, he abruptly stopped him, informing him that the internal affairs of the SAR were no concern of his and that ... he had complete confidence in the High Commissioner. The subject was never alluded to in any subsequent interview except by way of an occasional very guarded and very short reference, 'so short' as to give the S. of S. no opportunity of stopping it.[7]

Was Selborne rather than Grey correct in his account of the Chamberlain–Grey interview? The answer is no. Selborne was not present at the interview. His account was based on hearsay obtained from Chamberlain himself. Clearly Selborne had mixed up the Harris and Grey interviews and his evidence cannot be accepted against Grey's. (The reason why he used the key words 'allude' and 'guarded' was because he was in process of examining Dr Harris's notorious messages in which these words occurred.)

Returning to Earl Grey's private letter, in what sense could Chamberlain 'decline to receive' information which he had already heard? The important word here is 'officially'. (Grey said that Chamberlain rejected the confidential information because he would have to use it 'officially' if it were pressed upon him.) The new Colonial Secretary was admittedly in a difficulty. He recognized in the proposals to which Grey had just alluded a somewhat daring version of the Loch plan. This, he knew, had already been turned down, officially at least, by a previous Cabinet. Chamberlain felt that Sir Henry Loch had been right in his policy and the Liberal Cabinet wrong. Now he himself was faced with a chance to reverse that wrong decision.

It would be impossible for Chamberlain to strengthen the imperial troops without consulting the Cabinet, and there was no guarantee that with Lansdowne in the lead they would not refuse. But suppose the enlarged border force were composed of Company police? There would be no need to consult anybody, provided he did not sponsor the plan officially. His predecessors had miraculously made such a solution possible. Though this policy would demand a certain amount of finesse, it was not, he felt, intrinsically objectionable. Surely, if Rhodes's Elizabethan adventurers could fight their battles without always involving the home forces, so much the better?

It is the evidence of Earl Grey, Chamberlain's friend, rather than that of Harris, which really counts in a serious assessment of Chamberlain's complicity. If the fact is accepted that Grey did give Chamberlain a private account of Rhodes's plan, and that Chamberlain received it but only 'unofficially', the road becomes clearer to a realistic judgment upon the Jameson Raid. Chamberlain indeed 'knew nothing' *officially* about the private plans of Rhodes. 'I did not want to know too much,' he told Flora Shaw. In the complicated game of knowing and not knowing, of keeping official and unofficial knowledge strictly apart, he sometimes lost himself in the maze: 'The fact is I can hardly say what I knew and what I did not.' His left hand must not know what his right hand did; he would shut his eyes to the implications of carrying the promises of his predecessors to their logical conclusions. If handing over the Protectorate involved handing over the police too, he would not be the man to put a gratuitous spoke in the wheel of this fortunate development. There was almost a touch of that legendary 'absence of mind' in his attitude, through which the Empire was said to have been acquired.

Today, with every political move minutely examined by an Argus-eyed press, the resort to a distinction between 'official' and 'private' knowledge, though not unknown, is rare. The modern politician has little enough private life even in the sphere that is legitimately regarded as private. Rash indeed would be the Cabinet Minister who attempted to reserve a secret area of his official duties for 'unofficial' enterprise. When such a thing turns out to have been done, public opinion is uncompromising in disapproval.

But when Chamberlain was Colonial Secretary, this practice, though doubtless adopted with hesitation, was not uncommon. In 1889 Arthur Balfour wrote a letter headed 'Most private' to a correspondent addressed as 'My dear Duke'. As a result, certain encumbered estates in Ireland were bought up by a syndicate and a blow was struck against the Irish nationalists' 'Plan of Campaign'. Questioned in Parliament, Balfour denied all 'official knowledge' of the transaction.

The most interesting parallel, on a somewhat different plane, to Chamberlain's deliberate abstention from 'official knowledge' occurs in the story of the Raid itself. It will be seen in due course how Sir Graham Bower, faced with a difficult choice, decided to make Robinson play this same diplomatic game of 'private' versus 'official' knowledge. It brought disastrous results to Bower. For when something suddenly went tremendously wrong with the plans, the diplomatic subterfuge proved strong enough to protect the principals but was honourably rejected by the subordinate, Bower himself.

It would be a mistake, however, to suppose that Chamberlain's case rested entirely on a flimsy convention long out-moded and always of dubious validity; a convention indeed that today would be called double-think. His good friend Grey was hoping to build up with him an apparently more solid line of defence. His letter to Chamberlain of 10 December 1896 continued:

I most certainly can confirm you when you say that you did not know and could not know of any plan or intention of Mr Rhodes which could possibly lead to such an invasion of the Transvaal in time of peace as was perpetrated by Dr Jameson, for I did not know of any such plan or intention myself.[8]

Unfortunately for the Government and Company, this defence line crumbles just as the first did. There were similarities, of course, between the 'Loch Line' and the 'Rhodes Plan'. But it was the difference between them that was vital. Loch envisaged the troops as genuinely under Her Majesty's orders. This would have ruled out any raid – except as a purely personal adventure. Jameson's Raid could and did happen because of the very nature of Rhodes's planning. In the original Rhodes–Jameson plan, Jameson even proposed to start two days *before* the rising, just to make sure. This being so, the absolute distinction that Grey, Chamberlain and so many others tried to draw between the Rhodes plan and the Raid was tempting but untenable, a false dichotomy.

Paul Kruger, President of the Transvaal, holding the Book: Drawl cartoon from *Vanity Fair*

'Dr Jim': Spy cartoon of Jameson from *Vanity Fair,* 9 April 1896

Cecil Rhodes at about the time of the Raid

Joseph Chamberlain, Britain's Colonial Secretary in 1895

Dr Jameson and his officers. Back row, left to right: C Monro, K Kineaid-Smith, Dr Jameson, C H Villiers, Hon R White, J B Stracey and R Grey. Front row, left to right: C P Foley, Hon H F White, Sir J Willoughby, C F Lindsell and H M Grenfell

Jameson's men cutting the telegraph wires (from a sketch by Captain Thatcher supplied to *The Illustrated London News*)

Jameson's last stand at Doornkop, 2 January 1896 (from the painting by R Caton Woodville)

The surrender

# THE BRITISH SOUTH AFRICA COMPANY.

Telegram *from L. Harris* No. 1    Date 4 Nov 95

| Code Word. | Cypher. | Translation. |
|---|---|---|
| Umkleidung | | Mr Chamberlain 266 |
| Offerins | uppe | he does not return |
| uebergning | | London |
| ankrant | | until |
| schuftet | | to-morrow |
| steinbirke | | we have |
| | | spoken |
| Unnamung | | to Fairfield |
| augenwink | | and |
| transadios | | we have agreed to |
| bochischte | | if |
| lispelerin | | Colonial Office |
| sortearden | | they will transfer |
| schubwand | | to us |
| belegeld | | balance |
| nachrichen | | protectorate |
| spatrbot | | with |
| metzeneld | | police |
| stechheber | | 17th November |
| soprasoldo | | we will accept (agree to) |
| | | any liberal |
| lauchfarbe | | native |
| pflusajon | | reserve |
| aschmaul | | for |
| laubthaler | | native Chiefs |
| | | also |
| packschnur | | remain |
| schnaders | | under |
| | | imperial |
| polireisen | | rule |

One of the 'missing telegrams' from Harris to Rhodes, 4 November 1895 (as received in Cape Town)

# THE BRITISH SOUTH AFRICA COMPANY.

Telegram _____ No. 2 _____ Date _____

| Code Word. | Cypher. | Translation. |
|---|---|---|
| menmenkuft | | for a period |
| | | of |
| lambing | 2 | years |
| augenwink | | and |
| accattmuskante | | would give up |
| nebelitat | | Railway |
| saftreich | | subsidy |
| cameras | 03089 | £ 200,000 |
| kernhaft | | East bargain |
| ammanung | | E. Fairfield |
| sofrealsar | 11930 | he does urge |
| eukister | 14114 | if you cannot approve |
| ochauber | | let us know about |
| | | this as soon as possible |
| | | by telegram |
| beschicke | | we believe |
| ammanung | | E. Fairfield |
| serrabais | 17914 | he will carry out |
| muiresina | | Regret to inform you that |
| umpleidung | | Mr Chamberlain |
| sobonazo | 17930 | he does continue |
| gunchina | | Consult |
| ammafen | | Transvaal |
| rotterbaum | | with regard to |
| | | drifts |
| amrundert | | F Rutherfoord Harris |

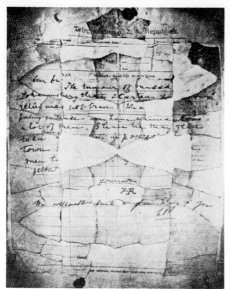

Fragments of the letter sent by Colonel Rhodes to Dr Jameson, which were picked up at Doornkop after the Raid

Jameson and his officers before Sir John Bridge at Bow Street

Contemporary print in *Vanity Fair* of Rhodes before the South Africa Committee, 1897. Left to right: Sir Richard Webster, Henry Labouchere, Cecil Rhodes, Sir William Harcourt and Joseph Chamberlain

Flora Shaw, Colonial Correspondent of *The Times*

Max Beerbohm cartoon of
Chamberlain

Léandre cartoon of Rhodes 'the
Imperialist' in *Le Rire*, 17 February
1900

Rhodes at 'the View of the World' in the Matopo Hills (later the site of his grave)

# 22

## *The First Three 'Missing Telegrams'*

Chamberlain wrote to the Prime Minister, after seeing Harris and Grey, that he would like a paragraph in the Queen's Speech on the affairs of the Cape and Bechuanaland.[1] His mind was racing ahead full of sanguine ideas for developing his 'estates'. The talk with his friend Lord Grey had done nothing to temper his optimism. But on the day after the interview, Harris dispatched the first of a notorious series of cables to his chief, Rhodes, in Cape Town, which would have frozen Chamberlain's blood.[2] They purported to be an account of the Protectorate negotiations at the Colonial Office.

Who composed these messages? They were sent as if from Harris alone, under his code name of 'Cactus'; it was perhaps a tribute to the prickly nature of his mission. But in fact many were drawn up in consultation between Harris and two of Rhodes's intimate friends in London, Rochfort Maguire and Earl Grey. Maguire, Rhodes's 'alternate' on the board of the Chartered Company, was an intriguing character. Married to a beautiful and aristocratic woman, a friend of the Prince of Wales and a member of all the right clubs, he was also a Fellow of All Souls and interested in philosophy and scholarship. He had been one of the envoys sent by Rhodes to do a deal with Lobengula.

The first cable was drafted by Harris and Grey. Together with seven other cables, it was withheld from the Committee of Inquiry, and the total batch of eight became known as the 'missing telegrams'.* At the time, of course, no one except Rhodes and his immediate confederates knew exactly how many telegrams were 'missing'; but certain allusions in other telegrams brought before the Committee made it clear that there were gaps in the series. On the interpretation and estimate of these eight telegrams depends much of Chamberlain's case. For these eight, as may be imagined, were the most incriminating and the least easily explained away.

The first 'missing telegram', sent on 2 August 1895 from Harris to

* The 'missing telegrams' were actually all cablegrams, but it is under the first name that they became famous and have gone down to history.

Rhodes, began with an accurate account of Chamberlain's refusal to transfer the whole Protectorate forthwith.*

His attitude on this point decisive. He states presence C. J. Rhodes England will not alter his mind; that C. J. Rhodes must leave him alone for the present. In his opinion he acceded to transfer Crown Colony in order to ensure immediate further Railway Construction, and much upset that it was not the case . . .

Incidentally, the last sentence shows that Chamberlain, when he eventually allowed Jameson's force to be posted on the border to guard the railway, was well aware and indeed was 'much upset' that no railway existed to guard!

The telegram continued:

We therefore decided to inform Secretary of State for Colonies guardedly reason we wish to have base at Gaberones and advisable our presence in Protectorate. Secretary of State for Colonies heartily in sympathy with C. J. Rhodes's policy, but he would not on this ground alter decision with regard to Protectorate . . .

A passage of some obscurity followed, which Garvin dismissed as irrelevant 'code jargon' and did not print. In fact it was highly relevant, though written in 'telegraphese', i.e. in words and phrases that happened to be in the code-book of the Company. (Any words not found in the Company's code-book, such as Flora until she became 'Telemones', had to be sent by the clerk 'open', meaning *en clair*.) The original text, as handed to the clerk for encipherment, was discovered in the Rhodes Papers by C. M. Woodhouse and was as follows:

Secretary of State . . . offered as alternate, to justify residents [*sic*] of BSA Co. in Protectorate, to consider favourably at once application for large land

* In two articles entitled 'The Missing Telegrams and the Jameson Raid' (*History Today*, June and July 1962) Mr C.M. Woodhouse analysed the striking discoveries he had made in the Rhodes Papers at Rhodes House, Oxford, in regard to this telegram and others of the mysterious batch. In brief, he found that the whole of the original text of this, the first 'missing' telegram, still existed. That this, and other telegrams of 1895 had three versions: I. The original draft by the sender. II. The version edited into 'telegraphese' so that the original draft could be enciphered and dispatched. III. The above as deciphered for the addressee. That Rhodes and Chamberlain did not always see the same wording owing to clerical discrepancies. That when the Select Committee saw a telegram it was in what should be called version IV, having been recovered from the telegraph company and deciphered in 1897 by a clerk different from the cipher-clerk of 1895.

grant in Protectorate in exchange for Railway Extension north. It is now for Mr C. J. Rhodes to decide whether large land grant with formation Township and sale of stands [sites] is practicable for October. This appears to be the only solution.

Chamberlain would have regarded this report to Rhodes of the opening skirmish in London as tendentious. His hearty sympathy was expressed for the railway aspect of 'C. J. Rhodes's policy', not for the further plan which Earl Grey had outlined to him. He had 'declined to receive it' though unofficially sympathetic. He felt no need to 'justify' the presence of the Company in the Protectorate, for the Liberal Government had already agreed to it, even down to the preliminary offer of a railway strip along the border, the 'large land grant' of the telegram.

Why then did Harris give a sinister twist to this telegram? Today there is no force in the argument that it was in order to blackmail Chamberlain later. To Harris the 'large land grant' had only one immediate use, and that a disreputable one: to form a 'jumping-off ground' for armed incursion into the Transvaal. The railway was mere camouflage. But to Chamberlain the 'large land grant' had a genuinely dual purpose and both purposes could be justified: first, to extend the railway; second, to keep a watch on the border. This second project, however, had inherent risks, because of which Chamberlain 'declined to receive' any details, and which in fact were to make him vulnerable after the Raid.

It would have been utterly impossible, however, in the excited state of foreign and home opinion after the Raid, for Chamberlain to explain the refinements of his true position. How define for Kruger's or the Kaiser's sceptical ear the line which separated Chamberlain's plan from that of Loch, or the Rhodes plan from Chamberlain's? The Colonial Secretary had good reasons for wishing certain telegrams to remain 'missing'.

Interviews and cables followed each other in dramatic succession. On 13 August Chamberlain saw Rochfort Maguire.* On the same day the second 'missing telegram' from Harris to Rhodes

* This fact is taken from a memorandum on Chamberlain's interviews written by H.C.M. Lambert, a junior official, and now among the *Chamberlain Papers*. See 'A Report on the Papers of Joseph Chamberlain relating to the Jameson Raid and the Inquiry', E. Drus, *Bulletin of the Institute of Historical Research*, Vol. xxv (1952), pp. 47 and 51–2.

emphasized Chamberlain's eagerness to 'assist', subject to two conditions: one, that the whole Protectorate could not be transferred yet, and two, that

he officially does not know of your plan.

Again the mixture as before, part accurate, part misleading: the insistence on Chamberlain's official ignorance was correct and was probably conveyed to Harris by Maguire; but the reference to 'your plan' was full of ambiguity.

In the third 'missing telegram' of 21 August 1895, Chamberlain's line of unofficial knowledge was again rubbed in. Moreover, a fresh cause for misunderstanding was introduced:

You are aware Chamberlain states Dr Jameson's plan must not be mentioned to him.

The words 'Dr Jameson's plan' did not refer to the Raid; the Raid was no one's plan but one man's madness. 'Dr Jameson's plan' simply meant Rhodes's plan, in so far as it revolved around the stationing of Dr Jameson on the frontier. Garvin, however, dismisses the third telegram altogether, on the ground that 'no human being' conceived that Dr Jameson's plan would one day include a raid. Of course not. But it was irrelevant.

Despite all the efforts of Harris and his colleagues, Chamberlain did not transfer the whole of the Protectorate until over three months had passed. Can this be used to prove that he knew nothing at all of Rhodes's plan, and therefore continued, unintentionally, to thwart and delay it? It seems not. For though Chamberlain was by no means in the full confidence of Rhodes, it has been shown that he knew enough to see in the negotiations an opportunity of killing two birds with one economical stone: cheap rail development plus border-duty at almost no expense.

Why then did he not toss the whole prize immediately to the clamouring Rhodes? Two excellent reasons held him back. First, distrust for Rhodes and his agents. Their sheer importunity, far from hurrying him, caused him to go slowly. A second reason lay in the alarm felt by the African chiefs at the prospect of spending their future under the Chartered Company. Chamberlain sympathized with this anxiety. Here in London, visiting the Colonial Office as

Rhodes's proxy, was Mr Rochfort Maguire; the very same Maguire who had sat in Lobengula's ill-fated goat-kraal canvassing for concessions. Chamberlain may not have been a paid-up member of the Aborigines Protection Society, but there was something of the old Liberal left in him. And public opinion had come out strongly in favour of Khama and against Rhodes; Chamberlain was never one to ignore public opinion.

The first three 'missing telegrams' bring the story up to the end of August 1895, when the prospect of a 'jumping-off ground' in the Protectorate for Jameson's force seemed rosy. After a lull for the September holidays, pressure rose again during the October drifts crisis and by mid-month Rhodes had his 'jumping-off ground', alias 'railway strip', signed and sealed. At the end of October and the beginning of November the 'missing telegrams' began again, in connection with the final transfer of the Protectorate.

In the meantime, a new series of fateful interviews took place. The scene was now the High Commissioner's office in Cape Town.

Chamberlain, as Rhodes understood from Harris, was in the bag. The time had now come for Rhodes to let into the secret his last potential accomplice, the High Commissioner. For it was a part of the Loch plan, adapted by Rhodes, that the High Commissioner, upon the outbreak of a Uitlander rebellion, should go up to Pretoria and mediate. But Rhodes would not approach Sir Hercules direct. He first confided the secret to the Imperial Secretary, Sir Graham Bower, his old friend and the man who had 'during three interregnums been practically High Commissioner and done admirably'.

The date was mid-October. Before he began to speak Rhodes swore Bower to secrecy. Rhodes then revealed his plans for the rising and his intention to bring down Company troops from Rhodesia to wait on the border and go in if necessary. Chamberlain, he said, knew already and so did 'a Liberal politician' – Lord Rosebery.* Rhodes then asked Bower the momentous question. Should he tell the High Commissioner?

Bower was in a dilemma. Tell or not to tell? He did not like the plan. He had no faith in a spontaneous rising of capitalists ('No one expects Rothschild to die waving a Red flag on a barricade and our local Rothschilds are not made that way'). He did consider some kind of engineered rising inevitable, but he did not want to encourage it. He was not at all sorry that the imperial authorities were 'infernally slow', as Rhodes contemptuously put it. If Robinson intervened as an accomplice, he would not in future be able to arbitrate between Boers and Uitlanders with 'clean hands'. Yet in his position of responsibility it would be wrong for him not to know. Bower described the tense scene in his *Apologia*: 'I turned my back on Rhodes and looked out of the window to think.' His thoughts switched to and fro, for and against. 'There is only a thin sheet of paper between previous knowledge and complicity . . . I was

* See pp. 309–11 below.

embarrassed by Rhodes's communication and the question was should I embarrass the High Commissioner?'[1]

In the end Bower turned back to Rhodes, having independently reached the same kind of solution as Chamberlain while listening to Grey. Bower decided Robinson should be told 'confidentially' and his knowledge should be 'kept secret'. He felt no qualms: 'For my part, though I laughed at these fine distinctions which savour of casuistry and self-deception, I always respected them.' Not only respected them in others but used them himself to further his own pacific policy. The end would justify the means.

While Bower had his back to Rhodes another thought came to him regarding the troops on the border. The imperialist Chamberlain was not the only one to consider troops at Pitsani to be useful and necessary; indeed, Bower thought it positively wrong not to have the troops available, because of Germany and the 'raw savages' in Johannesburg. He says he looked upon the railway guard much as manoeuvres, and acquiesced in this 'alternative pretext' for a border force.

Even after the Raid Bower could not bring himself to regard this part of the plot with disapproval. An extraordinary scene was to take place on the platform of Bloemfontein station when the High Commissioner, accompanied by Bower, eventually found himself on the way to Pretoria to 'mediate'. It was 3 January; members of the Free State Government and Press had assembled to wish the peacemaker *bon voyage*. But the peacemaker was gravely ill. His legs, swollen with dropsy, made him slow to get down on to the platform. His Secretary, Bower, 'disregarding etiquette', jumped out first, only to find himself faced at once with what he later admitted to be *the* question about the Raid: 'What were the troops doing on the border?' Bower, without any hesitation, rapped back: 'Watching Johannesburg.' But Sir Hercules had by now caught up with his too agile subordinate and sharply contradicted him: 'Guarding the railway.' The High Commissioner was decidedly put out by Bower's blunder. Bower apologized to his chief, but his *Apologia* records a significant fact: 'Sir Hercules and I had parted company in our answers to the key question.'

And so Sir Graham Bower advised Rhodes to enlighten his chief in private. Rhodes was shown into the High Commissioner's sanctum, and what followed, riddled as it is with contradiction, is still inspired guesswork. But there are marked indications that Rhodes fulfilled his mission. After all, as Bower himself wrote later, Rhodes only needed to say, 'The Capitalists have joined the National Union, there is likely to be a rising and I am moving the troops down to guard the railway,' and the High Commissioner would understand all. Bower believed he did so.

Though Sir Hercules never once mentioned the interview, Bower noticed that he immediately carried out the first item on Rhodes's agenda: he ordered the troops down to Pitsani. (It is significant that Grey also interpreted Chamberlain's attitude towards the rising through his actions: 'The subsequent act of the Government,' Grey wrote to Chamberlain, 'showed that you agreed with our view.')* So Bower now took Robinson's action to be his answer.

Furthermore, Robinson's remarks about the Colonial Secretary became increasingly vituperative after his interview with Rhodes. This strongly suggests that he had heard something to deepen his previous aversion. After the departure of Rhodes he referred to 'those damned conspiracies of Rhodes and Chamberlain'; later he echoed Bower's view that 'that damned fellow Chamberlain is always overriding the hounds'. When Bower told Robinson, shortly before the Raid, that Frank Newton had come to see him about the 'wild talk' among the Mafeking officers, he knew enough already not to want to hear any more: 'I won't see him. The whole thing is piracy. I know nothing about it.'

After Jameson's bolt Bower urged Robinson to recall the raiders immediately, to which Robinson objected: 'But perhaps Chamberlain has sent him in or may approve. He is such an extraordinary fellow he is capable of anything.' The same objection was at first raised to Hofmeyr's demand for a proclamation against Jameson: 'But I am afraid Pushful Joe is in it.'†

Rhodes and Jameson both assured Bower afterwards that Robinson knew all, Rhodes supplying a graphic note on his interview with the High Commissioner: 'The High Commissioner had taken it rather badly and did not want the subject mentioned.' Too much

---

* See p. 173 above.

† See below, p.223. All the above sayings of the High Commissioner are found in the *Bower Papers*, except for the remark about Pushful Joe which occurs in *The Life of Jan Hendrik Hofmeyr* by J.H. Hofmeyr, p. 490.

weight, however, must not be attached to evidence just because it is graphic. Bower himself, under the direction of the Colonial Office, adduced some equally graphic touches to prove that Robinson was never told:

It is clear Mr Rhodes omitted to tell him [Robinson] what he said to me. This Mr Rhodes voluntarily stated . . . in my room after the raid, saying that he was glad 'he had kept the Government out of it'.[2]

Dr Jameson was Robinson's physician. He told Bower, and also Lady Edward Cecil (afterwards Viscountess Milner), that he used his professional visits to keep his patient in the picture. The evidence of the late Lady Milner on this subject is some of the most intriguing that has come to light since the Raid. When J. L. Garvin brought out his *Life* of Joseph Chamberlain, Lady Milner was inspired to recount in the *National Review* of December 1934 (of which she was editor) her recollections of a conversation with Jameson in 1900. Just before the Raid, she said, Jameson had become so much worried about leakages in his plans that he almost decided to call the whole thing off. He described the situation to Lady Milner in the following words:

Rhodes, however, thought the matter had better go on and this was also Robinson's opinion. The High Commissioner knew every detail of the arrangements, and as the time approached, his train was kept in readiness for him to start at a moment's notice. The night before I left for Mafeking (a few days before the Raid started*) I went to see him. I was his doctor, and therefore private interviews were very easy to arrange on the score of his health. On that last occasion we went over the ground of our joint action again. Bower knew of the interviews and what passed at them. When the Raid failed, the High Commissioner let it be thought that Bower alone had information.

When Bower asked the High Commissioner to clear him, said Lady Milner, the curt reply was, 'I'll never speak.' This remarkable conversation with Dr Jameson was afterwards relayed by Lady Milner to Chamberlain whose comment was: 'I believe that to be substantially true.'

\* \* \*

---

* It was thirty days. See J. van der Poel, op. cit., p. 62.

Turning to Robinson's own testimony as to his part in the Jameson plan, the story is reversed. Up to the very last he denied any knowledge of the plot. Even in private to Bower he plugged the obstinate slogan, 'Remember, I know nothing about it.' South Africa and England both accepted his word. He was created Lord Rosmead between the Raid and the Inquiry, and when the Committee reported it gave him, as it gave Chamberlain, an immaculately clean sheet.

What is posterity to believe? It is inconceivable that the High Commissioner knew less than the Colonial Secretary. It is almost certain that he knew in much the same way – confidentially. But in whatever manner the Colonial Secretary may have come to adopt the policy of 'unofficial knowledge', the High Commissioner had it thrust upon him, against his will, by Bower. Is it surprising that when things turned out so disastrously, the feeble old man had just enough force left to stick to his guns and deny all knowledge? Bower organized the game for him and he played it only too well.

'He let me down in the end,' wrote Bower in sorrow rather than in anger. But Sir Hercules in the end was living the rôle for which he had been so unwillingly cast, living it with an almost frantic conviction. George Wyndham prophesied that at the Day of Judgment Robinson and Chamberlain, 'those two old men', would shake hands and congratulate each other on having done the right thing.[3] Bower, conscious of his own fortitude, was not afraid of the Day of Judgment and tended to regard St Peter with disapproval: 'My name is not Peter', he would say, 'and I am not going to run away.' But in the case of Sir Hercules, a hero only in name, it is probable that Wyndham was right.

Lord Rosmead, as he became, almost certainly persuaded himself by the end of his life that Sir Hercules had known nothing. Had not Rhodes said to him, as he passed through Cape Town in December 1896 on his way to the Inquiry, 'Well, you knew nothing about it?' To which Sir Hercules gratefully replied: 'Of course not, but I am glad you did not tell me anything for I would not have known what to do.'

But on his own deathbed Rhodes produced for his friend Sir Graham Bower, according to the latter, a very different account of the matter:

My dear fellow, I told him everything and the only questions he put to me
were: 'Is Beit in it and have you told Bower?'
He then said, 'I don't want to hear anything
more about it.'

Chamberlain was to maintain almost the same stubborn front as
Robinson, but for very different reasons. When Robinson reached
England to be tapped for dropsy, he found Chamberlain was not
going to admit anything and would therefore save him after all.
Immediately Chamberlain changed in the High Commissioner's
estimation from 'that damned fellow' into a very nice man 'with lots
of pluck'.

# 24

# Fairfield in the Toils

The 'jumping-off ground' did not satisfy Rhodes for long. With the drifts dispute working up to a crisis and playing into his hands, he aimed at scooping up all that Chamberlain's predecessors had promised, and quickly. He was soon ordering Harris to regard 7 November as zero hour for the completion of the transfer. Once again, code messages began to fly between Cape Town and London.

The fourth and fifth 'missing telegrams' were sent on 28 and 29 October 1895. Rhodes urged another private meeting between Grey and Chamberlain to press the importance of immediate transfer. Harris, in reply, acquiesced in this proposal but included the warning:

We dare not mention the reason.

This was the only one of the 'missing telegrams' which Chamberlain 'remembered' accurately enough to quote to the Tribunal. Harris's words, however, did not prove that Chamberlain was ignorant of 'the reason' for the transfer. They simply confirmed that the Colonial Secretary was sticking to his policy of the blind eye.

The next big date was 4 November. Things were moving fast. Chamberlain being away in Birmingham, Fairfield conducted the negotiations with Harris. An interview took place between them at the Colonial Office.

At the end of that day a letter went off from Fairfield to Chamberlain and a cable from Harris to Rhodes, giving their respective versions of the interview. The cable was to become the subject of much argument both among historians and members of the Select Committee, for whom it was produced. Though apparently most compromising, it did not go 'missing'. We shall soon see why.

Harris, in his cable, appeared to have trumpeted forth one clear, devastating note that stands out from the many jangling obscurities of his message:

I have spoken open E Fairfield.

The main text of the cable, as seen by the Select Committee (version IV)*, dealt with the transfer of the Protectorate, the drifts crisis and its effect on Johannesburg:

J. Chamberlain he does not return to London until tomorrow. I have spoken open E Fairfield and I have accepted if Colonial Office they will transfer to us balance protectorate with police 7 November we will agree to any liberal reserves for native chiefs ... Regret to inform you that J. Chamberlain he does continue punching Consul-General Transvaal with regard to Drifts. E Fairfield is anxious Johannesburg if they take steps in precedence of.

The meaning of the last sentence is still in dispute. According to one interpretation, Fairfield's anxiety was about the drifts, and was therefore quite innocuous. According to the other, it concerned the rising, and therefore went far to prove his complicity. When this cable was read out to the Committee of Inquiry, Chamberlain explained it from Fairfield's own notes written after the Raid at Chamberlain's request. Fairfield interpreted the sentence as:

Fairfield thinks that Johannesburg should take precedence.

In other words, said Fairfield 'the grievances of Johannesburg had a prior claim to those of the Cape Railway Department [i.e. the drifts] on the diplomatic services of the Imperial Government'. This explanation has been recently denounced as 'absurd, facetious, ridiculously far-fetched'. A so-called 'obvious rendering' of the last sentence in Harris's message is offered in its stead as follows:

Fairfield is anxious lest Johannesburg should take steps prematurely.[1]

According to this version, Fairfield's anxiety was lest some hasty act by the Uitlanders should prevent the planned rising from coming off successfully.

Neither of these explanations is entirely acceptable. A third possible interpretation could be:

Fairfield is anxious lest Johannesburg take violent steps which would prevent the drifts being settled.

* See footnote, p. 178.

In other words, Fairfield was worried lest the already exasperated Johannesburgers should break out over the drifts, thus ruining the chance of Chamberlain's 'punching' meeting with success. Harris at the Inquiry was to mention a *rumour* that the Johannesburgers would commit an act of violence, such as tearing up Kruger's rail track in reply to his drifts policy. Fairfield, also, in his explanation, noted that he had been passing on a *piece of gossip* to Harris.

So much for the possible meanings of the telegram's last sentence. But whatever it meant – and its exact meaning will probably always remain a mystery – a startling new fact has emerged about its fate. It was never seen by Rhodes. For this sentence, as well as the one before it, were never enciphered for version III, the version that Rhodes received. Thus, whether or not Fairfield was expressing sympathy with the rising, his words could not have acted as an incentive to Rhodes. For they never reached Cape Town.*

An even more extraordinary story attaches to Harris's most damaging statement – 'I have spoken open E Fairfield.' The obnoxious word 'open' (or 'frankly', as Harris was to explain to the Committee) was not in his own original message (version I). It got into the Select Committee's version IV through a series of accidents. First, the word 'spoken' had not been enciphered but written *en clair*, because there happened to be no code-word for 'spoken' in the Company's code-book. Next, the clerk who deciphered the telegram for the Select Committee, noting that the word 'spoken' was not in code, wrote 'open' alongside it. Finally, the word 'open', referring as it did merely to the code technique, became incorporated in the message itself.

Chamberlain's copy of the telegram was almost certainly version II, the correct one. It made no mention of 'open'. Hence there had been no need for it to go 'missing'. But when the compromising version IV was handed in 1897 to the Committee, Chamberlain dared not send for the correct version II from his own files, even though it would exonerate Fairfield and indirectly himself. Once his files became 'open', the game was up.

Fairfield's account of his talk with Harris and of the general

---

* This is another of C. M. Woodhouse's discoveries. See *History Today*, July 1962. But why these sentences were omitted by the cipher-clerk in London is another mystery.

situation went to Chamberlain in a five hundred word letter that same evening.[2] Thankfully Fairfield reported that the Protectorate business could now be polished off. It would be possible to transfer the border police immediately, and so get 'our people' off the scene before 'this ugly row' broke in the Transvaal. In return for obtaining this desirable date-line, Rhodes would give up his claim both to the native reserves and to the rail subsidy, that matter of £20,000 a year for ten years. Thus everyone, from chiefs to imperial authorities, would be 'in cottonwool', while Kruger would give way on the drifts. Fairfield wound up his letter with a significant sentence: ' . . . but that will not end the political "unrest".'

Chamberlain received this absorbing news at Highbury. Rhodes, though he authorized Harris to accept these terms, fumed at Groote Schurr. Having won the all-important point, immediate transfer, he began to complain to his long-suffering agent about the flies in the ointment. 'It is humiliating to be utterly beaten by these niggers,' he cabled. 'They think more of one native at home than the whole of South Africa.' He suspected that Lord Loch was at the back of it. However, Harris was right to take the credit and let the cash go: 'As to the £200,000 you can take high tone and let them have it' (12 November). But the victory of the chiefs continued to rankle, and eleven days later (23 November) Rhodes was cabling Harris again: ' . . . I do object to being beaten by three canting natives especially on score temperance when two of them Sebele Bathoen they are known to be utter drunkards.'

Would Chamberlain agree to the transfer at last? There was still one remaining anxiety in the mind of the Colonial Secretary, which must be settled before he would give the word. It was a matter which had exercised his thoughts for many weeks. As long ago as 2 October, while he was on holiday in Spain, he wrote a confidential letter to the High Commissioner asking him for information on this, among other subjects. But the High Commissioner's reply did not reach him for the best part of eight weeks. Meanwhile Chamberlain put the crucial question to 'many other gentlemen' (and perhaps to a lady, too, Flora Shaw). The question has since come to be summed up in the three words: Under which flag?

Under which flag were the Uitlanders in Johannesburg preparing to make their revolution, the Union Jack or the *Vierkleur*? Were they working for an independent Transvaal Republic dominated by continental capitalists, or for a Transvaal once more under the British flag? At first sight it seems a harmless and indeed sensible question for the Colonial Secretary to ask. And Garvin, Chamberlain's biographer, suggests that when Chamberlain put the question to those negotiating on behalf of Rhodes, namely Grey and Harris, no harm was in fact done. It was only the wording of Harris's telegram, in which he informed Rhodes of his answer to Chamberlain's question, which did the mischief. Known as the sixth 'missing telegram', this was Harris's message, dispatched to Rhodes on 5 November 1895:

We have stated positive that results Dr Jameson's plans include British flag. Is this correct?

Correct but not publishable. In the light of after events the words 'Dr Jameson's plans' were dynamite. The vast majority of the public at home and abroad would at once assume that 'Dr Jameson's plans' meant the same thing as Dr Jameson's Raid. Thus this message, had it not been mysteriously suppressed, would have convinced almost everybody that Chamberlain was 'in' the Raid plans 'up to the neck'.

But even the discriminating minority who had learnt to distinguish between Dr Jameson's plans and the Jameson Raid, might well have still felt uneasy about this telegram. For here, apparently, was their Colonial Secretary deeply enough involved with Cecil Rhodes to make an anxious inquiry of his agents: Would a Johannesburg rising bring back the Transvaal under the British flag? Unless he had a shrewd idea of Rhodes's part in what was afoot, why did he assume that Rhodes could influence the Uitlanders' aims? And why did he raise the 'flag' question on the very eve of the Bechuanaland transfer? Chamberlain's own notes on the 'flag' telegram imply that the subject happened to crop up in general conversation with Grey and was not essentially connected with the transfer. But who would believe that afterwards? The 'flag' telegram clearly showed that transfer and rising were connected.

With promptitude and a fine show of hurt feelings, Rhodes cabled back to Harris on 6 November 1895:

They must very much misunderstand me at home. I of course would not risk everything as I am doing excepting for British flag.

As Rhodes put it afterwards, more personally and more pithily to the Tribunal: 'You might be sure, sir, that I was not going to risk my position to change President Kruger for President J. B. Robinson.*

Dr Harris hastily sent off a propitiatory reply to the Colossus on 8 November:

Thanks they do not misunderstand you but feared if you should have power to insist on it.

---

* Robinson was one of the Rand millionaires opposed to the Rhodes group. Graham Bower agreed with Rhodes in preferring the devil he knew to some of the Randlords. He wrote to Buxton on 17 November 1922: 'I preferred Paul Kruger to Barnie Barnato.'

# 25

# The 'Fireworks' Telegram

Zero hour came on 6 November. A 'great indaba' was held at the Colonial Office. Boundaries were drawn with the wisdom of Moatlhodi, the man who puts things right. The chiefs who paid Chamberlain this handsome tribute were well satisfied with the extensive reserves which he, with his blue pencil, salvaged from Rhodes and marked on the map to remain under their mother the Queen.*

The rest of the Protectorate, apart from these reserves, was to swell the mighty dominions of Cecil Rhodes. Chamberlain felt it was a land of hope and glory, destined to be enriched and developed by the wealthy Chartered Company. 'God who made thee mighty make thee mightier yet . . .' Three months later it was touch and go whether the whole of Rhodesia would lose the services of her eponymous hero together with her special status under the Charter.

One can picture the final scene of the 'great indaba'. Khama, Bathoen and Sebele take their leave first, as befits distinguished strangers who have been received at Windsor Castle. Then the Secretary of State makes his farewells to the assembled directors of the Chartered Company. First a cordial hand-shake for the Duke of Fife, the Company's president. Mr Rochfort Maguire goes next, for Lord Grey is more intimate with Mr Chamberlain than the other directors and therefore lingers for a few friendly words while the room is emptying. Dr Rutherfoord Harris engages in last minute chit-chat with Mr Chamberlain's private secretary, Harry Wilson, who is assisting him in seeing off the visitors.

At some point during this informal scene a remarkable sentence passed the lips of 'the man who puts things right'. It was to form the basis of the seventh 'missing telegram' of 7 November 1895. For next

---

* This map can still be seen in the files, its vertical blue hatching representing Chamberlain's award, which is almost double the original area of horizontal hatching offered to Khama by Grey and Maguire.

day Dr Harris, who must have overheard the words himself or received an account of them from Lord Grey, dispatched the following cable to Rhodes:

Secretary for Colonies says you must allow decent interval and delay fireworks for fortnight.

'Fireworks' was indeed an explosive word. Used in this context it could only mean one thing, the Johannesburg rising. Chamberlain, having at last been persuaded to transfer Bechuanaland to Rhodes, was now apparently insisting that a decent interval, say a fortnight, should elapse before Rhodes sent up the balloon. Otherwise their mutual enemies might call attention to the suspicious proximity of the rising to the transfer.

No wonder this 'fireworks' cable was never published, until Garvin found a copy of it and parts of the other 'missing telegrams' among the Chamberlain papers. After going through the whole batch of cables Garvin's trenchant comment was, 'This is the worst.' It was the worst in two senses. First, because it was most harmful in its implications: here was the Colonial Secretary actually fixing the date of the rising from Downing Street. Second, it showed Harris at his worst, maliciously fabricating, according to Garvin, out of an 'open jest' made by the innocent Colonial Secretary 'a calculated message sent behind his back'.[1] For during the month of June 1896 a most innocuous explanation of the words in the 'fireworks' cable turned up. This is Chamberlain's own account of the matter in his *Memorandum*:

... I have no recollection of having used any such expressions, but I am reminded by Mr Wilson, my Private Secretary (who was present during the interview with the native chiefs and the Directors), and was standing by my side, that as Lord Grey was bidding me good-bye, I laughingly observed to him, apropos of the fact that he had been bombarding me with telegrams, on Mr Rhodes's behalf, on the subject of the Khama negotiations for some time past, 'that I wanted a fortnight's holiday, and that I hoped that for that time at any rate Mr Rhodes would not let off any more of his fireworks'. Mr Wilson has no recollection whatever of the use of any such phrase as 'you must allow a decent interval' ...[2]

The word 'fireworks', it seemed, did not refer to the rising at all.

Instead, it only meant the crackling fusillade of the negotiators' cables demanding the transfer, a fusillade which had been going on for weeks and had reached its peak two days before the transfer was made. (On 4 November Fairfield wrote to Chamberlain that Rhodes 'has been telegraphing all day . . .'.)

If Garvin's explanation is the true one and Harris did indeed twist the Colonial Secretary's jest in order to blackmail him later, it is somewhat surprising to find such a double-dyed villain accepted in a team which included 'chivalrous' Lord Grey and 'admirable' Lady Lugard (Garvin's adjectives).

Is one driven back on the view, then, that both Harry Wilson and Garvin were wrong and that Chamberlain seriously meant the rising when he spoke of 'fireworks'? Such is the conviction of his critics who, exonerating Harris, plant the blame squarely on Chamberlain's back. Not only was he speaking of the rising, but according to his severest judges he was directing Rhodes as to the date on which it should occur.

The question of what Chamberlain meant by 'fireworks' has been answered by a piece of evidence that came to light in Bower's papers at Rhodes House. According to Bower, Chamberlain gave Beit a message for Rhodes, to be delivered verbally when Beit reached Cape Town in December 1895. That message was virtually a repeat of the 'fireworks' telegram. This is how C.M. Woodhouse summarized the message, which he discovered among the Bower MSS at Rhodes House. It was an order to Rhodes to 'postpone his "fireworks" till at least a fortnight after the transfer of "the Crown Colony of Bechuanaland" to the Cape Colony'. Mr Woodhouse admits that, 'Later the Colonial Office denied the authenticity of this message.' But he himself accepts it with the words, 'neither Beit nor Bower is likely to have invented it to deceive Rhodes'.

Chamberlain's defenders might conceivably argue that Bower's memory was at fault and he was confusing Beit's message with Harris's telegram; but this, too, is unlikely.

Nor is it likely that Chamberlain used the arresting word 'fireworks' twice over, while attaching to it no other meaning than a bombardment of telegrams. He meant the rising each time. No doubt his emphasis was on the postponement of the rising ('at least a fortnight') rather than its date. Nevertheless on these two occasions

Chamberlain seems to have thrown over his hitherto firm policy of 'unofficial knowledge' and 'not knowing too much'. His only concession to the old policy was to speak metaphorically of 'fireworks' rather than openly of the rising.

# 26

# The Sick Man of Cape Town

While the sinister Harris–Rhodes cables flew back and forth between London and South Africa, two important letters were exchanged on another front. In their own way they were no less interesting than the 'missing telegrams'. One is in point of fact missing. But unlike the telegrams, no copy of it exists or has ever been published and the reason for its complete disappearance can only be guessed.

On 4 November 1895 the High Commissioner dispatched an extremely lengthy and able document to the Colonial Secretary from Cape Town. This is how it began:

Dear Mr Chamberlain,
 I will now reply as far as I can to the questions you put to me in your confidential letter of the 2nd of October as to the state of affairs in the Transvaal between the Uitlanders and the Government.[1]

The actual contents of that confidential letter from Chamberlain, to which the High Commissioner's reply refers, find no place in the voluminous pages of Garvin's *Life*. Garvin, however, though he does not quote Chamberlain's questions to Robinson, does say that he wanted to 'know the High Commissioner's whole mind' and 'begged Sir Hercules to be full and frank in reply'.

Why did not Garvin reveal Chamberlain's 'whole mind' by quoting his whole letter? History would give no clue but for the fact that among Bower's papers, opened in Cape Town eleven years after Garvin's volume was published, a phrase from Chamberlain's letter is mentioned. In Bower's eyes it was a highly objectionable phrase. It is possible though perhaps unfair to conclude that Garvin also found the phrase a dangerous one and therefore refrained from publishing the letter in which it occurred.

According to Bower, Chamberlain requested Robinson's views on the prospects of a rising in Johannesburg *with or without assistance from outside*. 'From outside . . .' These words at once aroused the suspicions and hostility of Bower. Having recently been taken into

Rhodes's confidence about his plans, Bower assumed Chamberlain had in mind the same kind of military 'assistance from outside' which he knew Rhodes intended to provide. Chamberlain's letter of 2 October, now 'missing', seemed to Bower a confirmation of his collusion in the plot to oust Kruger.

Without seeing the letter it is impossible to be sure what Chamberlain's phrase meant, though Garvin's apparent suppression is a suspicious factor. Chamberlain explained the phrase innocuously enough when questioned by Bower in London. What did 'outside assistance' mean? Chamberlain replied that he did not know; he was probably thinking Johannesburg might be assisted by the Free State. Bower dismissed this explanation as 'absurd'. Perhaps the most that can be said for it is that when Chamberlain was writing to Robinson (2 October 1895) the Free State did seem likely to 'assist' Johannesburg, at least over the drifts.

But even if Chamberlain was not specifically thinking of the Free State, is it necessary to conclude that Jameson's force was the only other 'outside assistance' he had in mind? It is at least possible that *with or without assistance from outside* was one of those intentionally vague, portmanteau expressions so much favoured by politicians and departments of state. Put in cruder language, Chamberlain may have simply meant: 'What is the form in South Africa? Tell me all you know about the different circumstances in which the Uitlanders might hope to succeed.'

Bower, in his capacity of *éminence grise*, drafted a reply to the Colonial Secretary which he considered as diplomatic as the other's was rash. He gave an objective account of conditions inside the Transvaal, including the paradoxical fact that the capitalists, though coining money by the million, were unable to endure Kruger's taxes any longer. In case of an outbreak, he suggested that the High Commissioner should proceed instantly to Pretoria in order to forestall any appeal by Kruger for German intervention. At the same time HM Government should be prepared to send 'a large force' from home to his assistance. Was this some echo of Lord Ripon's alleged promise of 10,000 men? However that may be, the sentence about reinforcements from home may well have seemed to Chamberlain part of the answer to his question about 'assistance from the outside'.

In his *Apologia*, Bower described how he dealt with the 'assistance' question:

I omitted all reference to 'with or without assistance from outside'. I never meant to give any assistance at all and I had not made up my mind how the troops were to be used. But I did refer to the High Commissioner going up as arbitrator.

Bower's casualness about the border police is a constant source of astonishment. His reference to the High Commissioner's mediation, however, causes no surprise. For elsewhere in this account he reveals the fact that Rhodes lent a hand in drafting the answer to Chamberlain, and Rhodes's own plan was to send Robinson up as a tame dove of peace to bring the Transvaal under his imperial wings. Other sections of the letter are redolent of Rhodes's ideas, so that there is no difficulty in accepting this portentous document of 4 November as the joint work of Robinson, Bower and Rhodes. They were surely a strange trio to be putting the British Colonial Secretary wise about the Johannesburg revolutionaries, of whom one was the instigator, another the accomplice and a third the dupe. J.L. Garvin comments with *empressement* on the startling fact that a pro-Afrikaner High Commissioner, 'the most moderate of men', could describe the Uitlanders' case so sympathetically. It is not quite so startling if Rhodes himself inspired the description.

What was Chamberlain's reaction to the letter of 4 November from Government House? To begin with, how did he take Bower's silent rebuff over his inquiry about outside assistance? The answer is almost certainly that he did not even notice it. When he and Bower met in London it was the latter who brought up the subject, not Chamberlain, and it is obvious from Bower's account of the interview that Chamberlain answered his question with unconcern. He had no sense of guilt over his remark about outside support for the rising, since his remark was not specifically aimed at Jameson's police.

Chamberlain cabled an answer to the letter of 4 November on 6 December 1896. This message has attracted attention, some admiring, some critical. The first paragraph ran:

Agree generally with your idea in private letter of Nov. 4th . . . I take for granted that no movement will take place unless success is certain, a fiasco would be most disastrous.[2]

Chamberlain's assumption that there would be no rising unless success was certain seemed to Garvin to exonerate him of any complicity in the subsequent débâcle. Therefore in Garvin's eyes they were 'words deserving to be marked'. Yet does not something too much like a staccato command from GHQ issue from this telegram? The tone of 'I take it for granted that . . .' has been interpreted by later critics in a sense that would have dismayed Garvin. Even the mention of a 'fiasco' lends weight to the view that he condemned the Raid because he feared it would fail and not because he feared it would succeed. Nevertheless Chamberlain's tone and words can be explained without resorting to any theory of collusion more extreme than the one which has already been advanced in these pages.

Chamberlain's style was often somewhat lordly, and the brevity of the telegraphic form adds to the impression that it was an order from 'the boss'. But though Chamberlain was very much 'the boss' in the Colonial Office, he was never willingly a director of the revolutionary movement. He had rightly asked for full and frank information from his own subordinate; he had received it and was making a legitimate comment. He did desire an end to Kruger's policies and power, but only on certain conditions; and a fiasco would settle Kruger more firmly in the saddle. Once again, this telegram was no deviation from Chamberlain's considered policy towards the rising – no encouragement and no discouragement.

Among Sir Graham Bower's private papers is found the statement that Chamberlain's telegram ran to a second paragraph in which was contained an offer to the people of Johannesburg. This was something important; yet something of which Garvin appears not to have heard. If the Johannesburgers would accept the English flag, Chamberlain promised that they should be allowed to elect their own Governor, a touch characteristic of Chamberlain's policy of encouraging local self-government. It is intrinsically sensible. But though the promise may have been sound, the act of making it was perilous.

Chamberlain meant that *if* there were a rising and *if* they decided to hoist the English flag, they would still be free to choose any Governor they liked. But Chamberlain's words could be interpreted very differently. They seemed to say, not '*if* there were a revolution', but '*make* a revolution, and all these privileges shall be yours'. His bribe, if it must be so regarded, was to ensure the right flag, not to ensure a revolution. But the daring pilot was steering too near the rocks. The paper-thin lines between non-intervention, encouragement and instigation had at this point become indistinguishable from one another. It was better that the second paragraph should fall into as few hands as possible.

Sir Graham Bower showed the telegram to the High Commissioner but refused to show it to Rhodes. To him, Chamberlain's offer, apart from the implications involved in his making it at all, was in itself neither sound nor sensible. Who could tell what kind of man that mixed crowd on the Rand would elect? Rumour afterwards had it that Joubert and Shippard were in the running. But Bower, with his strong feelings against international Jewry and a 'Stock Exchange Government', was not going to risk the election of a Governor from among the Barney Barnatos and other similar 'Randlords'.

As November passed and the revolutionary pot began to boil, the fatal results of this friction in the Chamberlain–Robinson axis became more evident. Mistakes Chamberlain made; but he was not helped to travel smoothly and safely along the difficult road by the taciturn hostility of his men-on-the-spot. What happened when Bower wished to report to the Colonial Secretary on the dangerous turn he felt events were taking? The High Commissioner stopped him at once. 'It is useless,' he moaned. 'Remember you are no longer dealing with Lord Ripon and Buxton. They [Chamberlain and Selborne] won't listen to you. Your duty is to stay where you are and do your duty; keep clear of the mess and don't desert me when my health is failing me.'[3]. Abysmal advice. They were in the mess already and absence of confidence between London and Cape Town made it worse.

Bower felt he could not press his ailing chief. 'The doctors had warned me', he wrote, 'that Sir Hercules's heart was getting worse. His legs were swelling from dropsy, and he could not sleep at night; everyone knew he was a dying man except himself and the doctors told me it would kill him to know it.' Chamberlain had been right to oppose Robinson's reappointment, though he could not foresee the full calamity. Robinson turned out to be worse than a 'Rhodes man'; he was a half-man.

On one occasion Bower, instead of getting in touch with Chamberlain direct, wrote to Edward Fairfield, his trusted friend in the Colonial Office. He had at last called a spade a spade for the benefit of Fairfield and roundly said the Empire must be peace-maker not peace-breaker. But the High Commissioner was aghast at Bower's temerity. 'You must be mad to write like that to the Colonial Office,' he quaked. 'In any case Chamberlain will have to submit his plans to the Cabinet, and they will sit on him.' Bower was sceptical: 'I had my own views as to the Cabinet sitting on Mr Chamberlain, but it was useless to argue with a sick man so I tore up my letter in his presence.'

It was the same wretched story when correspondence travelled in the opposite direction. Robinson strongly disapproved of a letter from Chamberlain to Kruger announcing his intention of setting up a Joint Commission to inquire into the alleged atrocities at Woodbush, perpetrated by the Boers against the Africans.* Bower regarded Chamberlain's action with 'despair'. According to his view, such interference with the internal affairs of the Transvaal amounted to a breach of the London Convention. But the High Commissioner, declining to reason with Chamberlain, sent the letter on to the British Agent in Pretoria. Grumbling, he called himself 'a mere Post Office'. The Raid prevented its delivery.

---

* During hostilities a burgher was said to have ordered a wounded child to be cut down with an assegai and then to have raped its mother. Sir Ellis Ashmead-Bartlett raised the matter, it was taken up by the *Daily Chronicle* and created deep feeling in England.

# 27

# *Hurry Up! For Pity!*

Towards the end of November and during December a number of remarkable 'hurry up' messages succeeded in adding new elements of falsification, muddle and feverishness to the last six weeks before the Raid.

On 19 November Dr Jameson went to Johannesburg to see the leaders of the National Union. A provisional date was fixed for the rising – 28 December – but more important, the undated letter, imploring him to hurry to the rescue, was extracted from the reluctant revolutionaries.* Jameson said he did not want to cross the frontier 'like a brigand'; but this letter enabled him, after changing punctuation and inserting a false date, to act not only like a brigand but also a forger. Perhaps Charley Leonard felt a premonition of its misuse, for he tried at the last moment to get the letter back. The story is Edmund Garrett's:

'Awfully sorry, old man,' said the Doctor drily, 'but it has gone down to Cape Town by the last train.' Mr Leonard protested and hesitated but the Doctor took him by the arm and gave vent to his usual interjection – an abbreviation of the word balderdash – and managed the Chairman of the National Union in his usual style.

As a result of Jameson's 'management', this notorious message, written by the Uitlanders more or less under duress, was first dated by Dr Jameson *20 November* and then, after it had been 'kept stewing for a month in some man's pocket',[1] it was re-dated by Dr Harris *28 December*. The letter was well and truly doctored.

Meanwhile the ardent manager of *The Times*, Moberly Bell, was secretly working away in England to present the Johannesburg rising in a favourable light. On 15 November he invited Captain Younghusband, a *Times* special correspondent, and Miss Flora Shaw to dinner at his house. Since the beginning of the month he had contemplated sending Younghusband out to Africa as a liaison

* See p. 66.

officer between the revolutionaries and his newspaper. That evening
the three conspirators finally tied up their plans and next day Bell
mysteriously informed his wife that he held 'more responsibility
than any man in England'.[2]

On 21 November Moberly Bell gave Younghusband the Harris
code for transmitting revolutionary news from Johannesburg. At the
same time Bell instructed him to pass on an urgent message to
Rhodes:

I want to impress upon Rhodes that we hope the *New Company* will not
*commence business* on a Saturday.
PS. Because of Sunday papers.

The manager of *The Times* was not above combining business with
patriotism. He did not wish his paper to miss a scoop. Moreover, if
the 'flotation' took place on Saturday, 28 December (the date that he
had heard was provisionally fixed), the 'Thunderer' would not be
able to give a lead to the press by welcoming the rising with a
jubilant peal.

The question of the date continued to worry the *Times* group. On
10 December Flora Shaw, using a code name of 'Telemones' as
supplied by Harris, sent an urgent inquiry to 'Veldschoen' (Rhodes)
in Cape Town:

Can you advise when you will commence the plans, we wish to send at
earliest opportunity sealed instructions representative London *Times* European capitals; it is most important using their influence in your favour.

The cable was signed with Flora Shaw's name only, fortunately
for Bell and *The Times*, as it turned out afterwards. Even more
fortunate was the fact that the draft copy of this cable and its two
successors never fell into the Committee's hands. For in all three
cases the signature as well as the text was written out in Moberly
Bell's handwriting.

On 26 November Dr Harris informed Rhodes that 'Flora' had
suggested an earlier date for the rising: 'Flora suggests 16 December
celebrate Pretoria district 1880.'

Dingaan's Day (16 December) was the Boers' Independence Day.
Miss Shaw felt it would be timely if the Johannesburgers won their
independence from the Boers on the same date. To the Committee
of Inquiry she described this suggestion of a date as a piece of

'idle conversation'. Her wish to hurry on the revolution was far from idle.

Rhodes cabled on 11 December that the rising would come 'about the New Year'. So at last the great day was fixed. Bell felt he could wait till 1 January and no longer. Everything at his end was ready. He had even given 'sealed instructions' to the *Times* Brussels correspondent to remain in Holland until further notice under cover of studying Dutch domestic politics. Her name was appropriate – Madame Couvreur.

Rhodes's cable of 11 December was to remain 'daily if not hourly' in Bell's mind.[3] Prompted by his eager accomplice he replied on 12 December with another exhortation to haste:

Delay dangerous sympathy now complete but will depend very much upon action before European powers given time to enter protest which as European situation considered serious might paralyse Government; general feeling in the Stock Market very suspicious.

Rhodes at once (13 December) wired the sense of this message to his brother Colonel Frank Rhodes. The London *Times*, he said, had cabled confidentially that postponement of the 'meeting' would be most 'unwise'.

Dingaan's Day came and went. Next day, 17 December, Harris and Beit landed in South Africa from London, hoping to see the fun begin very soon. The same day Rhodes got another cable from Flora Shaw, sounding an even more urgent note:

Held an interview with Secretary Transvaal, [who] left here on Saturday for Hague Berlin Paris, fear in negotiation with these parties. Chamberlain sound in case of interference European powers but have special reason to believe wishes you must do it immediately.

The Transvaal Secretary referred to was Dr Leyds. Ostensibly he had come to Europe for a throat operation. But Flora Shaw believed that his real mission was not to consult a continental surgeon but to forestall a British doctor's military operation.*

Harris replied on behalf of a rather huffy Rhodes:

---

* Leyds had earlier explained that he was visiting Delagoa Bay for the sake of his health; upon which Fairfield minuted that Leyds must be a homoeopath, driving out the poison of cancer by inhaling the poisonous air of Lourenço Marques. Robinson telegraphed Chamberlain on 23 November that Leyds was genuinely suffering from a malignant growth which would surely have a 'fatal termination'. Sir Jacobus de Wet thought otherwise. Leyds lived to a ripe old age. (C.O. 417/152, 22363.)

*To Telemones* [Flora Shaw]. *20 December 1895*. Thanks. Are doing our best, but these things take time. Do not alarm Pretoria from London. R. Harris.

Evidently Rhodes feared that Miss Shaw's professional interview with Dr Leyds, which had taken place on 14 December, might do more harm than good. He saw the danger when other people tried to combine patriotism with business.

In the meantime, Captain Younghusband arrived in South Africa. He proved to be a disappointing correspondent. Bell waited in vain for cables announcing an imminent revolution. Younghusband would not waste money on describing what appeared to him a stalemate. He had seen Dr Jameson's sanguine messages saying that all on the border was satisfactory and ready, but Colonel Rhodes, in whose house he was staying, was busy pouring cold water on Jameson at Pitsani. Everything was far from satisfactory in Johannesburg. In a caustic comment made after it was all over, Younghusband pin-pointed the flaw in Rhodes's plans: 'The great mistake made was trying to run races with cart-horses.'

Disagreement and confusion spread among the Uitlanders. Labour was none too sound. No wonder. For £50,000 was said to have been spent on the workers. Kruger's distribution of largesse was having a visible effect. According to Bower, men who had never owned a vehicle before were now starting to ride in dog-carts and carriages. Apart from bribes, Younghusband told Moberly Bell that the miners were making too much money to be interested in a stoppage, even for the sake of the vote. If Labour will not fight, who will? Rothschilds are not built that way. Bower believed that most of the revolutionary speeches were 'pure bluff'. Orators, he sagely remarked, are not fighters. The most brilliant speech-maker of Johannesburg, who was living with an actress in the town, would be found under the bed if it came to fighting. A wisecrack which Sir Hercules capped with, 'Yes, and there would be a prostitute in the bed.' The speakers in Johannesburg 'began by declaring their loyalty to the Republic and ended by singing *Rule Britannia*'. It was Bower's considered opinion afterwards that if Jameson had not run amok, the capitalists would have made a deal with the Transvaal Government.

And so, during the last days before the Raid, a game was being played of '*Watching the Tortoise*'. The tortoise was the Uitlanders' Reform Committee, so slow to move. By now there were many players taking part. Kruger was watching for the tortoise to put out its head. The Germans were watching. A German cruiser was standing by at Zanzibar, ready to rush marines to Pretoria to 'guard the consulate' when the reformers attacked. (Bower was sure the British Mounted Police would get there first, even if they had to kill half their horses in doing so.) *The Times* was watching. So was the Stock Exchange; watching for a slump caused by the rising, followed by a glorious rocketing of 'Chartereds'. Then there were the Governors of the Cape Colony, Natal and the Free State, all playing the same game of watching and waiting. Even Dr Jameson was supposed to be playing it, sitting with his troops on the Transvaal border. Rhodes swore that he would sit on there 'for years, if necessary'. It was only afterwards that Jameson's friends realized he was physically incapable of sitting still, watching a tortoise.

Chamberlain was watching the tortoise, too. But the slowness of its movements was not always accurately reflected in the official reports which reached him at Highbury. On 16 December Sir Robert Meade gave the impression that the pot was rapidly coming to the boil. Everyone was talking about the rising, he wrote; *The Times* that day as good as announced it and another troopship might be diverted to the Cape.

But enclosed in Meade's letter was one from Fairfield giving a more up-to-date picture of realities in Johannesburg:

16.12.95 – Mr Maguire called on me today. He said that his information was that nothing would happen before the New Year ... in saying that nothing will happen *before* the New Year, his Cape friends may mean that it will happen a good deal after the New Year. He has to do with companies which are not in the Rhodes group ... and do not seem to expect any *immediate* crisis.[4]

Then on 18 December came the shattering blow of President Cleveland's ultimatum on Venezuela. Immediately Sir Robert sat down to write to his chief again, this time in a very different vein. Everything now pointed to the need for getting the pot off the fire: the US quarrel, Germany's menace, the lukewarm feelings of the Uitlanders. Should the Colonial Secretary reach out his hand to remove it? On 18 December he wrote to Chamberlain:

... Perhaps as we shall have to face German opposition you may wish the Uitlander movement to be postponed for a year or so. Fairfield thinks he could get this done through Maguire ... but if the movement is to be postponed it must be done at once. Fairfield is confident he could do this without compromising you – should you wish it to be done ...[5]

Chamberlain replied by return with his so-called 'hurry up' letter. Of all his written words these have perhaps been most criticized.

The task of composing this all-important letter taxed Chamberlain's diplomatic skill to the full. He had to meet what Garvin calls 'a poser such as even Chamberlain in his life of hazard seldom had to meet'. No one except his enemies would claim that the final result was successful in conveying his true wishes. (His critics argue that he did succeed, in so far as his true wishes were to hasten the trouble in the Transvaal: he deliberately 'pulled the trigger of the infernal machine'.[6]) The Attorney-General, Sir Richard Webster, afterwards said that this letter, and Maguire's 'hurry up' telegram which it inspired, were the only two things in all the correspondence which could not be explained away. Certainly the results of Chamberlain's labours turned out to be singularly unfortunate:

*Highbury, December 18.*
My dear Meade,

Thanks for your letter. The question is a serious one to decide.

It must be noted that the American affair cannot become serious for some time ... As long as the Venezuelans do not attack us we shall not attack them. Altogether it must be months before there is a real crisis.

Now as to the Transvaal. Might it not come off just at the critical time if it is postponed now? The longer it is delayed the more chance there is of foreign intervention.

It seems to me that either it should come *at once* or be postponed for a year or two at least. Can we ensure this?

If not we had better not interfere, for we may bring about the very thing we want to avoid.

If Fairfield can make the situation clear to Maguire I should like him to do so – then the responsibility must rest with Rhodes and we had better abstain even from giving advice. I again repeat, the *worst* time for trouble anywhere would be about 6 months hence. I cannot say that any time would be a good one, but can the difficulty be indefinitely postponed?[7]

The most compromising sentence in Chamberlain's letter is the first containing his own italics ('*at once*'). To this may be added the words, 'The longer it is delayed the more chance there is of foreign intervention.' It must also be noticed that the discussion of post-ponement *begins* with a reason against it. A straightforward writer like Chamberlain would tend to put his strongest argument first. The emphasis in these sentences is against delay, and therefore they seem to support the theory that the letter was intended to hurry up the rising. Salisbury could not permit Chamberlain to publish it. Not that he thought it intrinsically compromising, allowing for its being a private letter, 'hastily written'. It contained two 'essential phrases': that the worst time for a rising would be six months hence and that no time would be a good one. Did Fairfield 'tune his language' to Maguire in that key? If he did, and could say so, no harm would result. Better, all the same, to keep the letter in the files.

It would indeed be unfair to suggest that the urgent note in Chamberlain's letter was directed solely to an immediate rising. The real urgency was a negative one, to prevent the rising at all costs from coinciding with an Anglo-American crisis. This could be achieved either by persuading the Uitlanders to postpone it inde-finitely or by leaving them alone to bring it off when they themselves apparently wished, round about the New Year. Incidentally, the second course fitted better with Chamberlain's policy of non-intervention. An effort to get the date postponed would have cut across this policy by throwing the weight of the Colonial Office against the rising. In Chamberlain's own eyes (though not in Fairfield's who was against the rising anyway) this would have compromised him. Unfortunately Fairfield, after his advice to Maguire to postpone was rejected, tilted the delicately balanced scales too far in the opposite direction by finally recommending an early revolution. He could have left the Uitlanders to make that choice for themselves, since he had just been informed they were bent on rising at once, in any case.*

Fairfield cannot be blamed, however, for failing to appreciate all the nuances of Chamberlain's utterance.

What is to be the verdict on Chamberlain's 'hurry up' letter? Chamberlain himself passed judgment on his own performance. The letter was open to misunderstanding, he admitted to Bower after the

---

* 'What Fairfield . . . had failed to communicate to Rhodes was Chamberlain's intimation that Rhodes must decide for himself.' *Cambridge History of the British Empire*, III, p. 359.

Raid, but rightly understood it was quite harmless. Even if it is impossible to go the whole way with Chamberlain, it would be equally wrong to go the whole way with his critics. Today he has become the dog with a bad name. He is the exponent of the 'new diplomacy', of short cuts, no delays, action at all costs. He is the type who, in the words of Rhodes, 'will always come to a decision' – no matter whether or not it is the right one: the type who 'might be too quick', who 'overrides the hounds'. A 'hurry up' letter is just what one would expect of him. He has a bad name, so hang him.

Such a verdict would be unjust. Scrutinized with the greatest severity, Chamberlain's message is a 'hurry up' letter only in the sense that anyone might wish to get the inevitable over while the going was good.

Even Sir Graham Bower shared something of this feeling, though his attitude to the rising was very different from Chamberlain's. 'I would prefer it sooner rather than later,' he said to Rhodes, when the latter showed him Maguire's telegram, 'for Sir Hercules is failing and a new man would be without authority . . . If the Johannesburgers elect to take their pleasure in a Revolution that is their affair.' But Bower strongly deprecated any hustling from the Colonial Office. That would change the imperial authorities from arbitrators (his own policy) into partisans. Bower's attitude did not please Rhodes at all. This was the moment when Rhodes hurled at his old friend the accusation of disloyalty to his chief, Chamberlain. Bower retorted that Rhodes was mad. Then Rhodes threw Bower out of Groote Schurr. It was their first quarrel after working together for fifteen years.

Meade handed over Chamberlain's letter to Fairfield. He was the liaison between the Colonial Secretary and Rhodes's London agents. Fairfield invited Maguire round to the Colonial Office, as the proxy or 'alternate' of Rhodes on the Chartered Company. The two intermediaries then proceeded to carry into effect what they imagined would be their chiefs' wishes. Fairfield began by proposing indefinite postponement of the rising. He used every argument he could think of, he told Chamberlain after the Raid. But Maguire met him with an apparently solid front against postponement. He had heard by cable from Johannesburg that the movement would start in about ten days (the original date). It was too late to defer action for a year, as Johannesburg was so full of 'bad characters', out of work, that there was nothing to do with them 'except to set them fighting'. The capitalists were no longer in command of the situation. Maguire and his friends could see no alternative but 'early action'. Fairfield added that they did not base their urgency on 'the possible development of the American question, but Maguire agreed with what I put to him on that point'.[8]

Fairfield was not to know that Maguire's lively account of events in Johannesburg was misleading. Nor does he seem to have been struck by the frivolous nature of the reasons advanced by a Fellow of All Souls for making a revolution. Having listened to Maguire's narrative, he decided that a rising was indeed inevitable. Fairfield abandoned the policy of 'indefinite postponement' and switched to his second string, 'the sooner-the-better'.

After Maguire had gone, he sat down and wrote an account of the interview to Chamberlain in his best vein of sophisticated cynicism, ending with a postscript that 'Chartereds' had fallen so low in the City 'that the news of a row can have no other than a favourable effect'. The date was 19 December.

After his visit to the Colonial Office, Maguire acted with dispatch. In consultation with Lord Grey he composed a 'hurry up' message for Rhodes based on Fairfield's communication, which in turn was assumed to be based on the Colonial Secretary's wishes. Next day, 20 December, he sent it off. It is now known as the eighth 'missing telegram'. In its effects on the situation it was the worst of the 'hurry up' messages and the worst of the 'missing telegrams'. Its text is wholly missing to this day. But those who did see it realized its potency. Chamberlain was one of them. When it reached Groote Schurr it spurred the conspirators gathered there into frantic activity. Alfred Beit was made to flash a message to Lionel Phillips in Johannesburg:

. . . Our foreign supporters urge immediate flotation.

Chamberlain, examining all the messages that had passed before the Raid took place, wrote in the margin of Beit's telegram: 'I have no doubt that Beit and Harris were influenced by Maguire's telegram.'

But it was the influence of Maguire's telegram on Rhodes that really counted. Rhodes, as described above, used it to cut himself free at the critical moment from Bower's restraining influence. With Flora Shaw's message of 17 December already burning a hole in his pocket, he only needed what he thought was a second, more urgent prompting from Chamberlain, to recover all his faith in the rising. He had quarrelled with Bower for trying to extinguish his ardour with 'cold showers'. Now those red-hot cables from London had come to make the cold douches vanish in clouds of steam. Three days after Rhodes read the eighth 'missing telegram', he raised Jameson, the watcher on the border, from despair to ecstasy:

Company will be floated next Saturday . . .

# 28

# Tortoise and Hare

The 'hurry up' telegrams re-animated Rhodes and Jameson. But no amount of hurrying up was going to keep the revolution going, even at a jog trot. Despite the cries from headquarters for 'immediate flotation', mounting disagreements in Johannesburg showed that total collapse was not far off. With bad blood over Venezuela, the old quarrel over the flag had become acute. The distraught reformers decided to seek a personal interview with Rhodes. He must be informed of the new flag crisis. On no account must Jameson be allowed to move until it was settled. So on 19 December a special envoy was sent to Cape Town. He was none other than the *Times* special correspondent, Captain Francis Younghusband.

The correspondent turned envoy was taking no small risk in thus entering into the political struggle which he had been sent to observe. The existence of his mission leaked out afterwards but not his name. Though his name was just mentioned to the Committee of Inquiry, his activities were always referred to as those of 'the gentleman' or 'the messenger'. The reason advanced for this reticence was that 'the messenger', being in South Africa at the time of the Inquiry, might be endangered if his identity were revealed. What would have been in far greater danger was *The Times*. That Younghusband's considerable part in the affair escaped all notice is one of the many remarkable facts in the Raid story. Moberly Bell's activities also escaped attention, but they were confined to London. Younghusband operated at the very heart of the conspiracy.*

While Younghusband was in the train on the way to Johannesburg, Colonel Frank Rhodes whipped in a new query to his brother: would the High Commissioner definitely mediate? Rhodes wired

---

* Sir Francis Younghusband (1863–1942) seems to have followed Rhodes's familiar pattern of 'Take first, ask afterwards'. When sent on a government mission to Tibet seven years after the Raid, he was criticized for exceeding his instructions over the resultant treaty. He had to wait another thirteen years for the high honour (KCSI) that would normally have been his reward in 1904.

back that he would go up instantaneously. When Younghusband arrived and broke the news that in any case the 'flotation' was off, Rhodes was furious. An angry and sufficiently ludicrous exchange took place:

*Rhodes:* Is there no one in Johannesburg who will risk being shot and will lead the malcontents?
*Younghusband*: There is no one willing to do this.
*Rhodes:* Then won't you do it? Do you mind being shot?
*Younghusband:* I have no interest in the proposed revolution and would not dream of leading it.
*Rhodes* (after much heated argument): If they won't, they won't. I shall wire Jameson to keep quiet.[1]

To keep Jameson quiet was only half of the request which the envoy had brought from his principals. The other half was that Rhodes should not insist on the English flag. Younghusband evidently thought Rhodes had conceded this too, for he took his leave and started walking to the station. Rhodes, however, sent a messenger – the inevitable Dr Harris – from Groote Schurr to catch him up and make sure that he gave the Uitlanders an uncompromising reply to their 'flag' question. Even if it meant waiting, their flag must be the Union Jack.

Younghusband reached Johannesburg again on 25 December and duly delivered his unwelcome Christmas message. But the reformers were not to be moved. They would not accept what Harris, in one of his telegrams, had referred to as 'English bunting'. Fearing Jameson's intentions, they sent him the strongest possible orders not to stir: 'Absolutely necessary to postpone flotation.' At the same time they dispatched two more distinguished emissaries, Charles Leonard and Frederic Hamilton, editor of the *Johannesburg Star*, to try to get sense out of Rhodes.

Leonard arrived at Groote Schurr on Saturday, 28 December, determined to put things straight at last. The Johannesburgers *would not have the English flag*. Two remarks by important members of their community stuck in his mind. On Christmas Day George Farrar (a signatory of the 'letter of invitation') had come round to his house at seven o'clock in the morning and said: 'I hear if Jameson comes in he is going to hoist the Union Jack. I have induced every man who has joined me and who is helping me in this business to go in on the basis that we want a reformed republic.'

Farrar then went on to make a solemn pledge, every word of which Leonard remembered: 'This is the Boer country; it would be absolutely morally wrong to do anything else and I will not go a yard further in this business unless that basis is maintained.'

At 11.30 A.M. on the same day Leonard met an American, Captain Mein, in the Club. 'If this is a case of England gobbling this country up,' said Mein, 'I am not in it; otherwise I am up to my neck in it.'[2] (Captain Mein afterwards found himself 'in it' with a vengeance. He was severely mauled by angry burghers on the way from Pretoria station to the gaol.)

In the middle of his Christmas dinner Leonard was again forced to give his mind to the 'flag' question. A message summoned him to a meeting of the reform leaders at Frank Rhodes's house, where he found they had already passed a resolution postponing everything until after the meeting on 6 January and forbidding Jameson to hoist the Union Jack.* Leonard made a little speech to the effect that reform of the Transvaal was morally right and 'to try to steal the Boer country' morally wrong. He was forthwith dispatched to Cape Town to repeat this speech to Rhodes. Meanwhile it was published under the guise of the Leonard Manifesto.

By the end of a tedious three-day journey to the Cape, Leonard and Hamilton were ready to pour out a whole torrent of reasons why the rising should be postponed. There was dissension over the flag, and the arms distribution had broken down. There was no chance of seizing the Pretoria arsenal and thus supplementing their own supplies of arms, since the Boers in their covered wagons had irritatingly failed to go home to their farms after the Christmas and before the New Year Communions, but camped in Church Square instead. Leonard ended with the wail that 'everything was mis-fitting' and they were 'absolutely unprepared for a revolution'.

Rhodes took his cue. He reassured Leonard about 'the basis' of the revolution and ordered Harris to send a telegram to his brother Frank:

* Hays Hammond says that a new provisional date of 4 January was fixed for the rising, and the meeting of 6 January was a 'blind' to deceive the Boers. (J. H. Hammond, op. cit., l, p. 334.)

Charles Leonard says, flotation not popular and English bunting will be resisted by public ... Is it true?

In the evening Leonard and Hamilton returned to Groote Schuur for further discussion. This time Rhodes was more definite. He seemed to take the lead in postponing the rising. The reformers, he said, should continue their preparations 'without any sort of hurry' – a rare command in this story. He would see that they got their arms and would keep Jameson on the border for six or nine months or longer 'as a moral support'. 'Go on with your meeting on 6 January', he concluded, 'and await the development of events.'

On that same Saturday, 28 December, Younghusband sent Moberly Bell an expensive and penetrating cable laying bare the unsatisfactory state of affairs in Johannesburg. The Uitlanders recognized, he said, that they must be under the aegis of England, but they disliked 'government from London'. Provided England did not force herself upon them they would become a British colony in all but name; 'eventually name may come too'. Then, as if he and Bell were directing the conspiracy, he asked: 'Is not best policy to let matter follow present course?' Bell had no choice, for Younghusband's last words were, 'action postponed for present'. Bell, assisted by Flora Shaw, cabled approval of 'your policy'. But he then asked, somewhat contradictorily, 'will Paul [Kruger] grant franchise without fighting?' His final question showed the way his thoughts were still turning, despite all that Younghusband could say: 'What date expect now?'

Rhodes had seen the red light at last. But something, his own temperament or the cables from London, still prevented him from flashing it clearly and consistently to Jameson on the border. Even the desperate word 'Ichabod', with which Harris now sought to restrain Jameson, may well have conveyed to him the wrong meaning. Surely Rhodes must be desperate because of the way the reformers were procrastinating? And if the glory had departed, it had departed only from Johannesburg. Jameson would bring it back.

It was not till the evening of Saturday, 28 December, after the holiday crowds had gone home and the woods under Table Mountain were peaceful again, that Rhodes called Bower up to Groote

Schurr and told him in the twilit garden that all was over. (That went for their quarrel too.) Bower heard for the first time the full details of the Rhodes plan; that Rhodes was financing the rising; that it had 'fizzled out like a damp squib'; that Sir Hercules, contrary to Chamberlain's wishes, had insisted on the Transvaal flag ('but that Sir Hercules was right'); and that Rhodes would now give up the whole Johannesburg business and develop 'his North', leaving the capitalists to make the best terms they could with Kruger. Dr Jameson's force would remain on the frontier, but reduced in strength.[3] If anything, Rhodes seemed to be relieved at the 'fizzle'.

Bower stayed at Groote Schurr until half-past eight, gazing into the darkening woods and into Rhodes's future, which to him must have seemed brighter. Then he went home. Next day, Sunday, at about eleven o'clock at night, as he was going to bed, he heard the sound of a horse's hoofs approaching his house. It was Rhodes's coachman come post-haste to summon him back to Groote Schurr. The 'fizzle' had suddenly burst into flame. Jameson had taken the bit between his teeth and gone in.

The Doctor had been told many times to wait. But he never heard, as Bower heard on that Saturday night, Rhodes solemnly reading the funeral service over his precious rising. The messages to Jameson were only 'wait'. Rhodes could not bring himself to say flatly that the thing was dead.

Even if he had said so, would the Doctor have listened? He had listened to the sayings of Cecil Rhodes for over twenty years, and the one he laid to heart was 'Take all . . . ask afterwards'.

# 29

# *Catastrophe*

Graham Bower sat in Rhodes's bedroom, too stunned to read the telegram (written partly in cipher) which Rhodes had handed to him. It was Dr Jameson's last message: 'Shall leave tonight for the Transvaal.' Then Rhodes showed him the telegram he himself had sent, too late, to stop Jameson. 'I have sent to stop him, and Heany has also gone to stop him,' Rhodes spluttered, green in the face. 'It may yet come all right. Don't be alarmed. It may come all right yet.' He knew it would not come all right, and a little later he added: 'I know I must go. I will resign tomorrow. But I know what this means. It means war. I am a ruined man, but there must be no recrimination. I will take the blame.'

Bower, still too 'knocked over' to read or think, took the hand which Rhodes held out to him. As he said good-bye, he made what is probably the first of several references to St Peter's denial of his Lord: 'Well, Rhodes, others may do as they like but my name is not Peter and I am not going to run away. If you have to bear the blame I will take my share with you.'[1] Then they shook hands and the Imperial Secretary went out, 'thinking hard'. Well he might. He had spontaneously taken a pledge which was to cost him dear.

The time was midnight when Bower took his leave of Rhodes. He let something like five hours pass before making the next move. At five o'clock in the morning of Monday, 30 December, just as Jameson's two columns were joining up on the wrong side of the Transvaal border, Bower sent a note to the High Commissioner by his gardener:

My dear Sir Hercules,
    I hope you will come to Town early. There is, I fear, bad news from Jameson. He seems to have disobeyed Rhodes, and to have taken the bit between his teeth.

Yours,
Graham Bower.

Afterwards Bower was severely blamed for letting the old man sleep on a few hours longer instead of waking him up promptly to hear the bad news. Bower's critics strangely overlooked the real mistake he made. In his early morning agitation he gave the High Commissioner away. For how could Sir Hercules understand what order of Rhodes's Jameson had disobeyed, or what was meant by the 'bit', unless he knew a great deal more than he later admitted of the whole conspiracy? Bower's error was not in the timing by in the wording of his note.

At 11 A.M. that same Monday morning, 30 December, a group of Rhodes's friends arrived at Groote Schurr to help him entertain some English cricketers he had invited to lunch. They were shown into the billiard room.

'Well, Jameson's off. Read that!' Rhodes handed them the news. Then he added, thinking of the cricketers, 'God knows what I can say to them with this on my mind.' Turning to Frederic Howard Hamilton, editor of the *Johannesburg Star* at thirty, he said: 'You are young. You will see the end of it all – the end of this big thing.' But Hamilton was to die in 1956, five years before South Africa left the Commonwealth. And that event, if anything, was the real end of Rhodes's 'big thing'.

Rhodes had managed to conceal his anxieties from friends less intimate than Hamilton, but next day he seemed 'distraught'. Purple in the face, he told Hamilton of his plan to save Jameson.

*Rhodes:* I'll go to Pretoria to see Kruger.
*Hamilton:* He'll hang you.
*Rhodes:* Hang *me*! They can't hang me! I'm a Privy Councillor. There are only 200 of us in the British Empire.

But Rhodes dropped the idea of tackling Kruger in favour of turning the heat on Chamberlain.

*Rhodes:* Well, anyhow, I have got Chamberlain by the short hairs . . .

– though Hamilton noted that Rhodes used a stronger anatomical metaphor.

*Hamilton:* Then he really is in it, Mr Rhodes?
*Rhodes:* In it? Up to the neck!

Returning to the Monday, that afternoon W. P. Schreiner, Rhodes's Attorney-General, called on the Prime Minister at Groote Schurr for confirmation or denial of the news. The 'large lymphatic lawyer'* had talked with Rhodes during the previous Sunday evening. Knowing that Leonard and Hamilton had been at Groote Schurr the day before, he warned Rhodes against seeing 'too much of Charley Leonard'. It would be a great mistake, he said, to get mixed up with the Uitlanders and their movement. It was after seven o'clock when Schreiner left, unaware that the man he had warned against such small fry as Leonard and Hamilton was thoroughly mixed up with a whale of a dangerous character. Like many others, Schreiner had no inkling of the connection between Jameson and the Uitlanders.

Rhodes did not so much as mention to Schreiner the excited comings and goings of that Sunday, when Harris tried in vain to get a telegraph message through to Jameson. He allowed his Attorney-General to go home in happy ignorance. No doubt partly because of this interview with Rhodes on Sunday evening, Schreiner could not at first believe some dramatic news which he received on Monday from Mafeking. Boyes and Fuller both sent telegrams announcing that Jameson had crossed the border. Schreiner's first reaction was to accuse Boyes of spreading false rumours ('Your agitated telegram received . . .'[2]) until Fuller's similar message, arriving three and a half hours later, made him think again. He consulted the Colonial Secretary, Johannes Albertus Faure, who had heard a rumour at the Johannesburg races of Jameson's plan, and then called at Groote Schurr meaning to confront the Prime Minister with the disquieting messages.

But Rhodes did not yet feel able to face the world. He had taken to the woods. Later that evening Schreiner received a distraught summons from Rhodes. 'The moment I saw him,' Schreiner told the Committee of Inquiry, 'I saw a man I had never seen before. His appearance was utterly dejected and different.' Before Schreiner could say a word Rhodes burst out:

---

* Ian Colvin in his *Life of Jameson*, 1, p.268. Colvin added that Schreiner 'never kindled to an idea, least of all the idea of leading a lost cause'. Schreiner was in fact a high-minded pessimist who adored Rhodes but broke with him after the Raid.

Yes, yes, it is true. Old Jameson has upset my apple-cart. It is all true . . .

Could this be play-acting? Schreiner dismissed the suspicion.[3] He saw that this was genuine. Rhodes really was a broken man. Even so, the situation might yet be saved:

*Schreiner:* Why do you not stop him? Although he has ridden in you can still stop him.
*Rhodes*: Poor old Jameson. Twenty years we have been friends and now he goes and ruins me. I cannot hinder him. I cannot go and destroy him.

In point of fact Rhodes had just cabled Flora Shaw in a spirit of defiance, to prevent Chamberlain from stopping 'poor old Jameson':

Inform Chamberlain that I shall get through all right if he supports me but he must not send cable like he sent to High Commissioner in South Africa. Today the crux is, I will win and South Africa will belong to England.

A sharp rap on the knuckles for the Colonial Secretary. In the afternoon a long cable to his Company representatives in London, including sentences like, 'We are confident of success. Johannesburg united and strong on our side,' besides being inaccurate, clearly showed which way the wind had veered. The actions of Rhodes after he received the fatal news are not those of a man determined to stop the runaway. Perhaps for this reason the authenticity of a curious telegram which he and Harris drafted on Sunday afternoon has been questioned. But though expressed in a roundabout way it did represent an effort to prevent the Doctor from starting. Rhodes showed a copy to Sir Graham Bower late on the Sunday night when he broke the news of the bolt, and since Bower apparently made no adverse comments on its nature, it presumably satisfied the man who was violently opposed to the whole adventure. (It is just possible, however, that Bower was too 'knocked over' to take it in.) A copy of the message, produced for the Committee, has been described as so 'mystifying' as to suggest that it was 'bogus';[4] the implication being that Rhodes did not try to stop Jameson at all. This was the copy.:

*Unbegangen [Rhodes] to Jameson.*
Heartily reciprocate your wishes with regard to Protectorate, but the Colonial Office machinery moves slowly, as you know. We are, however,

doing our utmost to get immediate transference of what we are justly entitled to. Things in Johannesburg I yet hope to see amicably settled, and a little patience and common sense is only necessary – on no account must you move, I most strongly object to such a course.

The telegram reads like a genuine attempt to handle an obstreperous colleague tactfully: Rhodes was Jameson's brother-in-arms not his brother's keeper. 'Heartily reciprocate your wishes . . .' It is good psychology to find a point of agreement before launching an attack. The reference to 'things in Johannesburg' was in line with Rhodes's decision confided to Bower the night before: the rising had 'fizzled' and the capitalists must settle with Kruger. At the end comes the real point of the message: 'On no account must you move.'

It is perhaps worth noting that like Jameson in his last message ('Shall leave tonight for the Transvaal') Rhodes in his last telegram abandoned the camouflage of Stock Exchange idiom. He did not forbid Jameson to 'float' but to 'move'. Perhaps, therefore, the involved nature of this telegram was also partly a security measure.

How should the attitude of Rhodes be summarized? Though he sent a strong prohibition, his message was no thunderbolt from Olympus. After he had broken the news to Bower, slept on it (if he slept) and ridden on it for another night and day, he made up his mind that he would not put a spoke in Jameson's wheel. Though the line to Mafeking was open by noon on 30 December, he sent no more wires to stop the raiders but cabled instead the 'women and children' letter to *The Times*. He was a 'ruined man' but a gambler still. Jameson, if not fatally obstructed, might win through. And as if to crystallize his changing moods, Dr Harris suddenly burst in with a message that Jameson was in fact being unfairly impeded at that very moment. Jan Hofmeyr was even now drawing up a proclamation in the High Commissioner's name repudiating him. Having more or less forced his way into the High Commissioner's office, the angry 'Bondsman' had proceeded to dictate action at Imperial HQ:

*Hofmeyr:* You must send off a proclamation at once. Kruger sent one to stop Adendorff.'
*Robinson:* Did he? But I am afraid Pushful Joe is in it.
*Hofmeyr:* It is all the more reason. Do you remember he was the man who said you would be merely a tool in the hands of Rhodes, if you were

allowed to come out, and he [Pushful Joe] tried to prevent your being sent
out a second time.
*Robinson:* Yes, that is true.
*Hofmeyr:* Well, now it is your duty to prove you can go against Rhodes.
*Robinson:* I will send that proclamation. Will you write it out?[5]

Rhodes was galvanized into activity by Harris's report of what
was going on in Government House. He drove into Cape Town like
Jehu and reached Robinson in time to cause a considerable scene.
'It's making an outlaw of the Doctor,' he protested vehemently.
Bower and Garrett had already managed to get the potent wording
of Hofmeyr's draft somewhat watered down.

The relations between Hofmeyr and Rhodes never recovered their
old, valuable warmth. Hofmeyr was fond of saying that he felt like a
man betrayed by 'the wife of his bosom'. The simile was quoted so
often that in the end Rhodes lost patience and on one occasion
interrupted the familiar rigmarole with, 'Oh yes, I know – about the
wife and so on . . .' The marriage of the two white races had ended in
divorce.

The collapse of Alfred Beit provides a fitting postscript to the
story of Rhodes's ordeal. Unfortunate 'little Beit' received the news
at Groote Schurr, crumpled over a bottle of headache tablets. He
had a nervous breakdown and made his will, leaving a million
pounds to those who might suffer from the Raid. Said Bower, 'He
behaved splendidly.'

Joseph Chamberlain was spending his Christmas holiday at Highbury in a state of detached anticipation. He, too, was waiting for the
rising to occur within the next few days and on 26 December, while
Leonard and Hamilton were in the train steaming southwards to put
it off, he sent an important letter to the Prime Minister announcing
its approach:

My dear Salisbury,
   I have received private information that a rising in Johannesburg is
imminent and will probably take place in the course of the next few days.
   The state of affairs in the Transvaal has been threatening trouble of this
kind for some time, and I have given secret instructions to Sir Hercules
Robinson, after consulting him by letter, how to act in an emergency.
   The War Office has arranged that two regiments, one from Bombay, and

one from Barbadoes, shall call at the Cape about the middle of January. I think the outbreak will be at the end of this month, but we have, of course, our usual garrison at the Cape, and Rhodes has the Bechuanaland Police.

There is nothing more to be done but to watch the event, which we have done nothing to provoke. If the rising is successful it ought to turn to our advantage.[6]

This letter does not presuppose a basis of mutual understanding or a background of knowledge on Salisbury's part. Nor does the account of precautionary measures sound like a recapitulation of policy already agreed to by the Prime Minister. Must it be presumed that Chamberlain had not hitherto consulted Salisbury? This conclusion fits not only with the tone of the letter but also with Sir Graham Bower's explicit statement to Rhodes. When the latter assured Bower that according to Flora Shaw's telegram all the 'leaders' at home were with him in his plans for a revolution, Bower queried the word 'leaders'. To whom did it refer? 'The Cabinet, I suppose,' said Rhodes. This was a mistake, wrote Bower afterwards, as the Cabinet was never consulted. Garvin, however, asserts categorically that the Colonial Secretary consulted his colleagues throughout: 'Chamberlain consulted Lord Salisbury and other principal members of the Cabinet . . .'.[7] But no dates are mentioned for these consultations in Garvin's otherwise accurately dated story.

Did Chamberlain consult the Cabinet? As no minutes of Cabinet meetings were kept before the year 1916, it is hard to be absolutely sure.* But judging from Chamberlain's own temperament, his policy and the state of Salisbury's last Cabinet, it is probable that the consultations were minimal. Chamberlain's instinct was towards quick decision and independent action. Like a good demagogue, he was more concerned with the reaction of the public than of his colleagues.

Lord Salisbury's last Cabinet was one of those which gave plenty

---

* The Cabinet room before 1916 was singularly lacking in amenities. Not only was there no Minute Secretary, but there was no push-bell either. Ministers had to walk to the door to send a message. But even if minutes had been kept then as they are today, it would still have been difficult to decide exactly what each Cabinet Minister said, for the minutes are taken with a view to translating decisions into action, rather than recording individual opinions. On the other hand, it would have been possible to discover whether affairs in the Transvaal were discussed.

of scope to Ministers who wished to go their own way.* But since his son-in-law, Lord Selborne, was Chamberlain's Under-Secretary of State, it is unlikely that he knew nothing of Chamberlain's doings. Moreover, there is some evidence[8] that Chamberlain was in consultation with Salisbury over at least the general position in the Transvaal. A letter from him dated 12 November records an appointment to see the Prime Minister that day at 5 P.M. We do not know the subject discussed at this meeting, but there is a presumption that it was South Africa. For next day another letter, evidently continuing a previous conversation, came from Chamberlain:

My dear Salisbury

I have looked up the question of the Transvaal Convention. Alas! it all happened when Gladstone was consul and when I was in office.†

It is probable that on 13 November Salisbury and Chamberlain were mainly occupied in discussing the relations of the Transvaal with other European powers. But this subject itself was so closely connected with the Johannesburg rising that it may well have led on to the second. There are no other letters from Chamberlain among the *Salisbury Papers* which mention, even indirectly, the trouble in Johannesburg.‡

Let us assume that Chamberlain consulted Salisbury and the Cabinet only in the most general manner. It does not therefore follow that his relations with Salisbury were strained or that his

* 'Salisbury's interpretation of the rôle of a Minister was that he did not owe a personal allegiance to the Prime Minister, and accordingly he allowed his colleagues wider scope for their activities than is generally customary.' (R. Rhodes James, *Lord Randolph Churchill*, p.208.) This attitude in 1885, of which Mr Rhodes James writes, had become firmly established ten years and two Cabinets later.

† Under the 1881 Convention (Pretoria) the Transvaal was permitted no communications with foreign powers except through HM Government. But in 1884 British influence was confined to the power of veto on a Treaty proper. This was the important Article IV of the (London) Convention. Chamberlain continued: 'Lord Derby was Colonial Secretary when this change was made, and I doubt if Mr Gladstone ever noticed it.'

‡ On 4 September 1895 Chamberlain wrote to Salisbury that he was about to go on holiday and would like to know his wishes on Delagoa Bay. That is as near as he got to the Transvaal, though his department was much occupied with the negotiations over the transfer of the Protectorate. Of course, it is possible to argue that he already knew Salisbury's views on this matter. The other questions he raised on 4 September were Mixed Marriages in Malta and the Venezuela Boundary.

letter of 26 December presented the Prime Minister with 'a rather arrogant *fait accompli*'.[9] If Chamberlain did not consult his chief it was because he took it for granted that he was expected to handle matters himself. The Prime Minister liked things done in this way and did not wish to be bothered. In that *fin de siècle* atmosphere, allowances were surely made for 'Pushful Joe'. His fellow Ministers must have felt that a spice of the 'new diplomacy' was bound to appear in his handling of his colleagues as well as of Kruger. And one aspect of the 'new diplomacy', playfully defined by Sir William Harcourt, one of the Liberal leaders, was to 'refuse all information at all times'.

Two days after sending Salisbury the letter about the rising, so full of controlled optimism, Chamberlain received a report from Fairfield of the 'fizzle' simultaneously with a rumour that Jameson would force an outbreak:

*Fairfield to Chamberlain, 28 December 1895*
    ... I met Hawksley, the Company's solicitor,\* last night, who said that he and his friends were being much chaffed in the city about the 'fizzle' of the revolution. He seemed to think that Rhodes (whom he does not much like) might be driven into an attitude of frenzy and unreason, and order Dr Jameson to 'go in' from Gaberones† with the Company's police and manipulate a revolution, but Maguire, who has just been here, says this is absurd ... Were the Company's Police to go in filibustering it would be a breach of their Charter, which you might feel bound to stop under Article 8.[10]

    Chamberlain waited until next day (29 December) to inform Salisbury of the 'fizzle', but not of the Hawksley rumour which had been contradicted by Maguire:

I think that the Transvaal business is going to fizzle out. Rhodes has miscalculated the feeling of the Johannesburg capitalists, and it is now quite

---

    \* The fact that Hawksley's position needed explaining suggests that Chamberlain was not intimate with the Rhodes group.
    † It is an interesting reflection on the extent of Colonial Office knowledge of Jameson's plan that they never caught up with the fact that his camp was at Pitsani and not Gaberones. After the Raid, Fairfield set about clearing up what he called a 'mystery': 'Where exactly is Pitsani Potlugo and was Jameson there?' (C.O. 417/177, p. 253.)

possible that Kruger will make some concessions, in which case the affair would be terminated for the present at any rate.[11]

To Sir Hercules Robinson a 'strictly confidential' and decidedly more informative message went off from Chamberlain at 5.30 P.M. on the same day. It contained a reference to the possibility of a raid:

Strictly personal and Confidential. *There seems to be a fiasco at Johannesburg owing probably to Rhodes having misjudged the balance of opinion there.* It has been suggested, although I do not think it probable, that *he and Jameson* might endeavour to force matters to a head by *Jameson or* some one else in the Service of the Company advancing from Bechuanaland Protectorate with Police. In view of Articles No. 22 and 8 of the Charter *I could not remain passive* were this done. Therefore, if necessary, but not otherwise, remind Rhodes of those articles, and intimate to him that in your opinion he would not have my support, and point out the consequences which would follow *to his schemes were I to repudiate the action.**

Today the fact that Chamberlain thus dissociated himself at the eleventh hour from Rhodes, though interesting, is not the most interesting thing about the telegram quoted above. Those words and phrases printed here in italics will be seen at once to contain irrefutable evidence that Chamberlain was not a stranger to Rhodes's plans. His references to the 'fiasco', Rhodes's 'schemes', and especially to Jameson by name, are all extremely compromising. The implication that his rôle had hitherto been a 'passive' one supports the theory of his partial complicity advanced in this narrative. It is therefore not surprising to find that the Government Blue book contains a bowdlerized version of the message, omitting all the italicized words and changing some of the others. Even so the result is not entirely innocuous.†

* The italics are the present writer's. The letter is among the *Salisbury Papers* at Christ Church, Oxford.
† The revised version of the telegram reads as follows:
It has been suggested, although I do not think it probable, that an endeavour may be made to force matters at Johannesburg to a head by someone in the service of the Company advancing from the Bechuanaland Protectorate with Police. Were this to be done I should have to take action under Articles 22 and 8 of the Charter. Therefore, if necessary, but not otherwise, remind Rhodes of these Articles and intimate to him that in your opinion he would not have my support, and point out the consequences which would follow.

Thus Chamberlain, warned of the impending Raid, in turn warned the High Commissioner, requiring him to pass the warning on to the Prime Minister of the Cape. (The Prime Minister of Great Britain was not informed.) But it was too late. The next day, Monday, 30 December, came the announcement that Jameson had gone in. The Colonial Office heard it at four o'clock in the afternoon. It was Flora Shaw who came round and broke the news to Sir Robert Meade. Whatever the Colonial Office may have revealed to her in the past, she certainly repaid her debt now.

Chamberlain, dressing for dinner before the annual servants' ball at Highbury, received the news by special messenger. He clenched his hands and to the intimate circle of his family expressed the personal impact of the disaster: 'If this succeeds it will ruin me. I am going up to London to crush it.' Hurried consultations followed, including one with his brother Arthur who was fetched over from Moor Green Hall, the other Chamberlain mansion just across the road. The family could be relied upon to rally round; on with the dance. A cab took him to the 12.50 A.M. train, so that the family coachman should not miss the ball. The cab arrived late; he himself almost missed the train. He reached his empty London house at 4 A.M. on Tuesday to face a very different kind of music.

At 10 A.M. that morning he was round at the Colonial Office to meet his officials and also Miss Shaw, back on the doorstep. This time she had brought the 'letter of invitation' to show them, together with a covering message from Dr Harris: 'You can publish.' Miss Shaw informed Chamberlain that she was about to take the 'letter of invitation' round to *The Times* for immediate publication. Neither she nor Chamberlain had any reason to think that it was a deception. He knew very well that its publication would have a profound public effect. He seems also to have thought up to the last

---

Sir Graham Bower's statement that this telegram was doctored is thus fully corroborated. Hitherto it has been supported by inherent probabilities. (See J. van der Poel, op. cit., pp. 198–9.) Bower's recollection of the deleted passages was reasonably accurate and so strengthens his general claim to be a reliable witness.

Of course some selection for Blue books is inevitable; Bower himself requested the Colonial Office to omit one of his own letters in the interests of 'harmonious healing up of old sores'. (C.O. 417/184, 12 September 1896.) Chamberlain doubtless justified the doctoring of his telegram on grounds of national interest.

that Johannesburg might still rise and so justify Jameson's madness. For he sent a telegram to the High Commissioner late on New Year's Day suggesting that Jameson's movement might be a feint to draw off the Transvaal forces, while the Uitlanders rose and seized Johannesburg and Pretoria. Yet despite all these hazards he did not hesitate to denounce the Raid.

# 30

# *The Premature Dispatch*

The Debate on the Queen's Speech of 13 February 1896 gave Parliament its first opportunity to discuss Chamberlain's handling of the Raid. It was applauded by both sides, though even more vigorously by the Opposition. Sydney Buxton and many other Liberals congratulated him on his pluck and promptitude. 'I do not know any one who could have acted better,' said Leonard Courtney. Sir Henry Lucy, the parliamentary diarist, thought it was just like Chamberlain's incredible luck to run into the Jameson affair so soon after taking office and to deal with it so brilliantly.

Chamberlain's speech excelled in self-confidence. So much so that for the first and last time he publicly admitted, by implication, that the troops on the border were not there solely to guard the railway. Boldly citing the Loch plan as an honourable precedent, he clinched his argument with a metaphor later to become famous:

When your neighbour's house is on fire, you are quite right to get out your apparatus in order to extinguish it and nobody can accuse you unless they can prove that you are bringing it out, not with the object of stopping mischief . . . but with the deliberate intention of promoting the mischief that you profess a desire to prevent [Cheers].

Chamberlain had 'got out his apparatus' and his conscience did not prick him; the troops had indeed been intended to stop mischief, not to promote it. He could not be expected to regard the rising itself as 'mischief' and to stop that. But for all that his conscience was clear in February 1896, he dared not make the same admission in May 1897. In front of the Tribunal he said he knew of only one reason for the border force: to guard the railway.

Part of Chamberlain's early confidence was due to the expected visit of Kruger to England. This was to be a genuine attempt at reconciliation, though Chamberlain quipped to his wife, 'if he will walk into my parlour it will be very nice of him', and Lord Salisbury hoped to see him 'drowned in turtle soup'. Sir Graham Bower, himself a senior KCMG, believed that Kruger's entourage positively longed to be deluged in honours, if not in soup. 'They thought they saw decorations, KCMGs, etc, in prospect,' he wrote, so they were 'anxious' for Kruger to go. Off his own bat Bower encouraged them, relying on Sir Robert Meade and his friend Fairfield to produce the swag once Kruger and his advisers were safely in London.

Yet a letter from Chamberlain to Salisbury on 24 January 1896 had shown how fundamentally unrealistic was the attitude of the British Government towards the Kruger visit. Chamberlain reported the arrival of a cable from Pretoria,

... to the effect that Kruger will accept our invitation to come here and discuss all matters of common interest. It is understood that any modification of Article IV is excluded. I think it will be a great 'coup' to get the old man over here and we have much to gain from him while he has little to ask from us.

Kruger would have laughed sardonically at this account of his requirements. The 'little' he had to ask of the British Government was no more and no less than his people's absolute freedom.

There were two powerful reasons why the President of the Transvaal was not to come. Kruger's pro-German State Secretary, Dr Leyds, advised him against the visit, though Kruger's own judgment had always been in favour of arguing things out. 'Young man,' he once said to President Steyn, 'you don't know the English. I do. You should argue with them – dispute with them – negotiate with them – but don't fight with them.' The London visit would have been a fine opportunity for argument. On previous visits to London Kruger had done well and learned much. The right decision would have been to go. But Chamberlain himself contributed another reason, perhaps the decisive one, against his going. It all hung on a diplomatic *bêtise* known as the 'Uitlander dispatch'.

In pursuance of his aim to achieve justice for the Uitlanders, Chamberlain drew up a scheme of municipal reform for Johannesburg which he described as 'Gas and Water Home Rule'. But he published his plan first and sent the draft of it to Kruger afterwards. The full dispatch appeared in the *London Gazette* on 7 February, while a mere summary of the proposals reached Pretoria. To Kruger it was a deliberate slight upon such sovereignty as he enjoyed. Chamberlain tried to explain it in Parliament as an attempt to give the House all the facts of his scheme, and of the position in

Johannesburg, at the very beginning of the session. 'If I have done wrong,' he concluded wryly, 'it is a lesson to persons who endeavour to diplomatize on new methods [Laughter].' There was more laughter, this time unintended, when he rounded off his written apologies to the offended President with a touch of the 'new diplomacy' at its most naïve: 'How is Mrs Kruger?' he suddenly inquired of the President, whose wife had been ill.

Were Chamberlain's new methods really to blame or was his blunder due to some other more recondite cause? Unknown to the world an attempt had been made on 4 February 1896 by Rhodes's solicitor, Bouchier Hawksley, to blackmail Chamberlain. It has been suggested that the publication of the premature 'Uitlander dispatch' was in fact the Colonial Secretary's response to pressure, his effort to buy off Rhodes by rushing to champion the Uitlanders. It is time to return to the 'missing telegrams'.

Rhodes arrived in England on 3 February 1896, an angry St George bent on saving his precious Charter from the dragon of parliamentary inquiry. He was met at Southampton by Rutherfoord Harris and Bouchier Hawksley. The three travelled up to London together. By the time they reached the capital the finishing touches had been put to a plot to defeat the Inquiry. St George's weapon was to be blackmail. Chamberlain would be warned through Fairfield that a series of telegrams, implicating the Colonial Office in the Rhodes plan, were held by Hawksley. At a word from Rhodes they would be published. No Inquiry, no telegrams; it was as simple as that.

When Rhodes got out of the train he had a pleasant surprise. 'I found all the busmen smiling at me when I came to London,' he said afterwards, 'and then I knew I was all right.' There were other signs that things might be all right for Rhodes and his Charter, even without Hawksley's drastic action. His friends in England had already taken steps on his behalf. In his journal for February 1896, the Hon Reginald Brett (Lord Esher) noted that he told 'Natty' Rothschild to meet Rhodes as soon as he arrived and make him see Chamberlain at once. There had already been anxious exchanges, in some of which the Colonial Secretary participated, as to how Rhodes's defence at the Inquiry could best be handled. (Mrs Brett tried to buoy up her husband by saying: 'You should never despair of a man like Rhodes till you see him swinging on the gallows.') On 1

February Brett received a letter from Chamberlain suggesting that it would be a help to Rhodes if he could find documentary or verbal evidence of a German–Dutch plot in the Transvaal, in order 'to divert the issue and to share the blame'. During his interrogation by the Committee of Inquiry, Rhodes did in fact take this tip and run the anti-German line hard. The continuation of Chamberlain's letter to Brett throws an interesting light on his own part in the plot:

If Rhodes were able to say (and to stand examination upon it) that he was, like everyone else, aware of the possibility of revolution in Johannesburg and that he thought it his duty to be prepared, and even to have a force in observation, but he had no intention that this force should be used except upon emergency and with the consent of the High Commissioner, I think it would be difficult to find serious fault with him.[1]

It is impossible to resist the impression that in this rather muddled rigmarole Chamberlain was thinking of his own position as well as Rhodes's. He knew nothing of Hawksley's telegrams and believed at this stage that even if all came out he would live down the 'serious fault'. As for Rhodes's prospects, Chamberlain's over-rosy view of them was partly due to the fact that he did not yet know whether the rumour of Rhodes having financed the rising was true.

There was no lack of helpful plans for letting Rhodes down lightly. But in the early days of February the Colossus was not interested in how to defend himself before the Tribunal. He intended to scotch it. Without delay Hawksley paid his sinister visit to Fairfield at the Colonial Office. The existence of the cable correspondence between Harris, Maguire, Grey and Rhodes was revealed. Fairfield at once informed Chamberlain and was immediately instructed to write to Hawksley asking for copies of the cables. Hawksley's reply arrived on 5 February. In silky but ominous language he refused Fairfield's request to see his dossier:

I think perhaps enough has been done, and we may leave matters at this point. Mr C. [Chamberlain] knows what I know and can shape his course with this knowledge.[2]

Hawksley went on:

You know and I do not what has passed between the High Commissioner and his Secretary and the Colonial Office.

Having thus protested his inability to blackmail the Colonial Office, even had he wished to do so, Hawksley continued smoothly:

As I hope I made clear to you there is not the slightest intention to make any use whatever of confidential documents.

Hawksley described himself as Fairfield's 'very great personal friend'. But on this occasion Fairfield must have felt that his very great friend was submitting him to a very great strain. Hawksley's letter finished up with a significant remark:

If you can hurry up the dispatch about the Uitlanders it would do much good.

Again the all too familiar 'hurry up' motif. Hawksley was hinting as to how his client might be appeased. Chamberlain was not the man to be moved by threats, but the suggestion of quick action, by way of compromise, was one to attract him.

Next day, 6 February, Rhodes came to see the Colonial Secretary. It was the first time these two had played opposite one another during the whole course of this tense drama without understudies or intermediaries. But the procedure had already been discussed between Rhodes and Brett, and Brett and Chamberlain. Should Rhodes tell Chamberlain the whole truth? Brett saw Rhodes on 5 February, the day that Chamberlain was digesting Hawksley's behaviour over the cables, and discovered that Rhodes wished to reveal everything. Brett then carried this news to the Colonial Secretary, whom he found, not surprisingly, in poor shape. He was very tired and also worried at the prospect of hearing 'too much' from Rhodes. Suppose he should be compelled, as a result, to arrest Rhodes as well as Jameson? 'He could see no advantage in receiving Rhodes's confidence.'

There were no fireworks at the interview. Between the principals the discussion, though lengthy, did not get down to bedrock. Chamberlain's Private Secretary, Harry Wilson, noted in his diary: 'They were closeted together for an hour and forty-five minutes and went over the ground very thoroughly.' Over the ground, but not beneath the surface where the telegrams were temporarily buried. 'We looked in whenever we got a chance,' continued Wilson, 'and . . . the discussion seemed to be proceeding amicably enough.'

Chamberlain would do his utmost to save the Charter, though Rhodes's hard-won, short-lived control of the police must end. And the Inquiry? If Parliament demanded it no power on earth could stop it being held. Rhodes thought of the power of blackmail; said nothing. During this interview, not a word was mentioned of the telegrams.

It is clear that nothing occurred during Chamberlain's first interview with Rhodes to justify a theory that he brought pressure to bear on the Colonial Secretary resulting in the premature publication of the 'Uitlander dispatch'. If anything, the screw was put on Rhodes. That loyal observer, Harry Wilson, noted that Rhodes arrived looking 'flustered and worried, his face red and his hair rather tumbled. One instinctively thought of certain visits in one's schooldays to the Headmaster – and there is something schoolboyish about C.J.R. which bears out the comparison.' Wilson added: 'Lord Selborne told me afterwards that it had been most satisfactory, and that Rhodes had shown a great amount of common sense.' (Selborne was present at the interview.) What probably harassed the red-faced visitor was the thought of his own doubledealing. He had promised his friends to be good in the Headmaster's study, but he could not forget the drawing-pins he was preparing to put on the Headmaster's seat.

If the Chamberlain–Rhodes interview furnishes no evidence that the 'Uitlander dispatch' was hurried up under pressure, the same cannot be said of a letter which reached the Colonial Office just before the red-faced visitor arrived. On the same day, 6 February, Reginald Brett sent a friendly letter to Chamberlain preparing him for the visit of Rhodes. Rhodes would be discreet and go home to South Africa, said Brett, 'but he wants something to show for his visit here'.[3] Chamberlain had already decided to tell Rhodes he would fight for the Charter. But the Uitlanders' grievances were still not met. Attention to this matter as well as to the Charter would probably count as the 'something' which Rhodes wanted. The very next day, 7 February 1896, Chamberlain's 'Uitlander dispatch' was published. Brett, acting for Rhodes, had hurried it up.

The 'hurry up' theme persists with ill effects throughout the course of this story. There is no support, however, for the view that it was the blackmailing telegrams, any more than Rhodes's interview, which achieved the hurrying up of the dispatch. At this juncture

Chamberlain had not seen them. He had no reason to think that they were lethal. He had been told that they would not be used. He believed that Kruger's forthcoming visit would in any case render their use unnecessary.

Kruger declined in the end to go to London. But the Colonial Secretary could not altogether blame himself, despite the fact that Dr Leyds made the most of his diplomatic blunder to poison Kruger's mind against the visit. Bower, in his *Apologia* of ten years later, asks the question, Why did Kruger allow himself to be overruled by Leyds? In Kruger's own character Bower finds the answer. Though Kruger's judgment was still good his will was weak. He was old and tired. Leyds, young and charming, dominated Kruger much as Bower himself controlled Robinson. Each made crucial mistakes. The abortive visit was a setback not only to Chamberlain but to the cause of peace.

# 31

# 'War-Mongering'

As the spring of 1896 advanced the political climate grew more wintry. By early April it was just possible to hope that Kruger might come to England but not to expect it. And unless he came it was good-bye to a settlement without an Inquiry. Those who were already convinced of Chamberlain's complicity – Sir Graham Bower and Dr Leyds, for instance – detected a reckless resolve in the Colonial Secretary to paint out his own guilt by printing the map of Africa red: red in the blood of the two white races.

Rumours of these alleged intentions reached the Governor of Natal as well as the Cape, and telegrams from both Colonies urged Chamberlain not to try to win concessions from Kruger by sending him an ultimatum.* Sir Hercules Robinson, at loggerheads with Chamberlain over his handling of Kruger ever since the Raid, dispatched many pleas against strong measures and at the end of April summed them up in a phrase reminiscent of the reformers' advice to Dr Jameson: 'Sit still and wait patiently.'

During the time that cables were arriving from South Africa, Chamberlain cleared his own mind by an exchange of letters with Fairfield, the latter putting the point of view of Government House, Cape Town. In what Chamberlain called A STATEMENT OF POLICY 1896, sent to Fairfield on 5 April, he argued that previous generosity to the Boers was a piece of Christian chivalry which had brought no reward in this world:

The Boers (and Mr Fairfield) believe that we gave way because we were afraid of them and they (the Boers – not Mr Fairfield) have been intolerable ever since.

* On 8 April 1896 the *Cape Times* published a cartoon representing an interview between 'The Man on the Spot' (Robinson) and Chamberlain, who is pulling a gun marked 'Ultimatum' from a bag marked 'Diplomatic Outfit'. 'Better not take that with you,' says Robinson, 'if you are going to call on Kruger. Might annoy the old man.' Chamberlain: 'Sh! It's all right. It isn't loaded.' Robinson: 'All the more reason not to show it then. We've had enough in South Africa of fire-arms which don't go off.'

Sir Evelyn Wood, he went on, had told him a few days ago that reconquest of the Transvaal would not be a very difficult thing. All the same, he appreciated Mr Fairfield's remarks about the serious risks of a conflict:

I shall never go into such a war with a light heart, and at the present time we have no reason – either of right or of interest – which would justify the enterprise.

Towards the end of his 'statement' the Colonial Secretary allowed himself a short burst of intense irritation against both Uitlanders and Boers:

I cannot feel the least sympathy with either Kruger or his antagonists.
    The former is an ignorant dirty cunning and obstinate man who has known how to feather his own nest and to enrich all his family and dependants.
    The latter are a lot of cowardly selfish blatant speculators who would sell their souls to have the power of rigging the market.

After this he felt better and finished up more calmly:

In spite of all this our business is to bring about a fair settlement.
    We shall not do it, I admit, by a policy of empty menace or arbitrary impatience – neither, I think, shall we succeed if we underestimate our reserve force and allow Kruger to have it all his own way.[1]

Fairfield replied on 7 April that the inner circle of 'the extreme war party here' were confident of making a *casus belli* either out of Kruger's refusal to negotiate in England or out of his failure to satisfy the Uitlanders. The Colonial Secretary at once lashed out again on 8 April 1896, this time at the 'extreme war party' in England:

*Secret.* I quite understand the little game. But I do not mean to carry out a policy for the benefit of these gentry and I entirely agree that we have no *casus belli* at present and shall not have even if Kruger definitely refuses our invitations and declines to make any changes in his precious Constitution.
    I do not think it wise, however, to explain this to the housetops and I do not mind the noisy exaltation of the Jingo party, since it does not commit me and *may* put some pressure on the people in the Transvaal who are afraid of war.[2]

Despite Chamberlain's testiness with almost everyone involved in the Transvaal, he had closed his mind, for the present, against war.

Therefore, when Sir Graham Bower arrived in London on 13 April
with a special message that the High Commissioner would resign
rather than support Chamberlain in war, his mission was successful.
Bower's two interviews with Chamberlain at the Colonial Office
make fascinating reading, but the clash was not so much over differences of policy as of temperament. There is even an occasional
hint that the great Joe charmed away some of Bower's resentments,
though this may be due to Bower's pleasant sensation that he
himself scored the final victory as well as offering to make the final
sacrifice.

Bower returned to Africa on 25 April convinced that he had been
instrumental in preventing the mad bull in the Colonial Office from
breaking out and goring his enemies. But Bower had misjudged the
situation. Chamberlain was not out to convert Bower from a peace
to a war policy and was quite ready to receive ammunition against
the extremists on his own side. It was not in the least surprising that,
as Bower put it, 'he took it all very well and bore no malice'.[3]

They had finished by discussing the obvious alternative to war
against the Transvaal – conciliation. To Chamberlain, this involved
the 'full inquiry' into the Raid which he had promised Hofmeyr,
with exposure and punishment of the guilty men. In the cause of
peace, Bower now made an important offer. He was prepared to put
himself forward as one of the guilty men, to 'accept the rôle of
scapegoat'. He had already told Rhodes, on the memorable night
when he first heard about the Raid, that he would shoulder his share
of the blame. Bower, however, was by no means certain that his
sacrifice would be called for or that an Inquiry was the only
alternative to war. His policy was to stop 'rubbing in the Raid'. Back
in South Africa he worked hard but in vain to get Hofmeyr to
abandon the Inquiry and shake hands with Rhodes.

How to handle Kruger was one of Chamberlain's increasingly
awkward problems. But it was not at present his worst. The major
anxiety was how to handle Rhodes. Ever since the Raid, Chamberlain had pursued a policy towards Rhodes of mingled helpfulness
and severity. As regards the Charter, he would do all he could to
assist; as regards the Inquiry, Rhodes must do all he could to accept.
One thing Chamberlain had to insist on: that he resign from his
position on the Chartered Company. The board of directors were
showing great reluctance to get rid of him, thereby jeopardizing the

Charter's future. On 6 May Fairfield gave Hawksley a 'private assurance' by letter that Chamberlain would speak up for the Charter in the House. But next day Fairfield wrote again to say that Chamberlain's 'private assurance would be withdrawn' unless the board accepted Rhodes's resignation.[4] They did so in June.

This, however, did not mean that all differences between Rhodes and Chamberlain were removed. Ever since Hawksley revealed to Fairfield at the beginning of February that he had in his possession a batch of cipher telegrams, Chamberlain was aware of danger. At first there were only vague rumours. But as the spring months passed a growing whispering campaign by the London friends of Rhodes insinuated into a widening circle the belief that Chamberlain was Rhodes's accomplice. He was 'in it up to the neck' they hinted; the secret cables proved it. London was full of people who would 'wag their heads' and imply that if they had not actually seen the cables with their own eyes, they knew what was in them. At last, at the beginning of June, Chamberlain could stand it no longer. He decided to hit back. Hawksley received a demand from the Colonial Office for the immediate production of the cipher telegrams.

# 32

# Blackmail

Chamberlain received the cables at the Colonial Office on 6 June 1896 'for confidential perusal and return'. Great was his wrath against those 'blackguards'. He felt bound to offer his resignation but when Salisbury refused to accept it, his first instinct was 'to tell Hawksley what I think of him and his fellow-conspirators and defy him to do his worst'. But on second thoughts he decided that though the insinuations might be completely discredited in this country they would be used against Britain in the Transvaal and on the Continent. His policy should therefore be to prevent the cables from being published; to fight the 'dishonourable lot' and their 'blackmailing scheme' to the death by threatening reprisals against their Charter. 'I don't care a twopenny damn for the whole lot of them,' he told Edmund Garrett, 'but if they put me with my back to the wall they'll see some splinters.'

There were at least fifty-nine cables in all.* For ten days they were kept at the Colonial Office, examined by the Attorney-General, annotated by Fairfield, Meade and Chamberlain and sent back to Hawksley on 17 June. The protracted correspondence which followed makes a painful impression. Chamberlain remained for months torn between outraged feelings of injured innocence, which he yearned to prove, and a conviction that this would be impossible if he resorted to a public show-down. The following are extracts from some of the letters written during 1896 by the main combatants in the battle of the telegrams:

---

* Fifty-four is the number which Bower gives: forty-six were produced at the Inquiry, and there were eight 'missing', according to Chamberlain's memorandum of 12 June 1896. But Lord Blake's conclusion – which must be the correct one – given in his chapter on the Jameson Raid (*History and Imagination*, p.334, 1981), is that there were at least thirteen 'missing telegrams': four from Rhodes and one from Maguire making five, plus the eight noted in Chamberlain's memorandum; and as the five were all November telegrams, there may have been others 'missing' from other months. Garvin (*Life of Joseph Chamberlain*, III, p.110) says there were fifty-one, including *seven* 'missing'. He consistently ignored Maguire's 'hurry up' telegram, and may have miscounted the three in Appendix 15 of the *Report*, p. 598.

*Fairfield to Hawksley. 17 June 1896.*
... Mr Chamberlain feels the greatest surprise that such telegrams should ever have been sent ... If they should be made public – to which Mr Chamberlain makes no personal objection whatever – he will be prepared to deal with them in full detail and as they deserve.[1]

Would Chamberlain's fear of the telegrams stop him from appointing the odious Committee of Inquiry? Rhodes and his friends fervently hoped so. They were disappointed. Chamberlain moved for the Committee on 30 July, but when the end of the session caused it to be postponed, Hawksley weighed in with renewed charges of collusion. The following letter might induce the Colonial Secretary to postpone the Committee indefinitely:

*Hawksley to Fairfield. 20 August 1896.*
... responsibilities were undertaken in the honest belief that they were undertaken with the approval of the Imperial Authorities ... I very respectfully submit that ... reasons other than the ostensible ones were intimated to him why the acquisition by the Chartered Company of the Bechuanaland Protectorate was urgently necessary.

Chamberlain shot back angry comments on 22 and 23 August:

... The letter from Hawksley is characteristic. It is impossible now to resist the conclusion ... that there was a deliberate plot to commit the Colonial Office involuntarily and by partial confidence to a general approval of Rhodes's plans, and then to use this afterwards as a screen for the whole conspiracy. What is there in South Africa I wonder that makes blackguards of all who get involved in its politics? I should like to tell Hawksley what I think of him and his fellow-conspirators and defy him to do his worst ...

... It is time to have done with him and this blackmailing scheme ...

The same conflict, though in a poignant rather than bitter form, is reflected in an exchange of letters between Grey (now out in Rhodesia as Administrator in place of Dr Jameson) and his friend Chamberlain. On 20 August Grey wrote:

... Rhodes thinks his own dignity and self-respect will not allow him to appear before a Committee of Inquiry of which Labby* is a member ... he is being tried a bit too far. He knows that the publication of these miserable cables would do him good, not harm.

* Henry Labouchere, radical MP.

Chamberlain's reply on 13 October was in the nature of an *et tu Brute*:

. . . You, at least, are in a position to confirm me when I say I did not know and could not know of any plan or intention of Mr Rhodes which could possibly lead to such an invasion of the Transvaal in time of peace as was perpetrated by Dr Jameson . . . Personally I do not shrink from the fullest publication of anything that has taken place, although I believe that the disclosure of the telegrams to which you refer would be the death-blow of the Company.

The battle of the telegrams was fought from February 1896 to February 1897; it broke out anew, as we shall see, between various combatants during the sittings of the Committee of Inquiry and flickered angrily for several years afterwards. There is no doubt that by the end of 1896 the atmosphere inside the Colonial Office had become extremely oppressive. Many things combined to put the Colonial Secretary thoroughly on edge: Willoughby's letter from Holloway to the War Office,* disintegration among Chamberlain's own officials, a progressive embitterment of the struggle with Kruger and a sudden turn for the worse in the war over the 'Hawksley' cables. As already pointed out, Chamberlain cordially disliked many of the groups with whom he was in uneasy alliance: Willoughby was a 'Stock Exchange hero', the financial backers of the Raid were 'blatant speculators' and the right-wingers at home were 'noisy jingoes'. What had now gone wrong inside his own department?

Towards the end of June, Chamberlain heard that Sir Hercules Robinson was asking for a peerage. That meant a glad good-bye to his debilitated henchman. But who was to succeed him? 'I am afraid that the Press and the Telegraph are killing all ability and original-ity in the Civil Service,' wrote Chamberlain to Salisbury on 29 June 1896.[2] Lord Grey, Chamberlain continued a week later, must be rejected for the post, though he was the obvious choice, owing to his connections with the disgraced Chartered Company. 'Sir Hercules has surprisingly improved (I do not know whether it is the prospect of the peerage) and is talking of going back in August.' In the end Chamberlain decided he must look outside the Colonial Office staff

* See p. 125.

for the dual post of Governor and High Commissioner.* On 8 January he wrote again to Lord Salisbury: 'The personnel of the Colonial Office has gone to pieces altogether. Meade intended to retire last year but I persuaded him to stop another twelve months ... I fear he will never do any more work [after an accident]. Fairfield has had two strokes ... If he returns he will certainly not be fit for much.' Fairfield had collapsed during the previous November: he was to die in April 1897, a few months after Chamberlain's letter to Salisbury.

A vivid glimpse of the other side of the picture is furnished by Bower in his *Apologia*. Chamberlain's officials must have felt they were in charge of a bull who was being teased in his stall before he went forth to be baited in the public arena. His two anxious attendants, Bower and Meade, alternately tried to lower the temperature of their irritated charge and to raise their own spirits. Bower, who had come back to England for the Inquiry, found Chamberlain in more combative mood than during his first visit. Chamberlain, he says, swore to be even with Kruger 'and was prepared to carry matters very far if the telegrams came out'. After a disquieting interview with the chief, Bower called on Sir Robert Meade, laid up in bed. They discussed Chamberlain's bellicose attitude and Meade tried to reassure his agitated visitor. The Inquiry, he insisted, was 'not the formidable thing the world supposed'. Chamberlain and Harcourt understood one another. Bower would be only mildly censured and moved to another post. 'Good-bye, Bower,' concluded the optimistic invalid, 'we have, I think, saved the china from our mad bull.' Whether or not the bull was mad, Meade was tragically wrong in believing that Chamberlain would be able to save Bower from the Liberal picadors on the Tribunal.

About Christmas a book was published which may well have driven the Colonial Secretary into one of those truculent moods witnessed by Bower. It was a misguided attempt by two journalists friendly to Rhodes and Chamberlain to inoculate the public against sinister revelations at the Inquiry by giving them a light-hearted preview of the 'Hawksley' telegrams. The journalists, of whom something has already been heard in this story, were Edmund Garrett and William

* He appointed Alfred Milner, Chairman of the Board of Inland Revenue.

Thomas Stead. Because Garrett had at first opposed the Uitlanders' rising, Fitzpatrick dubbed him a 'scorner and slanderer of his own flesh and blood'. Fitzpatrick went on, however, to pay tribute to Garrett's vitality and gay, laughing courage, which redeemed his psychological and physical defects. He was a consumptive with 'long wavy hair, long ugly face and sunken grey eyes'.

Stead had a brilliant facility with his pen and nothing could be more lively, even today, than his sallies in *The Review of Reviews*.* He had a talent for prising up stones under which nasty things were hiding. But an obsessive vindictiveness seized him if ever one of his swans turned out to be a goose or worse still a bird of prey. Sir Charles Dilke, Chamberlain's friend of old radical days, was hounded relentlessly by Stead over the Crawford divorce case. Stead would later serve Chamberlain in the same way. But just now he was prepared to assist the great collusionist for the sake of the imperial cause.

*The History of the Mystery or The Skeleton in Blastus's Cupboard* was the stimulating title of Stead's story, to be published as the *Christmas Annual* of *The Review of Reviews*. A surprisingly accurate account of the Raid leading up to the 'Hawksley' cables, it was placed in a melodramatic, semi-fictional framework and crowned with a superbly happy ending. Stead sent the proofs to Fairfield, who saw no harm in mentioning cables which he believed were bound to come out in any case. Fairfield wrote to Bower: 'I think we are all rather glad it has come to this. Nothing could be worse than the system under which Rhodes's partisans were all to go into raptures over their patriotic silence whilst all the time spreading their own version of the matter far and wide.' It is noteworthy that Fairfield here distinguishes between the Harris–Rhodes 'version' of the affair and, by implication, the true one; he also evidently thought that the Colonial Office could make out a good case for themselves even if the

---

* His contemporaries, however, deprecated his methods and regarded him as something of a charlatan. The *Quarterly* wrote: '*A fin de siècle* Peter the Hermit, he preaches crusade after crusade, conducted with headlines, leaded-type, sensational paragraphs, and all the artifices of latter-day journalistic advertisement.' When the title of one of Stead's later anti-Boer War diatribes, *Are We in the Right? An Appeal to Honest Men*, was mentioned in the House of Commons, it was greeted with a roar of laughter. Even Rhodes had to revoke Stead's appointment as one of his executors because of his 'extraordinary eccentricity'. (L. Michell, *Cecil John Rhodes*, Vol II, p. 325.)

telegrams were published. All too full of irony is his remark to Bower about 'patriotic silence'.[3] Patriotic silence was to be Bower's fate for the next fifty years.

The frontispiece of *The History of the Mystery*, described as a sequel to *Blastus the King's Chamberlain*, depicts a stage on which an immaculate Chamberlain and a sleek ring-master, Rhodes, are introducing the jaunty little skeleton of Dr Jim. The face of Lord Salisbury peers pleasantly from the wings while an enormous serpent, representing an Atlantic cable, hisses into Rhodes's ear. The caption reads: 'Not Such A Bad Skeleton After All', and the motto of the book is '*Tout savoir c'est tout pardonner*'. All the characters have easily recognizable names. 'Jeanne Leflo' (Flora Shaw), 'a delicate and beautiful girl' with a touch of Edmund Garrett's consumption, is the first woman editor of a great newspaper, the *Johnstown Sentinel*, and is also the Jeanne D'Arc of the revolution. In his preface, Stead bemoaned the fact that there was no Jeanne D'Arc in the real story: the fiasco of the Raid and revolution, he thought, was quite possibly due to its being 'so exclusively a one-sex show'. Rhodes appears as the 'Hon. Robert J. Cecil' (Lord Robert Cecil was to defend Harris at the Inquiry), Kruger is 'Uncle Saul', Jameson is 'Dr James Zahlbar', Harris is 'Dr Cactus' and poor Sir Graham Bower finds himself turned into 'Sir George Crawler'.

But at the last moment Stead's motto of '*Tout savoir*' was rudely assailed. A strong intimation came from the highest quarters that if Stead published unexpurgated copies of the telegrams the world would know more than it could pardon. Stead's story and Stead's alone would prevent the obnoxious cables from being totally suppressed. Panic measures ensued. Groups of large black oblongs like coffins suddenly appeared in the text of the *Christmas Annual*, wherever references to 'Cactus', 'Blastus' and the telegrams were thought to be too pointed. But the attempted deletion of the telegrams from Stead's '*History*' merely left the '*Mystery*' more exposed than ever; nothing, said Garrett, was 'as bad as the blots',[4] particularly as several incriminating passages came through unscathed. The November visit of 'Dr Cactus' to 'the frigidarium of Downing Street' (the Colonial Office) concludes with an admonition from 'Joseph Blastus': 'Don't let your fireworks off too soon' – a direct quotation from the seventh 'missing telegram'. However, the next chapter made up for any inadequate blotting: rows of enormous black coffins covered every column.

Alas for Stead's eleventh hour black-out. A similar command to drown the telegrams in printer's ink did not reach Garrett in time. Stead's totally expunged chapter entitled 'The Serpent in Eden' appeared sparkling and unsullied in Garrett's review in the *Cape Times*, together with all the other passages which in London had been erased. Garrett's subsequent apology only drew attention to his *faux pas*. Though Stead hotly denied it, the general opinion afterwards was that the activities of himself and Garrett finally removed all chance of Chamberlain dropping the Inquiry.

Hawksley, Willoughby, Meade, Fairfield, Stead and Garrett all contributed to the pressures. So did society, in its solicitude for Jameson and his officers. On 16 December, for instance, the Home Secretary had the delicate task of answering a request from the Dowager Lady Dudley to release for Christmas the Raid officers still in prison. He was obliged to refuse – 'But it is very hateful to me.'[5] Some six weeks later Mrs Richard Chamberlain wrote to Bouchier Hawksley about her brother-in-law, Joe.

I quite agree with you that very little good, if any, can be done with J.C. now. He knows what he has to expect, and will have had plenty of time to think it over by the time C.J.R. arrives.

The flirtatious, volatile Mrs Chamberlain went on to raise some hares about her beloved 'Doctor' and his future. Unlike the rest of Chamberlain's fanatically loyal family, her sympathies strayed somewhat outside the clan and she wrote to *The Times* after the Raid defending 'that gallant and unfortunate gentleman', Dr Jim. Now she asked Hawksley whether Rhodes intended to 'sacrifice' the Doctor; she was sure that at one time he contemplated doing so. She ended with a rush of sentiment: 'I think you can perhaps partly understand how much it means to me to feel he has got a friend like you.' Hawksley was no 'friend' to Chamberlain and his voice was loudest throughout the summer of 1896 in urging the publication of the cables which Mrs Chamberlain's brother-in-law was determined to suppress.

\* \* \*

The reformers also added to the pressure with an unremitting barrage of letters from Pretoria gaol; and so did Dr Harris, publishing articles on Kruger's new ring of forts round Johannesburg and the 'Jack-boot of the German mercenary'. So did the Cape music-halls, celebrating in song the transit of these same mercenaries through South Africa:

> Strange German faces, passing to and fro,
>   What have you come for, we should like to know;
> Looking mysterious as you join the train.
>   Say now, you Uhlans, shall we meet again?

Above all, so did Kruger. Chamberlain's sharp attitude towards the Transvaal had been much criticized as well as applauded and towards the end of the year Kruger replied with his provocative Aliens Act. Chamberlain described it to Salisbury as a 'clear breach of the Convention' which would 'cause great heart-burnings here'.*

Must it be assumed, because of these many fierce pressures, that Chamberlain was contemplating a war policy towards the end if not during the early part of 1896? There are no conclusive proofs, but he was certainly drawing nearer to a policy involving force. At the beginning of November 1896 he wished to send reinforcements to South Africa, but a combination of Meade and Robinson supported by the Cabinet prevented him.[6] Five months later, however, the Cabinet rather reluctantly reversed their decision and a show of force in Delagoa Bay achieved the repeal of Kruger's Immigration Act.

One more misfortune occurred, this time to Rhodes, at the end of the black year 1896. His beloved house, Groote Schurr, was burned down. It fell to Lord Grey to break the bad news. Grey put off the evil hour until they were riding together over the veldt. Then he told his friend to be prepared for 'an ugly knock'. Rhodes turned

---

* *Chamberlain to Salisbury, Salisbury Papers, Oxford*. In a letter of 1 January 1897, however, written by Chamberlain to Lionel Phillips, he distinguished between the Aliens Law and the Immigration Law. The former he believed was popular with the working classes and therefore perhaps should not be denounced from home; but the latter was a violation of the Convention. (See E. Drus, *The Bulletin of the Institute of Historical Research*, Vol. xxvii (1954), p. 165.)

white. Instead of Groote Schurr's end, he expected the news of Jameson's. When he heard the truth, relief flooded his drawn and agonized face. 'If Dr Jim had died,' he said, 'I should never have got over it.'[7]

# PART III
## Probe

Rhodes came to England 'to face the music' (his own phrase) flushed with the applause of his admirers in South Africa. As the man who had twice conquered the terrible Matabele proceeded from Rhodesia to the Cape, vast crowds came out to show him their loyalty. The hero could not face the music without striking one strident note himself. He was about to submit himself, he said, to the verdict of his fellow-countrymen's 'unctuous rectitude'. Rhodes has put his foot in it again, wailed his horrified friends. One of them suggested that he should say he had been misreported. '*Anxious* rectitude' was surely the phrase he had really used? But no. The Colossus had spoken. Let it stand. Rhodes assured them he would cut off his right hand rather than withdraw it. Actually he was delighted by this as by many another of his own *bon mots*. He quoted it frequently in after years, facetiously deciding that 'unctuous rectitude' should be one of the qualifications for a Rhodes Scholar.

*The Times* reported that Rhodes arrived in England in excellent health but desired no formal reception, banquet or interviews. He wished to be regarded as 'a man who has come home on business' and is eager to return to his affairs. His tactics were eminently successful and probably accounted for the Committee's alacrity in acceding to his request to return to Africa the moment his initial interrogation was over.

Rhodes found himself sitting opposite to Chamberlain in the Colonial Office on 26 January 1897. Lord Selborne has left a shrewd account of the Rhodes–Chamberlain interview.[1] It shows the two men still sparring, despite the assurances of Earl Grey. 'I think you will find on his arrival in England', wrote Grey on 10 December from Africa, 'that he will wish to follow any advice you may think it right to give.'

Chamberlain's advice was simple. The Committee of Inquiry was inevitable, the telegrams lethal. Face the one; suppress the others. But Rhodes, once again snuffing the Colonial Office sawdust, could not resist a last attempt to make Chamberlain dish the Committee.

In dramatic language he vowed that he and his friends would suffer imprisonment – go to the Clock Tower underneath Big Ben – rather than give the cables to that Committee. Let Chamberlain be ready for a comparable sacrifice: suffer eclipse rather than allow such a Committee to come into existence. Stung by Rhodes's high moral tone, Chamberlain retorted that to abandon the Committee was now utterly impossible. Impossible precisely because of Hawksley's blackmailing tactics and the whispering campaign conducted by Rhodes's partisans.

After these demonstrations the atmosphere became more friendly. In a short while the antagonists were assuring one another they had never really believed the hard things each was supposed to have said about the other. They were 'working together', Chamberlain announced, over ends, if not over means: 'they were both big Englanders'. Selborne's notes towards the end of the interview depict both men in characteristic attitudes: Rhodes vivid and emotional, stirred to eloquence by his own deep feelings; Chamberlain faintly ironic, sparely practical:

*Mr Rhodes* said he wanted again to lay stress on the necessity for personal sacrifice if needs be *pro patria*. What was his reputation or Mr Chamberlain's compared with the interests of the country? 'In twenty years you will be gone, snuffed out, but the country will remain.' The moral of this was that the Committee should be stopped even now and let the world say what it liked of Mr Chamberlain or of himself.

*Mr Chamberlain* replied that he took no objection to the principle but very much to the particular application, because (1) it was not possible; (2) if possible it would in the end produce more evil to the country than the inquiry would.

*Mr Rhodes* said 'Nothing is impossible; everything is impossible until you are confronted with something more impossible still, and you must choose between them.' It is better to lose your arm than to lose your life. . . . What he did fear was Sir William Harcourt on the scent of the cables: personally he was a charming man, but he had not an ounce of patriotism in him and for a party advantage he would go all lengths.

*Mr Chamberlain* reiterated his policy was to keep the Charter as far the best method of developing the country.[2]

Something had finally developed between these two which amounted to a state of mutual blackmail. Chamberlain was using his power over the Charter to prevent Rhodes from publishing the cables; Rhodes was using his possession of the cables to prevent

Chamberlain from abrogating the Charter and from holding the Inquiry. Ultimately both were looking beyond the immediate struggle to the safety of the Empire. But in the immediate struggle Chamberlain held the stronger hand.

On 29 January 1897 the Committee of Inquiry into the Raid was duly reappointed, after being nominated on 11 August 1896 and allowed to lapse three days later when the parliamentary session ended. Chamberlain proposed its reappointment in a speech which showed he had a gift for tact when he chose to use it. It brought forth from Sir Henry Lucy the ecstatic comment: 'What a rare leader is here in store!'[3] His mild, matter-of-fact statement lasted only fifteen minutes, so that the motion slipped quietly through, despite the threat of an explosion from Rhodes's many friends in the Tory Party. The Committee's terms of reference, which fell into two parts, were as follows:

... To inquire into the origin and circumstances of the Incursion into the South African Republic by an Armed Force, and into the Administration of the British South Africa Company, and to Report thereon ...

In the second part, which the Committee never in fact reached, they were required to:

... Report what Alterations are desirable in the Government of the Territories under the Control of the Company.

The Committee was to meet under the chairmanship of W. L. Jackson, a Yorkshireman, a Conservative and a former Irish Chief Secretary. He had a plumpish face, moustache and fluffy hair; Harcourt described him as a 'judgmatical man'. This was perhaps the kindest thing to be said of the future Lord Allerton, for he turned out to be no match for the wily witnesses he called. His son, a famous cricketer, on being congratulated upon a big score, replied: 'Yes, I'm glad to think it will give the guv'nor a leg up.' The governor of the Committee was soon to need every 'leg up' available. Jackson's poor showing as Chairman, however, was amply compensated for by his masterly activity behind the scenes. He 'severely edited' one or more of the forty-six telegrams which were produced before the Committee.*

* Conversation with Rhodes recorded by Rosebery in his betting-book, May 1898. (C. M. Woodhouse, *Rhodes*, p. 379.)

A galaxy of talent was assembled at the Committee's horseshoe table. On the Chairman's left sat the Leader of Her Majesty's Opposition, the formidable Sir William Harcourt. He was said to look like an elephant but surely, on this occasion, the wisest of elephants who would forget nothing. He had written to Morley that though he did not believe the 'ridiculous stories about Joe's complicity' he would 'take care that the whole story comes out without fear or favour'.

To the right of the Chairman sat one with 'a foxy face, the eyes being singularly close together giving him a deceptive look'.[4] When he enters to take his seat 'he walks like Brer Fox – pad, pad', and his name is Joseph Chamberlain. With a fox on one side and an elephant on the other Mr Jackson should be able to handle all comers.

Besides the Colonial Secretary there were two other Conservative ministers: the Attorney-General, Sir Richard Webster, and the Chancellor of the Exchequer, Sir Michael Hicks Beach. The former, having prosecuted Dr Jameson, knew all the facts of the case. He was a stalwart, portly, bewhiskered figure, but he contributed more to the Committee in distinction of appearance than of performance. Hicks Beach was a man with few friends or enemies but universally trusted. He was therefore an asset to the Committee. Five back benchers, George Wyndham, Alfred Cripps, Sir William Hart-Dyke, J. C. Bigham and J. L. Wharton made up the Conservative team. Wyndham and Cripps were both known to be friendly to Rhodes and their names were in fact put forward by Rhodes's solicitor, Hawksley.

The five Liberal MPs, including Harcourt, were Labouchere, Campbell-Bannerman, Sydney Buxton and John Ellis. Labouchere, known to be violently hostile to Rhodes, introduced a touch of French *chic* to the Committee, with his trim figure and beard. Aged sixty-five, the brilliant founder and editor of *Truth* was a wittily cynical politician with the unique gift of presenting to the public in an acceptable form the most uncompromising radicalism. He had quarrelled irrevocably with Chamberlain over Home Rule and could be counted on to hit hard.* Campbell-Bannerman, afterwards Liberal Prime Minister, was said by Stead in 1897 to be more

* Sir Shane Leslie called him 'a pure wire-puller'. (*The End of a Chapter*, p. 34.)

interested in the future than in the past. Certainly he dug out nothing of importance about the Raid. Ellis was the odd man of the Liberal team, expected to pick up any scraps overlooked by Labby or Blake. Edward Blake, MP for South Longford, represented the Irish nationalists. He was three years older than Chamberlain and one of the Committee's ablest members. A Canadian lawyer and politician of Irish extraction, no one expected him to be soft with aggressive imperialism. Indeed, he was regarded as leading 'Counsel for the Prosecution', with Labby as his Junior.

How did it come about that these fifteen eminent men failed so abysmally in their task? The answer lies partly in the bizarre story of hand-to-hand combats between Committee members and witnesses or even among Committee members themselves. The rest of the answer lies in the operations of a united patriotism, which overrode personal vendettas and party feuds in order to repel a threat to national survival from the outside. Nothing else can explain the strangest fact of all connected with this Committee of enigmas. Joseph Chamberlain was a member.

The rumours and writings of the past twelve months had made it clear to everybody that Chamberlain and his ministry were under suspicion. Yet here was the suspect invited to inquire into his own past. As Fairfield put it: 'It is very awkward for a witness in a case affecting himself to examine and re-examine himself.'[5] Fairfield therefore wanted the Colonial Secretary to be represented by Counsel, except that Rhodes and his friends had already retained all the best men!

Chamberlain, to his credit, demurred at his own appointment. (Harcourt actually proposed him for Chairman.) No one else involved in setting up the Committee protested against his membership. With Chamberlain a member, it should have been obvious from the start that nothing derogatory to the Colonial Office was likely to emerge from the findings of a Committee whose motto was 'Loyal' rather than 'Thorough'.

# 34

# Cross-Questioning Rhodes

The first public session of the Committee was held on 16 February 1897. At last the public were permitted to take a longer, deeper look into the Raid. The Committee met twice weekly, on Tuesdays and Fridays, in Westminster Hall; not of course under the hammer beams of its great roof (no hammer blows were destined to be struck by the South Africa Committee) but in the adjoining Grand Committee Room, which was neither spacious nor handsome. Against its panelled walls stood an array of padlocked cupboards.

The room's drabness did not prevent society from crowding into it, nor the press, except for *The Times*, from treating the Inquiry as the hottest of hot news. Such was the competition for press seats that applications had to be weeded out; eventually there were thirty-three press representatives instead of the twenty-one originally proposed.

The fifty-four-year-old Prince of Wales entered by a side door, escorted by the Duke of Abercorn and the Earl of Selborne; he thus seemed to have under his wing both the Chartered Company and the Colonial Office. Mrs Richard Chamberlain was also among the visitors. Her presence created an unfavourable impression, since she was known to idolize Dr Jim. To end the scene, the Colonial Secretary sensibly suggested that the Serjeant-at-Arms should clear the room of all but representatives of press and Parliament. The Prince, as a member of the House of Lords, continued to attend the morning sessions, only leaving at the luncheon adjournment. He found court cases an agreeable change from his dull public duties. Many people, however, suspected that he attended the Committee to keep an eye on his own interests. Afterwards it was rumoured that some of the white-washing in the Report was laid on by a royal hand.*

*****The Investor's Chronicle*, for instance, hinted that the Report was shielding the Prince. Wilfrid Blunt went further and wrote in his diary on 15 July 1897, after the Report was published: 'The Queen is at the bottom of half the Imperialistic mischief

The first day was one of overpowering excitement. Cecil Rhodes, accompanied by Alfred Beit and Lionel Phillips, preceded His Royal Highness into the Committee room and seated himself in the witness chair between the horns of the horseshoe table. He had evaded the earlier Cape Committee and everybody was intensely curious to see how the Colossus would react to a spell in the pillory. A big man dedicated to a big crusade was the picture he treasured of himself. That was the part he instinctively tried to play throughout the Inquiry. However, Chamberlain had assigned him a different rôle: that of a guilty man let down by his friend and in turn letting down his country. This rôle was utterly repugnant to Rhodes. He never believed in it. He never threw his heart into it. Hence the editor of the Liberal *Westminster Gazette*, J. A. Spender, who attended all the public sessions for his paper, saw the Inquiry in terms of 'a stubborn but extremely obscure duel'[1] between Rhodes and Chamberlain. He acutely described Rhodes as looking like a great child who had eaten something unwholesome and was suffering the pangs of indigestion. Rhodes had in truth tasted something indigestible: the humble pie set before him by Chamberlain in the Colonial Office at their last meeting, and now due to be publicly consumed.

As Rhodes, on the first day, took a few bites, everyone thought he had stage fright. The fact that Harcourt (the hound 'on the scent of the cables') was Rhodes's first interrogator, added to his anxiety. He tended to answer in monosyllables – 'Yes', 'No', 'Quite true'; or hesitantly – 'I think not', 'I think so'. Twice he gave no answer at all and five times his reply was 'Oh'. Before the hundredth question, a crisis was reached. Rhodes had said that in placing troops on the Transvaal frontier to be used in certain eventualities, he was *acting within his rights*. Seizing on this phrase, Harcourt demanded to know exactly what kind of 'rights' Rhodes thought he had:

*Harcourt:* If you were acting within your rights in placing that force there, is there any reason why you should not have informed Sir Hercules Robinson that you were so doing?

---

we do abroad. She is pleased with the title of Empress, and likes to enlarge her borders. I should not be surprised if she was really in the Jameson affair with her Ministers, indeed this is the best explanation of the extraordinary manoeuvres of the Government and the connivance of the official opposition.'

Here was Harcourt already right on the target. Rhodes had only to say, 'I *did* tell Robinson', and the balloon would go up. The accusing finger would inevitably swing round from the High Commissioner to the Colonial Secretary, and with the one trapped it would be difficult for the other to escape. Chamberlain's heart must have been in his mouth as Rhodes went at his first big fence, but his face remained impassive as ever. Very clumsily Rhodes took it:

*Rhodes:* You want an answer?
*Harcourt:* Yes.
*Rhodes:* I think you should get the answer from the High Commissioner.
*Harcourt:* I have had the answer from the High Commissioner . . .

Harcourt then read Robinson's account of what Rhodes had told him, which naturally did not include his intention to use the border police to tip the scales.

*Harcourt:* Is that a correct account of what you told Sir Hercules Robinson about the matter? . . .
*Rhodes:* I am sorry that the High Commissioner is not here. I think he was aware that there was trouble likely to occur in Johannesburg, and he knew that there was this force on the border. I do not like to say anything. I would prefer that the High Commissioner himself made the statement . . .

Rhodes's performance was due to nervousness and also an impish impulse to answer dangerously; as dangerously as possible without actually giving the game away. Already he was beginning to feel better. Soon he would show his Prince how the uncrowned king of Africa dealt with an inhibited muster of mere MPs. Before the morning was out, Rhodes had twice replied to Harcourt in a distinctly arrogant fashion. Asked whether guns were run into Johannesburg by Captain Holden, an officer of the Chartered Company, Rhodes replied:

Yes, and he has been punished for it. I suppose you have noticed the trial in Cape Town, have you not?

Harcourt wisely ignored this piece of rudeness. He got some of his own back over the 'women and children' letter. Rhodes could only put up a weak . defence, though in the process he hit upon a technique which he later developed to a high pitch of usefulness.

Harcourt asked whether Dr Jameson had not based his invasion on the forged letter:

*Rhodes:* I really cannot say: I was not with the Doctor.

*I was not there* became one of Rhodes's favourite ways of side-stepping an awkward question. Harcourt strengthened his attack by bringing up some of the incriminating telegrams already published in the Cape Blue book. How did Rhodes explain his message to his brother Frank (endearingly disguised as 'Toad, Johannesburg') urging no postponement of the rising, because *The Times* cabled it would be most unwise? This was the first time the accusing finger had pointed at *The Times* and at Flora Shaw, sender of the cable. Rhodes, clearly uneasy, felt around for the correct method of reply. He soon found it. Afterwards developed with devastating effect, it consisted in naming no names and in refusing to discuss matters involving third parties:

*Rhodes:* It is one of those cases where other people come in, is it not? . . . Well, it came from the person who dealt with the Colonial articles of *The Times*.

Harcourt accepted Rhodes's explanation that this cable had been sent on the 'person's' own responsibility. But he immediately brought up an even worse telegram: the one which Frank Rhodes sent so urgently on 21 December to know whether 'the Chairman' was definitely coming up on the day of the rising. Now who was this 'Chairman' on whom the success of the revolution depended?

*Rhodes:* (No answer.)
*Harcourt:* I must ask you, did that mean the High Commissioner?
*Rhodes:* Would you just read the telegram again? I did not quite catch the hang of it . . .

Harcourt put the telegram into plain language and repeated his question: was it Sir Hercules Robinson?

*Rhodes:* I think I should like to think over my answer to this question, if you have no objection. I think I should like to think it over. I did not even know that that telegram was here.

Feeling he had got Rhodes on the run, Harcourt agreed to postpone the identification of the 'Chairman' until next session. It was a major tactical error. For Rhodes used the interval to repair his defences. And even on this first day, though rattled, he had not done so badly. In a letter of 20 February from Hawksley to Lord Grey out in Rhodesia, Rhodes earned a good mark from his anxious confederates: 'He was nervous the first day, though his evidence was good even then.'

Rhodes had laid the foundations for two vital defence measures: the right to plead ignorance of all matters of which he was not a personal witness ('I was not there') and the right to exclude all discussions involving third parties ('other people come in'). Rhodes spent Wednesday and Thursday most profitably working out his 'third party' tactic with his Counsel, Messrs Pope and Pember, both QCs and leaders of the Parliamentary Bar. When on Friday, 19 February, the Committee reassembled, no one was spry enough to forbid Rhodes to use it. The Chairman did indeed make one feeble attempt to postpone a decision on the 'third party' principle ('I think we had better leave that question until it arises'). But the Colossus stood firm:

*Rhodes:* I do respectfully submit to the Committee that they should consider . . . whether I should be forced to give answers which may affect the position or drag in the names of third parties.

It was Harcourt himself who actually sold the pass:

*Harcourt:* I can assure you I entirely accept the situation, and if you think that any question I am asking you does not affect yourself, you will certainly find I shall not endeavour to press it.

If Harcourt could have foreseen that not only Rhodes but Harris, Hawksley and Flora Shaw would all make use of the ground he had ceded, he would not have been so chivalrous. As for the High Commissioner's part in the revolution, Rhodes now agreed that Robinson *was* the 'Chairman'.* He had discovered, he said, since the previous session that it was all right to admit Robinson knew

---

*When the 'Chairman' telegram first came out in the Transvaal Green book, Robinson hastily informed Chamberlain that he believed the 'Chairman' meant Dr Jameson! (C.O. 417/181, 4 May 1896.)

*something* about the rising – the Cape Blue book, which he had hitherto not bothered to study in detail, had already made that clear – but when asked whether the High Commissioner knew of the active part Rhodes was playing in it, he replied with mock horror: 'Oh dear, no, of course not.' But finally, with Chamberlain's intimidating monocle glinting in his direction and Harcourt and Blake both pushing him, Rhodes was compelled to subscribe to Robinson's statement without further equivocation: 'Quite so. I do accept it.'

In the meanwhile, the second session had seen Rhodes's defence tactics extended in two new directions. First, he painted himself as a big man ready to assume responsibility for overall planning, but who could not be expected to remember trivial details. Second, he found a difficult question could often be handed on to some future witness. In this tactic he was assisted by Chamberlain, who was always ready to help when the Colossus was behaving properly:

*Chamberlain:* I think Mr Rhodes has given a sort of speculative account of the thing; he cannot give us actual information, whereas Dr Harris, when he comes, will be able to give us actual information.
*Harcourt:* Then I will postpone that point.

Harris would indeed be able but not always willing to oblige; and 'actual information' proved as difficult to come by throughout the Inquiry as Rhodes and Chamberlain together could make it. It is significant that before the end of the second day they were already collaborating, when necessary, against Harcourt. A question was put to Rhodes by the latter as to what he had told Chamberlain during their first interview at the Colonial Office. For the first, but not for the last time, Chamberlain decided to jump in:

*Chamberlain:* I must interpose here. Should not I be examined about my speech and not Mr Rhodes? . . . our conversation was, as Mr Rhodes has said, entirely devoted to the consideration of the present situation and the future situation. I did not go into the past.
*Harcourt:* So I understand.

Chamberlain had given an intimation that Colonial Office conversations were not to be among the subjects for inquiry.

The battle swayed back and forth, and as the second session wore on Harcourt regained some of his ascendancy. Finally he found himself on the trail of the telegrams. Did Rhodes have any communications, direct or indirect, with any of the directors of the Chartered Company on the subject of his support for the rising? Rhodes was made to reply to each name individually. First came the two dukes. Rhodes gave a prompt 'No' to each. Then came Earl Grey, over whom he hedged. He fell back on his geographical defence line:

*Rhodes:* No, I would point out to you that I was not in England. I could not do it.
*Harcourt:* But there are means of communicating without being in England.

Pressed harder, Rhodes tried in vain to bring his 'third party' principle into play again:

*Rhodes:* I would rather you asked these questions of the people themselves.
*Harcourt* (exasperated): No, I beg your pardon, not at all; I am asking [about] your conduct, not theirs.

In the end Rhodes said 'No' to the name of Grey. But there was more trouble over Rochfort Maguire's name. Rhodes had told a lie over Grey: he was not going to do it again for his own proxy. So he stalled: 'I have made my reply . . . I communicated with my agent and I will not go further than that.' Harcourt was obdurate: 'But I ask you the question; and I must ask for an answer.'

*Rhodes:* I do not remember sending any cable to Mr Maguire.
*Harcourt:* Or letter?
*Rhodes:* No, I never write letters.

That last little score must have pleased the audience; it was in character for the Colossus to move faster than the post. But in trying to by-pass Maguire, Rhodes in fact made a fatal slip. Harcourt pounced on the word 'cable' introduced by Rhodes ('I do not remember sending any cable to Mr Maguire'). There were many cables, he said, which did not come out in the Cape Inquiry. Had Rhodes any objection to these cables being produced now?

Rhodes was facing his second big fence. The eye behind the monocle was colder than ever. He decided to take this fence loyally:

'I consider that they were of a confidential nature and should not be produced.' Logically Harcourt pointed out that all the telegrams, whether published at the Cape Inquiry or not, were equally confidential. But Rhodes would not budge: 'That is the view I take of it, that they were confidential, and I do object to their being produced.' Harcourt thereupon picked up the Cape Blue book from the horseshoe table and brandished it before the witness: 'You would have objected, of course, to these being produced?' he jeered. 'Yes, I certainly would,' retorted the man in the chair. And then, with that spice of genial contempt which the spectators were beginning to expect from Rhodes: 'Would you not have?' 'I quite understand,' said Harcourt bitingly. But he threw in the sponge none the less. 'Now I am glad to tell you,' he said, 'that I am coming to an end,' and forthwith he dropped the subject of the telegrams.

It was another victory for Rhodes, and when Harcourt returned to the old question of Rhodes's 'rights' to foment a revolution, he felt able to inflate his ego to the full. While engineering the rising, in what capacity did he act? As Prime Minister of the Cape Colony? As managing director of the Company? 'No,' returned the Colossus, 'in my capacity as myself.' What could even a Select Committee of both Houses of Parliament do against the great *I Am*?

Harcourt's temper began to fray. He and Pope had a set-to, terminated by cries of 'Order, order; we are getting irregular' from the Chairman. The day ended badly for Harcourt with another vain attempt to establish the connection between Rhodes, Flora Shaw and *The Times*. After a pointless wrangle with the Attorney-General as to whether Flora was a 'lady' or a 'person' – 'I leave out the question of sex,' snapped Harcourt – he hoped at least to prove that Rhodes had imparted knowledge of his plans to the sexless sender of the 'hurry up' cable to *The Times*. But no. Rhodes thought that his communication with the 'person' may not have been *direct*. And so he could not answer that question either.

Hawksley gave Grey a joyful report on this session: 'Rhodes has done very well, and I think will come out on top . . . Yesterday he was simply splendid.'[2]

Popular belief attributed Rhodes's spectacular recovery from his early nerves to the size and nature of his luncheon. Sir Henry Lucy has described the Falstaffian scene:[3] 'Members, timorously looking in, apprehensive of the smell of blood, beheld a strange sight.' Did they expect to see Rhodes in the witness box, if not in the dock? 'What really happens is that Mr Rhodes, taking his luncheon about his accustomed hour, is good enough to allow a number of members of the House of Commons to cluster round him. These he, in intervals of munching sandwiches and imbibing stout, lectures . . .' His mound of sandwiches was enormous; his bottle of stout 'looked like a Martello tower, black with age and the smoke of battle'. His tumbler was of a size 'fit for a colossus'. And according to that irrepressible journalist, Frank Harris, the Attorney-General himself was proud to help Rhodes to a whisky and soda 'like a waiter'.

The third session opened with Campbell-Bannerman examining, but the future Prime Minister was not a tough inquisitor. John Ellis, the next Liberal, made an effort to approach the target. He asked if Rhodes had a London agent after Harris returned to the Cape. Remembering '*Telemones*', Maguire and Grey, Rhodes resorted to one of his stock evasions: 'I cannot remember . . .' Did he tell any colleagues in the Cape Cabinet about his plan? 'No.' Did he tell the press? 'No, I never go near the press.' The remark was good for a laugh, and Rhodes used it to laugh off Flora Shaw and Francis Younghusband of *The Times*, not to mention Edmund Garrett and W. T. Stead. Then came the key question – the question that lay at the heart of the whole Inquiry. Ellis was the first to put it squarely. But he introduced it in a way that told Rhodes and Chamberlain they need not worry overmuch:

*Ellis:* Perhaps I need hardly put the next question, but I will do so. Did you communicate to the Colonial Secretary or anyone within the Colonial Office these views of yours?
*Rhodes:* I only communicated with my agent in London . . .

The obvious follow-up, Did your agent communicate your views to the Colonial Office? was conveniently precluded by the 'third party' rule.

When Blake took over from Buxton, Rhodes was in rollicking form. Did he give general rather than detailed instructions to his agents? 'Quite so,' he swaggered, 'I just said generally "Do this" or "Do that".' The '*verb. sap.*' entry in Bobby White's diary was read aloud to shame him. Rhodes merely commented saucily: 'That shows how very careful you have to be in what you say.' At one point Blake began to examine him in a penetrating manner about the transfer of the railway strip: 'All that fits in in a most wonderful way . . . with the secret scheme that you had in your mind . . .' But the great man no longer needed to bestir himself to steer his interrogator away from the shoals; the Colonial Secretary did it for him. Like Harcourt, Blake failed to make him speak about the 'Hawksley' cables. 'That I do not think I am entitled to answer,' was Rhodes's reply to questions on the subject. 'I do not say I do not know . . . I think that is a sufficient statement for me to make to the Committee. I think there I should stop.' Thwarted, Blake turned into the maze, ever seductive to the Liberals but profitless to the Inquiry, of the millionaire's financial operations. During the remainder of Blake's cross-examination, he twice managed to get Rhodes up to the fence again, but with the assistance of the Chairman he ran out each time.

Labouchere was the last shot in the Liberals' locker. He got off to a false start by suggesting to Rhodes that the German menace in South Africa was fictitious. Immediately Chamberlain fed to the witness an astute question, calculated to win sympathy for Rhodes while alienating popular support from Labouchere: Did Rhodes ever see Lord Kimberley's dispatch of February 1895 in which he criticized the German attitude towards the Transvaal? Yes, Rhodes was shown it by one of the colonial governors.

*Chamberlain:* It would appear from that, that Lord Kimberley took the same view of that [the German menace] as you do.
*Rhodes:* I think so; I think any Englishmen would.
*Labouchere:* Well, I do not.

Chamberlain had adroitly made it a case of Labby *v.* the rest. After that Rhodes went from strength to strength. He turned out epigrams ('Protection is when you create bastard factories and make bad articles' – 'Governments spend their whole time in making conventions and then tearing them up') and blew off yet another thousand words on the Uitlanders' grievances, which must have caused many heads to nod in sympathy with gallant Dr Jim. Labouchere, through his fanatical hatred of 'big business', allowed himself to wander far from the trail of the cables, and the Committee found itself discussing, under his guidance, how on earth the millionaires could complain of being ruined by Kruger's taxes, and whether Kaffirs should have more or less than twenty-five lashes for running away the second time. It was magnificent propaganda but it was not investigation. When at last Labouchere got back to the matter in hand, he, like Ellis, put the question in a manner which invited defeat:

*Labouchere:* You are not prepared to tell us who knew in South Africa about your intentions with regard to the rising?
*Rhodes* (complacently – the game was getting too easy): No, I have said that before. I think it would be unfair.

During the rest of the day Labouchere tried manfully to make up for lost time. He 'punched' Rhodes (to use one of Dr Harris's expressions) on the '*Telemones*' cables from *The Times* to such an extent that Rhodes protested rather wickedly: 'You began with *The Times*, and then you went to the Colonial Office, and you will be in the Imperial Secretary's Office [Bower's] before we know where we are.' This possibility did not deter Labby. He only tossed more and more names into the arena: Flora Shaw, Fairfield, Chamberlain, Younghusband. The Attorney-General had already intervened to stop one of Labby's questions and the Colonial Secretary began to get thoroughly restive. What was this madman from *Truth* going to ask next?

*Labouchere:* You absolutely then acquit Mr Chamberlain of all knowledge beyond the general knowledge that disturbances might take place in Johannesburg?
*Rhodes:* Yes, so far as I am concerned. I was out in Africa at the time. . . . I was not then at home . . . and had never seen the Colonial Office on any of these questions.

Chamberlain saw that Rhodes, riled by Labouchere's onslaught, was back at his old, mischievous innuendos. That radical scoundrel was clearly nagging him into disloyalty. The monocle glinted towards the Chairman and at last the 'judgmatical' man judged it time to end the farce with a straight question to which Rhodes would have to give a straight answer. Did he tell Chamberlain about his plans or not?

*Chairman:* Your answer is that you did not?
*Rhodes:* I did not.

Chamberlain felt it prudent to smooth over this moment of crisis with a suave offer to assist the Committee himself: 'I shall be very happy to answer any questions on the subject.' This hint, however, did not curb his colleague. He was about to bring in Willoughby's letter to the War Office when the Attorney-General interrupted his question in mid-flight and was upheld by the Chairman. Labouchere plunged on. Had Rhodes heard of Hawksley's letters to Mr Chamberlain? The Colonial Secretary barked, 'What about?' Once more the Chairman intervened to deflect the stream of Labby's curiosity, but the editor of *Truth* at once produced yet another dangerous name:

*Labouchere:* Have you read Mr Garrett's book?
*Rhodes:* No I have not.
*Chairman:* I think we cannot go into that.
*Rhodes:* And may I add I have not read *Blastus*?*
*Chairman:* I think we had better finish here for today.

It was a wise decision.

Labouchere's second innings (2 March) was unsuccessful compared with his first. As with his colleagues, the interval of several days between sessions seemed to make him lose the hot scent and stray into less rewarding paths. What was Rhodes's precise 'pocket interest' in the Chartered Company? Immediately Labouchere's colleagues rounded on him. Rhodes patronizingly interposed on Labby's behalf, promising to give all the financial answers when he came back for the second part of the Inquiry. But the second part was never held, Rhodes never came back and Labby's attempt to twist the lion's tail left the impression that while the questioner was harbouring mean suspicions, the witness was a sea-green incorruptible:

*Labouchere:* Then that [share-pushing] was not one of your objects in promoting the revolution?
*Rhodes* (with enormous self-righteousness): Certainly not.

* King Herod's Chamberlain in Stead's *History of the Mystery*.

That was the end of Rhodes's Liberal enemies. The rest of his cross-examination was plain sailing. He managed to reverse the point of the Inquiry by expounding to Bigham and Wyndham all the sins of the Boers. As the recitation proceeded, Harcourt lost patience. 'Really, Mr Chairman!' he expostulated, when Rhodes asked the Committee which side they would take in a British civil war. 'We had better get on,' said the Chairman miserably. It was to become a familiar moan. But the bickering between Harcourt and Wyndham got worse until Rhodes had the delightful sensation of turning to Wyndham and saying: 'I do not know whether you are examining me or Sir William Harcourt.' There was little use in questioning Rhodes further. What the Committee were clearly longing to do was to get at each other's throats. When Cripps's turn came to examine Rhodes he chose the safe course: 'I do not propose to ask Mr Rhodes any questions.'

At last it was Mr Secretary Chamberlain's duty to wind up. Would the session end in a duel with Rhodes or a combined operation? Smoothly the Colonial Secretary conducted Rhodes through the Protectorate negotiations. But before he had finished, the big child was finding it irksome to be good so long. Suddenly the sprite inside him popped out again, giving Chamberlain a last unpleasant surprise. Rhodes had chipped the Colonial Secretary with getting a good bargain over the transfer. 'And perhaps you were all the more ready to make a good bargain,' teased Chamberlain, 'because you had some other views?' Rhodes did not like being needled, even playfully. If he had 'other views,' why, his interrogator had been given a shrewd hint of them. So he fired back: 'I am afraid you took advantage of them.' It was a deadly innuendo; for how could Chamberlain take advantage of Rhodes's secret plans unless he knew what they were? Prudently letting the innuendo pass without comment, Chamberlain promptly changed the subject.

That was farewell to Rhodes. The Committee let him go home to Africa at once, and when he was later desperately needed to produce the 'missing telegrams', they had not the nerve to haul him back. But though the Colossus hastened away, he intended his image, like that of King Ozymandias, to remain with the Tribunal as a salutary reminder to his enemies that he had worsted them: 'Look on me, all ye mighty, and despair.' As the six days of his cross-examination drew to a close, his duel with Chamberlain, though it flared occasionally, was gradually petering out. The eyes of Rhodes were not really fixed upon the immediate issues: imperial collusion, Johannesburg intrigues, Jameson's mad dash. He was looking beyond the Committee of Inquiry, beyond Chamberlain, Kruger and all living politicians to the federated British South Africa of his dream. Upon this vast horizon the Jameson Raid appeared to him as but a speck.

Rhodes could indeed see far, but not far enough. He did not see the speck growing into something even vaster than the landscape in which it lay. For the Raid, and the Boer War which followed it, were to put an end for ever to time-honoured methods of empire-building and tear the heart out of lusty, free-booting Britain.

# 35

# *Trials of a Tribunal*

There was no doubt that when the Committee reassembled on 9 March for the seventh session, they were in a tetchy mood. That Rhodes had got the better of them was now widely known. Whoever succeeded him must expect rough handling. Rhodes's successor was Sir Graham Bower, and he duly received a grilling that even today is painful to read about. The *Annual Register* summed up his evidence as 'most startling', but Bower made the initial mistake of trying to pass it off casually. He was led astray by the mistaken belief that since Chamberlain knew of his intended 'confession' he would inform Harcourt and both would let him down lightly. Chamberlain did indeed intervene several times to save Bower from the merciless bullying of the Liberals, and at the beginning gave him a chance to think better of his determination to confess:

*Chamberlain:* I put it first to you, is Mr Rhodes willing that you should state what happened, which he stated to you under seal of confidence?
*Bower:* Well, I told him I was going to say it to the Committee, and he offered no objection . . .

Chamberlain's idea was that Rhodes, having established so many defensive rules while present, should be granted yet another in his absence – 'the seal of confidence' which cannot be broken. But Bower had made up his mind to speak and said so.

Harcourt took over from Chamberlain and the tone at once changed. It is true that as the Liberal attack developed, Bower automatically attracted some help from the Conservatives, but it was not enough to save him from a terrible drubbing. He recorded afterwards that at times the strain became so great he did not know whether he was standing on his head or his heels: sometimes he suspected he was about to lose his memory altogether.

His story was that Rhodes had put him on his honour not to tell the High Commissioner of his plans; he regarded this charge as sacred and kept his chief in the dark. How could he make this tale sound plausible? How could he cover up Robinson, remain loyal to Rhodes and yet at the same time defend himself? It proved to be impossible. In fact, that aged invalid, Lord Rosmead (Robinson), was so frightened by Bower's clumsy efforts at covering up, that he sent a furious telegram denying all collusion and demanding that Bower should unequivocally corroborate him. Abjectly his Imperial Secretary complied. After many pitiful attempts to extricate himself from the web of contradictions he could not avoid spinning, he was finally battered by Labouchere into saying that Rhodes had never really intended a rising at all; hence no communication with the High Commissioner was necessary. At this absurdity Labouchere lost his temper and a general fracas ensued:

*Labouchere:* I am asking these questions because I consider that Sir Graham Bower is not telling the truth. I say it openly –
*Chairman:* Order, order.
*Labouchere:* I claim to examine this gentleman. If the Committee like to stop me they can.
*Chairman:* I really think the Committee are bound to protect witnesses against insult.
*Labouchere:* Very well, that is my opinion . . . He has entirely altered his evidence.
*Chairman:* Surely this is entirely out of order. If you have a question to put, put it.
*Labouchere:* Then I shall clear the room on each question I ask to which objection is taken. I want to see if this Committee is to be a sham.
*Chairman:* Surely that is not the way to facilitate the business of the Committee.
*Labouchere:* The way to facilitate the business of the Committee would be to let me ask my questions.

Accusations and counter-accusations flew between the members of the Tribunal, Bigham rather pathetically saying that he too, but for Labouchere's threat to clear the room, would lodge an objection. He did Bower the courtesy of assuming that he would speak the truth, and hoped that 'most of the gentlemen of the Committee' would assume the same thing. But the moment had long passed when poor Bower could give any impression of truthfulness. He staggered to the end of his ordeal having achieved his aim: to cover Rosmead without smearing Rhodes. But he achieved it with the maximum of damage to himself. This sorry episode may be concluded by quoting one' of the rare occasions on which Bower scored.

Chamberlain, though he did his best for Bower during the Inquiry, was in the latter's eyes prime mover of the catastrophe. Hence Bower could not resist one sharp thrust at him. When it was a question of why Bower did not warn Robinson that Rhodes would 'act' on behalf of the Uitlanders if the British Government proved 'infernally slow', Bower replied meaningly: 'I had very little doubt as to who would intervene on that occasion . . . I did not think we had a very slow Secretary of State.' To the many who knew Chamberlain's reputation for brash impetuosity, this was a palpable hit. To those few who knew the full story, it was a daring reference to his 'unofficial' activities.

When Jameson was called to give evidence it seemed at first that the Doctor would this time ride through without opposition. But Labouchere was on the alert. 'Did you', he asked Jameson, 'in any way inform any of the officers who were going with you that the imperial authorities approved of the action?' A ghastly kaleido-scope suddenly danced before Jameson's eyes – the troops on the Pitsani parade-ground listening to his speech; the assurances of Willoughby and Raleigh Grey; Willoughby's letter to the War Office and his own supporting statement. He could only splutter stupidly, 'The imperial authorities!', blurt out something about 'private conversations' and finally take refuge in a refusal to speak.

Surprisingly, Labouchere at once relaxed his grip ('I do not wish to press you at all') and allowed Jameson to work his way out of his *impasse* amid such a turmoil of explanations that even with the lavish help of punctuation the reporters could scarcely make sense of his remarks. The upshot was that Jameson knew the High Commis-sioner intended to go up and mediate in Johannesburg; this led Jameson to tell his officers that the Government would back up their enterprise; it did *not* mean that Robinson had ever heard of or backed up Jameson's plan. This story, with the Doctor taking due blame for his verbal and physical short cuts, satisfied the Commit-tee. He was speaking for the mass of his fellow-countrymen when he summed up his case in blunt words:

*Jameson:* Of course in a thing of this kind I perfectly recognize that the proper thing would have been to tell the High Commissioner, but then I would never have entertained the subject if I was going to do a proper thing.

I know perfectly well that, as I have not succeeded, the natural thing has happened; but I also know that if I had succeeded I should have been forgiven. That was the position.

The Resident Commissioner in the Bechuanaland Protectorate, Frank Newton, was the next to sit in the witness chair. He must have felt decidedly apprehensive. With a parallel record to Bower's, would he meet with the same treatment? It cannot be said that Newton excelled himself, though he confessed his guilt. He could not tell the whole truth: that Robinson had declined to hear his news of Jameson's plans. So he began by explaining that Rhodes persuaded him to withhold the information from the High Commissioner, and later corrected this to an assertion that he did so on his own responsibility. But despite this contradiction, nobody trounced him. Harcourt was absent.

Johnny Willoughby, who followed Newton, was no Leander Starr Jameson. A telegram sent from Jameson to Hawksley five days before Willoughby's appearance, shows that special measures were thought necessary to bring him up to scratch. Jameson's confident words have a shaky undertone: 'Had an hour with Johnny. He will be all right. Wyndham promises not to leave it till he succeeds . . .'[1] The results of Willoughby's examination showed that the fears of the Rhodes group were amply justified.

After one or two skirmishes, Labouchere winkled out of him two important admissions. First, that he had given his officers assurances, based on 'private conversations' with Jameson, that the imperial authorities were behind the adventure; if the expedition succeeded 'they would not be bothered by anybody'. Second, that he had written a letter on the same subject to the War Office. Nothing, however, would prevail upon Johnny to produce this document. *Confidential* he had marked it and confidential it must remain. Enthusiastically championed by the Conservatives on the Tribunal, Willoughby was privileged to witness the development of a 'scene' so tumultuous between the Chairman and Labouchere that there is no record of it in the minutes, save for the euphemistic phrase, 'After some discussion . . .' But the *Annual Register* was more revealing. It reported Labby as exclaiming that if the letter was not to be laid before them, 'the Committee was a farce and a humbug', having for its chief object 'to hush up everything'.

'After some discussion' Chamberlain, seeing that valour was the better part of discretion, boldly suggested that the War Office should be made to hand over the letter at the next session. The Committee were then compelled to hear Willoughby's 'honest and bona fide belief in the imperial authorities' collusion. The next question was obvious: Upon what did he base this belief? But Johnny was enough of a soldier to perceive that his enemies frightened one another more than they frightened him. Referring to 'private conversations' with Jameson, he again refused to specify further. In vain Harcourt thundered; in vain the Chairman cleared the room. Even the miracle of a unanimous decision by all fifteen members of the Committee that the witness *must answer*, failed to shake him. The session closed on a note of bathos:

*Chairman* (to Hawksley): Order! Order! (to Willoughby, in a last minute hope of wringing partial victory from defeat): Perhaps you might be able at all events to answer this question. You refer in your letter to the imperial authorities. Will you tell the Committee who the imperial authorities were to whom you referred?
*Willoughby* (game to the end): *I must decline to answer that question.*

Three days later Dr Jameson was recalled to try to square his own evidence ('of course I never told my officers') with Willoughby's bona fide belief. It was the last session before the Easter recess. Harcourt was more than ready to return to the daffodils of Malwood, his home, and Chamberlain to Highbury in the charm of its spring-flowering shrubs. The Committee co-operated with Jameson in blazing a trail out of the thicket by which 'Johnny' might be induced to retire.

Jameson put up two sign-posts: first, the letter was written not to cover the Raid but to save the officers' commissions; second, Jameson had sanctioned the general purpose of the letter but not the references to the 'imperial authorities'. He had seen it too late, however, to change the obnoxious wording. Would Willoughby accept this way out? The ex-prisoner, liberated from Holloway only a few days ago after serving eight of his ten months' sentence (the last two were remitted), was in no mood to make more than minimal concessions. He would go as far as saying he accepted Jameson's evidence, but no further. Sydney Buxton, however, insisted on another step. Let Willoughby specifically repudiate, as Jameson had already done, his use of the words 'imperial authorities'.

Willoughby writhed and wriggled. He recalled the conditions under which he had drafted the letter: in prison, 'in a sort of glass case with the door open, and warders listening to every word you say', and only twenty minutes for discussion with Jameson and Hawksley. He was still, he said, nervous and dazed; afraid, if he answered this question, of the next being so turned and twisted as to trip him up. Yes, he would have worded the letter differently, the phraseology was wrong, he would not use those terms now . . . But no one could make him be more specific than that. As Buxton pointed out, it was not a matter of phraseology but of fact; and Willoughby could not bring himself to say, in unequivocal fashion, that the fact he had alleged of the imperial authorities was untrue.

Willoughby established for those who succeeded him an important precedent. He was the first to defy the Committee. And he successfully defied them on the key question of imperial collusion.

In the House of Commons, Chamberlain regaled his colleagues with the details of Kruger's demand for a Raid indemnity. The one-time amateur actor made the most of the occasion by reading through the bizarre list of damages in a grave voice with a dead-pan face. The 'moral and intellectual' damage to the Boer Republic was estimated at one million pounds and the account for material damages amounted to £677,938 3s. 3d., making a grand total of £1,677,938 3s. 3d. Or it might be, said Chamberlain, that Kruger intended the grand total to be one million pounds, thus leaving £322,061 16s. 9d. for 'moral and intellectual' damage. (Loud laughter.) 'Commando services' cost Kruger £136,733 4s. 3d. and 'Compensation to be paid to the commandeered burghers for their services and the troubles and cares brought upon them' came to £462,120. The expense account sent in by the Orange Free State did not fall short of the Transvaal in exactitude: it was £36,011 19s. 1d.

W. T. Stead called this intriguing bill 'a screaming farce'.[2] The

Boers' expenses, he reckoned, in defeating Dr Jameson could not have amounted to more than £50,000: 'Any enterprising contractor would be very glad to move all the troops, spend all the ammunition, and provide for all the accommodation of the prisoners at that figure, and made a handsome profit on it.' The *Johannesburg Star* printed a cartoon of 'Professor Ch——' examining the bumps on 'Oom P——'s' cranium: Bump of Forgiveness, absent; Forgetfulness, ditto; Craft, highly developed; Self-esteem, abnormal; Combativeness, growing; Morality, worth a million . . .' Shortly afterwards the *Star* was banned but reappeared as the *Comet*, still trailing its tail though less flamboyantly. Chamberlain's officials computed that each day of the Raid must, according to Kruger, have cost him as much as Britain's whole Ashanti expedition – £170,000! – and his moral claim was 'preposterous'. Chamberlain repudiated the latter and demanded detailed vouchers for the material claim. Neither was ever paid; or rather, the Boer War was to put paid to both.

Everything now turned on the Committee's handling of Rhodes's 'big four': Harris, Hawksley, Maguire, and Flora Shaw. Rutherfoord Harris was the first of the quartet to appear. Like Rhodes, he had eluded the summons to the earlier Cape Committee and once again curiosity among the spectators was intense. He was represented by Lord Robert Cecil, one of the Prime Minister's sons, who afterwards helped to found the League of Nations. He defended with surprising vehemence (for which he apologized to the Tribunal) a cause greatly inferior to those which he was later to espouse.

The mystery of Harris's 'guarded allusion' to Jameson's plan which he claimed to have made to the Colonial Secretary, has already been discussed. It was a matter of life and death for Chamberlain to convince the Tribunal that Harris was interrupted before he could make it; and he was prepared to go to all lengths, even into the witness chair, to succeed. Nevertheless, Harris stuck to his story that the allusion was made; 'naturally', however, he accepted Mr Chamberlain's statement that he did not *hear* it. It was an offensive way to put the point: was Chamberlain as deaf as Fairfield? Throughout his interrogation Harris treated the Tribunal with the kind of insolence he had learned from his master; but where Rhodes was high and mighty, Harris was pert.

When Chamberlain was about to leave the witness chair, Labouchere detained him in order to elicit the interesting fact that he had seen the cipher telegrams. But the redoubtable Labby showed some weakness in tackling his masterful colleague, for he failed completely to ask Chamberlain what was in them. Harris, back in the box, jauntily conveyed to Harcourt that he did not intend to throw any light on them either. Suddenly Harcourt decided to stand no more nonsense. Ignoring the protests of Counsel, he extracted from an unwilling Harris ('I do not know why you should force me to give names when you have never forced Mr Rhodes to give them') that he had seen Fairfield at the Colonial Office and that both Beit and Maguire knew about the Jameson plan. The Tribunal conspicuously avoided pressing Harris on whether he had told Grey. Yet Grey could have been a key witness.

Meanwhile, enough had now been said to make it essential to get the Harris–Rhodes telegrams; it was clear that they were in the possession of Rhodes's solicitor, Bouchier Hawksley. At the next session, 4 May, Hawksley was made to hand over the cipher key and the Committee spent a happy morning unravelling, with Harris's help, a number of not very important facts: that Rhodes, for example, had the picturesque registered address of '*Veldschoen*,\* Johannesburg'. During the following session, after the Chairman had cleared the room, the Committee agreed unanimously to force the rebellious Eastern Telegraph Company to produce all copies of the cables which had not been destroyed in the normal course of business. The interval between their production and decoding was filled by some characteristically rowdy scenes between Labouchere and the directors of the Chartered Company. At length, on 18 May, Dr Harris was confronted with a batch of cables dating from 2 to 29 November 1895, and required to explain them. Fortunately for all concerned, the messages sent during the previous months had already been destroyed.

As these intriguing documents lay upon the horseshoe table, the name of Lord Grey, so long shielded, suddenly burst into the limelight. A message from Harris to Rhodes revealed the fact that

---

\* *Veldschoen*, the heavy boots worn by the Boer farmers, were Rhodes's favourite footwear.

Grey, endowed with the dignified code name of 'Gothical', had been chosen by Rhodes to be one of his London contacts when Beit and Harrison returned to South Africa. For what mission had Rhodes selected this popular aristocrat, hitherto beyond reproach and above suspicion? No one on the Committee put the question to Harris. Had it been put, Harris would almost certainly have refused to answer. The Committee would then have been compelled to hear Grey himself in evidence. With what result? Either a blank refusal to speak on Grey's part also, or a reluctant admission that he, like Harris, had earlier made a 'guarded allusion' to the Colonial Secretary. There could have been no arguing this time that the allusion was an illusion. Grey was not one to tell a lie. But despite the bandying about of his name, he was never summoned. Of course he was far away governing Rhodesia. That in itself seemed a valid excuse for not trying to reach him.

Harris's telegram of 4 November ('I have spoken open E Fairfield') brought up the part of Fairfield in the affair. Once again Chamberlain felt obliged to interrupt Harris, this time a good deal more abruptly than before, and to read out Fairfield's own explanation of the startling (because mistranscribed) words.* Chamberlain's colleagues listened to the rigmarole in silence, doubtless somewhat mystified. No further questions were asked on that subject.

A dangerous light now began to play over *The Times*. Two of the cables from Harris blatantly brought in the name of 'Flora'. It was evident that Dr Harris was being familiar for serious reasons. When a later cable disclosed that 'Flora' had been promoted to the registered address of '*Telemones*, London', no one could doubt but that the dynamic Miss Shaw would shortly be sitting in the witness's chair.

One cable from Harris to Rhodes (18 November) above all showed the public that the Committee was on the track of something sensational. In its subject matter there was nothing new. It merely noted Rhodes's extreme impatience to acquire the railway strip 'at any sacrifice'. Reference, however, was made in it to three previous telegrams sent from Rhodes to Harris: on 26 October, 3 November

---

* See pp. 189–90 above.

and 7 November. The Chairman admitted that the first of the three would have been destroyed in the normal course of business. But where were the other two? The date, 3 November, concealed the 'flag' telegram, while the 'fireworks' telegram was hidden under the date 7 November. The dilatory hounds had picked up the scent of the 'missing telegrams' at last.

Sir William Harcourt, as Rhodes had feared, showed a particularly sharp nose. He accused Harris of knowing perfectly well that some were missing, and by asking him point blank why this was so, he drove Harris into an obvious lie: 'I have not the remotest idea.' Labouchere's pin-pricks during the next session suddenly goaded Rhodes's exasperated agent into taking the offensive. Menacingly he informed Labouchere that he had long awaited the chance to make him prove certain allegations against the Rhodes group, which he, while a member of the Tribunal, had made in the pages of a foreign newspaper, *Gaulois*. With enormous relish, Harris read out Labby's highly-coloured account of financial sharks, rotten companies, a fleeced public and society ladies and gentlemen used as touts. Hastily the Chairman cleared the room. When Harris and his Counsel returned, they had the pleasure of hearing Labouchere's behaviour condemned by his own colleagues. And the allegations were yet to be proved.

Labouchere, however, was not the man to remain subdued for long; the instant an opportunity occurred he moved that Bouchier Hawksley and Flora Shaw should both be called upon to produce all the rest of the telegrams which had not yet been seen. The room being cleared, Labouchere was this time supported by the voting and Rhodes's solicitor Hawksley, holder of the telegrams, found himself in the chair.

Bouchier Francis Hawksley, though the rôle he played in the Raid story was not an attractive one, had a pleasant enough appearance. His eyes were set well apart, with rather drooping lids, and he had a shrewd, humorous expression. Sir Robert Meade, however, described him as 'rather foxy'.

Hawksley's examination was brief but pregnant. Although he was afterwards to make a habit of carrying the 'missing telegrams' about in his pocket, they were not on his person that day. But he agreed to seek Rhodes's permission to produce them at the following session, admitting 'frankly' that they had not been destroyed and even volunteering the reason why. It was due to a special request from the Colonial Office to preserve them, since certain 'gentlemen' there had embellished them with pencilled notes. Hawksley's 'frank' disclosure of unasked-for facts was a first hint of his subsequent methods.

There was little rest for anybody during that spring weekend. The intrepid Miss Shaw heard that she was to be grilled. In her friend Mrs Moberly Bell's diary occurred the following entry on Sunday 23 May: 'F. knows now she is called to S.A. Committee. She does not mind much and is still sure she did all things rightly, and thinking ditto again under same circumstances. She had a bad cold but is quite plucky.'[3]

Before the following Tuesday, 25 May, when the Committee met again, both Hawksley and Labouchere had important tasks to perform. Neither met with success. Hawksley cabled his chief, Rhodes, for leave to put in the 'missing telegrams'. He received no reply. Labouchere had to prove his allegations against Harris. He contacted the friend on whose information he had based them, 'a gentleman of high position and large business experience'. Would the gentleman allow Labby to publish his name and those of his witnesses? Despite or perhaps because of his exalted status, the gentleman refused to oblige. When Tuesday arrived, Labby's discomfiture was prodigious. In a lengthy letter to the Chairman he was forced to withdraw and apologize to Harris. George Wyndham tried to prolong the agony by getting Labouchere himself placed in the chair. As this would have meant another clearance of the room, the Chairman managed to stave it off.

Swiftly following on Labouchere's rout, another humiliation befell the Committee. Hawksley declined to produce the 'missing telegrams' until such time as his client should give him permission to do so; worse still, without being asked he read out the correspondence between himself and Fairfield in June 1896 when the existence of the fatal telegrams was first disclosed to Chamberlain. Deeply incensed, Chamberlain was compelled to listen once again to those serpentine phrases: 'Mr C. knows what I know, and can shape his course with this knowledge . . .' Bigham protested to the Chairman that he did not know what they were doing. Chamberlain was more explicit: 'The witness is volunteering the information,' he exploded; 'he has not been asked any question as to this.' Harcourt, who was examining Hawksley, did not relish being interrupted and a row broke out between him and his two colleagues which was only quelled by another clearance of the room.

Hawksley defied every attempt to make him divulge the telegrams. Finally, the Committee were asked to accept a position of grotesque paradox: were Rhodes himself present before the Committee, it was agreed by all including his Counsel that he would have to obey orders and produce the telegrams; but so long as Rhodes was absent, Hawksley insisted on obeying his client rather than the Committee and withholding them. The shadow of the departed Colossus was indeed almost more potent than his substance. After yet another clearance of the room, the Attorney-General lamely informed Hawksley and his own obstinate legal brethren, Pope and Pember, that the Committee would take until Friday to decide what to do about the 'missing telegrams'. Another fantastic detail in this farcical situation was that the Attorney-General had seen the telegrams and knew their contents perfectly well.

# 36

# *Lady into Fox*

It was not surprising that Flora Shaw's appearance before the Committee, which followed immediately after the Hawksley débâcle, went with a swing. She was the only woman to face the Tribunal and the Grand Committee room was packed. The firm line of her chin, steady rather deep-set eyes, pleasant youthful-looking face with a hovering smile, were not at all what the public and journalists expected. Most people were on the look-out for a middle-aged frump; for Flora Shaw was scarcely known to newspaper readers before her appearances at Westminster. The impression she gave of elegant, distinguished femininity took their breath away. Flora, however, was not without apprehension over the ordeal ahead. A Victorian lady, she blushed to think of her Christian name bandied about in Harris's vulgar telegraphese. What would the Conservatives on the Tribunal think of her? And what would the Opposition do to her?

As always, she wore her favourite black (black silk for the month of May) and was accompanied by her sister Lulu, wearing a hat which the press described as 'seasonable'. Chamberlain had had to break the news, through his secretary Harry Wilson, that Flora would probably be refused permission to bring her sister along, since Rhodes's sister was not allowed to be present at the Committee. Fortunately Lulu was admitted. Such a symbol of feminine defencelessness at once stirred the Committee's chivalry. They were delighted to have a reason for behaving once again as gentlemen.

For all her feminine impact, Miss Flora Shaw was well able to look after herself. Her sharp wits enabled her to score a bull point in the first few minutes. Harris, contrary to a statement in one of his messages to Rhodes, had certainly not 'sent her' to Chamberlain: 'I need hardly say I should not have accepted any mission from Dr Harris to go to Mr Chamberlain; he was not in the position to send me anywhere.' Such language about the odious Harris was heavenly music in the Committee's ears, offended as they had been hitherto by mingled uproar and innuendo.

But when it came to her own '*Telemones*' cables, sent after Harris had left England, Flora was on more dangerous ground. Without the cables in front of her (why did not the Committee accept Labouchere's motion to send for her cables and Miss Shaw together?), she earnestly advised the Committee that it would be wiser to let her give the 'drift' rather than supply actual words, which might be inaccurate. Wiser indeed. Miss Shaw was thus able to summarize her three cables to Rhodes without mentioning the name of Chamberlain, which appeared in the first and third. As for Rhodes's replies, the memory of the brilliant journalist failed her completely at this juncture. She vaguely recollected one answer from Rhodes, together with the 'women and children' letter; in point of fact Rhodes sent four other important messages in two of which occurred the name of Chamberlain.

In this skilful tactic Flora was following the advice of her editor George Buckle, who had told her on no account to quote the telegrams from memory. 'If they exist,' he wrote from the Athenaeum on 24 May 1897, 'the Committee can get them. If not, *tant mieux*.'[1] Buckle's letter went on to warn her against making speeches to the Committee. Her air should be that of a person 'called on to speak on one or two points', not of someone bursting with information. A clever woman does not like to be called governessy, even on Athenaeum Club writing paper. Miss Shaw's biographer tells us that Buckle's letter cast an indelible shadow over her relations with *The Times*. The truth was that Buckle in his heart did blame her severely for her part in the plot, and she knew it. (Partly owing to his wife's delicate health, the social life of *The Times* had come to revolve round the Moberly Bells, and the fact that Buckle, the editor, was kept in the dark so long must have added to his chagrin.) Moreover, like John Walter, the proprietor, and many others, Buckle did not believe that the Victorian spinster in her black silk dress could stand up to the barrage of legal stars such as Webster, Cripps and Bigham. Little did he know his Miss Shaw.

A totally new Sir William Harcourt blossomed forth when the Chairman handed Miss Shaw over to him. He was full of gallantry. Referring to Rhodes's remark that he never went near the press, Sir William was not surprised that he should have broken his rule in Flora's case: 'I can quite understand the exception he made.'

The Colonial Office, too, had apparently made an exception in favour of this remarkable lady. When she told Harcourt that she had been first 'allowed' to go there seven years ago, the picture of her trim figure gliding along those gloomy corridors seemed as different from Dr Harris's visits as day from night.

To a question from Sydney Buxton she replied with a lecturette on the difference between the Raid and the rising, imploring the Committee with a subtle mingling of flattery and finger-wagging to make an effort of imagination which could not be expected from the public. (Moberly Bell had previously suggested this line to her.) As a matter of fact, the Committee were already making that effort of imagination to a degree that the situation was far from justifying. For how could the Raid be materially distinguished from the rising? It was as much a part of the rising as an accident is part of the conditions out of which it springs.

Flora Shaw's great test was to come when Harcourt asked her whether she had inspired *The Times*' leading article that criticized Chamberlain for repudiating Dr Jameson. She knew it was now or never. Once the Committee got inside *The Times*, all would be lost. As if obeying professional etiquette, but in fact following the lead of Rhodes and her legal adviser, Sir Herbert Stephen, Flora gently but firmly intimated that the Committee would not wish her to discuss what went on in her office. Harcourt retreated as if, like the man in the moon, he had burned himself on her coolness; while Sir Henry Campbell-Bannerman, perhaps remembering his favourite French novels, rescued the lady with a most generous escape clause:

*Sir Henry:* I understand you would rather not answer questions as to your relations with or communications to *The Times* newspaper?
*Flora Shaw:* I would rather not.

What a sigh of relief must have gone up from Mr Monypenny, *The Times* observer, and his friends. It had been an unnerving experience, this business of having nothing between their newspaper and ruin but the wits of a woman. They had forgotten that the style of Flora Shaw had once been mistaken for that of a man. She was playing her part so brilliantly that they would have to forgive her in the end for getting them into this horrible scrape.

Labby was positively civil when he questioned her about her own messages. When Harris's telegram came up, in which she appeared to have actually suggested the date for the rising ('Flora suggests 16th December') the astute lady blamed herself for this 'conversational indiscretion'. It is always as well to apologize when one can. Once, indeed, the Attorney-General almost tripped her up:

*Sir Richard Webster:* In sending these three telegrams did you send them on your own responsibility altogether?
*Flora Shaw:* Entirely.
*Sir Richard Webster:* They were not written in consultation nor dictated to you by anybody?
*Flora Shaw:* No.

Shades of Moberly Bell! Three days later, Miss Shaw took the opportunity to send a little note to the Chairman. She had not heard the Attorney-General use the word 'consultation'. Now she must correct this small matter: 'I am not in a position to say that I consulted no one.' But the man she consulted was 'a personal friend, who but for his friendship would not have discussed the matter with me'. Surely the Committee would not be so discourteous as to wrest from this defenceless woman the name of her sole male adviser? Miss Shaw hinted boldly that in any case her code (transmitted by Rhodes) would not permit her to reveal a 'new name' belonging to a third party. She only mentioned the matter at all because of her scrupulous regard for truth: 'I cannot allow an inaccuracy to stand in my sworn evidence.' No move could have been more shrewd. In one brief note she had put on record her consuming desire to answer truthfully and the Committee's duty, should they need to interrogate her again, not to press her too hard.

The session ended with a bouquet for the scintillating leading lady:

*Chairman:* We are much obliged to you for the very clear way in which you have given your evidence.
*Flora Shaw:* Thank you.

It was a case of thanks all round. Back in Printing House Square, *The Times* staff thanked their skilful protector and Flora Shaw thanked her lucky stars.

\* \* \*

The Committee were prepared for the blow that fell on the following Friday, 28 May. But they were still not at all sure how to deal with it. Bouchier Hawksley once more occupied the witness chair. Sonorously the Attorney-General informed him that the order of the Committee must be obeyed. For this purpose, the Committee was a court of law. The Chairman, in ringing words that belied his cracked hopes, proceeded for the third and last time to demand the 'missing telegrams': 'We therefore call upon you, Mr Hawksley, to produce the telegrams.'

As they feared, Rhodes, at last deigning to speak, had issued another 'No'. His solicitor, with 'very great respect' thrice expressed, made it clear that he did not intend to obey the Committee. He emphasized his defiance with a double-edged thrust at the Committee's rapidly vanishing prestige: 'I think, with regard to what the Attorney-General has just said, that this can scarcely be described as a judicial tribunal.'

The Chairman announced that Hawksley's defiance would be reported to the House of Commons, adding: 'We will not go further with you today.' The language was the language of menace, but the spirit behind it was vacillating and defeatist. 'I suppose Mr Hawksley still remains in the box, technically?' asked Labouchere of the unfortunate Chairman. *Technically* was the appropriate word. *Technically* Hawksley was about to be dragged before the bar of the House; *technically* he would be condemned to the Clock Tower. *Technically* his days would be desolate with prison fare and his nights hideous with the strokes of Big Ben. But all these technicalities withered away in the light of harsh facts. After all, who was Bouchier Hawksley? Just another 'Rhodes man'. If anyone was for the Clock Tower it should be Rhodes himself.

Yet who could guarantee that the Colossus, if summoned, would obey? There was the time factor, too. Rhodes had jeered at the Committee for its snail's pace: 'At the rate you are going on, this thing will take two years.' 'This thing' was due to wind up with the current parliamentary session. If the Report were again postponed there would be further suspicion in Africa, criticism in Britain. And to what end? To the end that a bedraggled Tribunal should be flouted a second or third time by the Right Hon. C. J. Rhodes. The Select Committee on South Africa prepared to write its Report without once setting eyes on the 'missing telegrams'.

As the last few witnesses appeared, the atmosphere in the Grand Committee room was so embittered that new brawls were constantly developing. Alfred Beit, accustomed to seeing himself described in the pages of *Truth* as 'Herr Beit', challenged Labouchere to substantiate his 'vile attacks' and charges of stock-jobbing; Chamberlain intervened to support Beit, Labby flourished his favourite weapon (clearing the room) while the Chairman uttered his plaintive and familiar cry, 'I think this is getting very irregular.' It was a supremely undignified ritual, which was fittingly lampooned by a member of the House of Commons:

> This is, I think we may assume,
>   An incomplete affair;
> For whilst they often 'clear the room',
>   They never clear the air.

Rochfort Maguire, when his turn came, made not the slightest effort to co-operate. His cynical manner indicated that it was now quite in order to treat the Tribunal like dirt. When Labouchere, seeking to prove blackmail, put a series of questions about the notorious telegrams, Maguire replied with curt offensiveness.

Why did he tell the Colonial Office about them in February 1896?

*Maguire:* It was thought to be right that they should be told about them.

Why did Hawksley show the telegrams to the Colonial Office in June?

*Maguire:* They were asked for.

Was there any object to be gained by showing them?

*Maguire:* No.

It was Maguire's way of saying, This whole thing is a put-up job. We blackmailed Chamberlain to stop the Inquiry, he blackmailed us to sit on the telegrams. He knows all the answers. He is on the Committee. Why should I join in the game?

Maguire's performance, on the top of Harris's accusations against

Fairfield and the Committee's failure to subdue Hawksley, made another statement from Chamberlain essential. It was obvious that the telegrams had been used to blackmail the Colonial Office. It was obvious that Fairfield's part in the affair had somehow assisted the blackmailers and needed explaining. What was in the 'missing telegrams'?

Chamberlain went back into the box, but on this key question he was as resolute in withholding information as the Committee were irresolute in demanding it. Sydney Buxton's method of examination was typical of their whole attitude: 'It is, of course, for you to say whether you are able at this long distance of time to charge your memory with them, and whether you would care to give your impression of them?' Chamberlain cared only to give the most general idea: they were very similar to those already produced. Presumably he would welcome their appearance? asked Labouchere. The impassive Minister was 'quite indifferent'. Would he make a request to Rhodes for them? Rhodes would pay no attention, said Chamberlain. Would he mind making it? 'Not in the least' – but all the same he would not make it. So that was that.

These answers are the more intriguing when it is remembered that Chamberlain's memory had no need to be 'charged' at all. Locked in his files lay his own *Memorandum*, containing copies of the 'missing telegrams'. What is perhaps even more remarkable is the fact that none of his colleagues asked him whether he had taken copies. Only one explanation is possible: Chamberlain's colleagues did not desire to know more than he desired to tell.

As for Harris's allegations against Fairfield, the general feeling was that the Colonial Secretary finally succeeded in laying his sad ghost. During his last intervention, he paid a tribute to Fairfield's character: he was 'absolutely truthful, absolutely honourable'. But he was also, if not absolutely incapable of hearing what was said to him, at any rate very deaf indeed. Chamberlain had to shout at him, and like all deaf people, he was sensitive and did not like saying, What? If he had heard and understood Harris's confidences, he would certainly have passed them on to his chief. Therefore, since he did not pass on any such information, argued Chamberlain, he did not receive any.

It was no great strain on Chamberlain's conscience to swear that

Fairfield did not mention the Jameson plan to him. The true inference, however, from this fact was not that Fairfield knew nothing about the plan, but that he believed his chief knew enough already. Such scrupulosities would have been ruled out in Chamberlain's mind by overriding reasons of state.*

By the beginning of June a delightful Whitsun holiday lay ahead and all seemed to be over bar the shouting, which, in the form of Pope and Pember's legal eloquence, the Chairman hoped would be 'kept well in hand'.† Little did anyone guess what a dramatic encounter awaited the Tribunal a month later. After Maguire's stone-walling, the Committee felt bound to ask for the '*Telemones–Veldschoen*' (Shaw–Rhodes) cables. They were demanded by the Chairman on 1 June and then decoded. Flora Shaw knew at once that she would be recalled. After Whitsun all sorts of wild rumours began to fly around. *The Saturday Review* commented with some asperity that it was just as well Miss Shaw was recalled; the mystery over her telegrams must be cleared up for *The Daily News* and *Daily Chronicle* had evidently seen them, no doubt thanks to Labouchere.

On Friday, 29 June, the Chairman handed in the decoded telegrams; not merely the three or four that Flora had already been able to charge her memory with, but a daunting pile of ten. On Tuesday, 2 July, after a nerve-wracking weekend, Flora Shaw made her second appearance before the South Africa Committee. Buckle and Bell must have felt it was too much to hope for another miracle; and yet it seemed that nothing less could save Flora now. There lay those appalling telegrams on the horseshoe table, with the name of *The Times* sticking out and that of Chamberlain lavishly spattered about. Perhaps that was why the Colonial Secretary arrived half an hour late for the start of the proceedings. The Opposition, on the

---

* A week after the Raid collapsed, Fairfield wrote a minute to the effect that 'the innocence of our local officials' was proved by certain 'humdrum details' in their dispatches. He actually named Newton as one of the 'innocent' officials, thus at least proving that there were many gaps in his own knowledge. (C.O. 417/145, 9 January 1896.)

† In his diary for 3 June, Wilfrid Blunt wrote: 'The South Africa Committee is virtually, but not virtuously over.'

contrary, were there in force. Buckle and Bell shuddered. But there was no faltering in Flora Shaw.

She was one who warmed both hands before the fire of life and if her fingers were occasionally burned, *tant pis*. Her approach to this second cross-examination seemed to be one of positive welcome. She was delighted to have these telegrams published at last: it would end all the 'mystery-mongering'. Of course two of the messages from Rhodes had completely slipped her memory (an excellent ploy, suggesting how innocent they were) but she would throw in for good measure an additional cable sent by herself to Rhodes on 1 January, that the Eastern Telegraph Company appeared to have omitted. It was Flora's account to Rhodes of the Colonial Secretary's reaction to the Raid, and she brought it out triumphantly: 'Chamberlain is awfully angry.'

Splendid Miss Shaw. She was soon in a fair way to dominate the fifteen politicians before whom she was arraigned. Who could have guessed this would happen again? Perhaps only those who knew her whole history. There was a story that in 1893, at a dinner-party in Australia, she had sat between a Dutchman and a Belgian who were astounded to find a woman '*si forte dans la question de l'Afrique*'. The Belgian chaffed the Dutchman, '*Elle vous a bien roulé, mon cher.*' But he was afterwards consoled to find he had been worsted by '*la grande Miss Shaw*'.[2]

It was now time for her to offer some general explanations of her three main messages. They were intended for Rhodes's eye, not the public's. They were sent from her own private address (130 Cambridge St, SW) at her own expense. Hence they were as short as possible. Extreme brevity produces crude language. She would be pleased to expand them and show what they really meant. What about the 'sealed instructions' to *The Times* correspondents? That was a case of the wrong translation from cipher: it should have been 'confidential information' sent, of course, purely on her own responsibility, and shown to Bell only *after* it was dispatched. (Flora had to juggle with time here, to protect Bell. She showed it to him *before*.) Her second message – 'Delay dangerous sympathy now complete' – was entirely her own work. (It was written out in Bell's handwriting, even down to Flora's signature!)

The Chairman, wishing to put on record Flora's sole responsibility for these telegrams, began a question with the clumsy words: 'Would you tell the Committee frankly?' It was a measure of her moral ascendancy that he immediately apologized for using such language. Her last message to Rhodes before the Raid began with the words, 'Chamberlain sound in case of interference European Powers . . .' Flora's explanation of this phrase was one of her great successes. It was for South African consumption, making it clear that Mr Chamberlain was no longer a Little Englander. Imperialist Joe a Little Englander? The whole Committee, including the subject of the telegram, smiled, enchanted by this touch.* Later on Labouchere returned to this sentence: Would not Rhodes have received the impression that Miss Shaw found out about Chamberlain's 'soundness' from her Colonial Office contacts? Flora Shaw replied: 'I do not care very much whether he did, because Mr Chamberlain *is* sound.' Triumph, and no doubt more smiles.

The second part of that telegram was more difficult to explain, but the Committee were in a receptive mood. Why did Miss Shaw say she had a 'special reason' for thinking Chamberlain wanted the rising to take place at once? Rather severely Miss Shaw pointed out that it was contrary to her normal practice to discuss Colonial Office conversations, and she would only do so now in order to put an end to 'idle and wholly useless chatter'. Her 'special reason', then, was based upon an entirely hypothetical and casual remark dropped by Mr Fairfield. He had said to her: 'Well, if the Johannesburg burghers are going to rise it is to be hoped they would do it soon.' Added to this was her own special knowledge of the Government's difficulties over Venezuela. Putting these two things together, she felt justified in sending that telegram. Labouchere helpfully pointed out that in that case she should have said 'special reasons'. Flora agreed with alacrity: 'Yes, perhaps I did say that. It may be possible the code word meant either.'†

* *The Times*, on 3 July 1897, reported that Chamberlain had generally appeared totally unconcerned by the whole proceedings, but for this once, 'the perfectly impassive expression of his face for a moment gave place to a broad smile'.

† In the light of after-knowledge, one curious fact connected with this cable emerges: Flora Shaw sent it to Rhodes on 17 December; Chamberlain did not send his 'hurry up' letter to Fairfield until 18 December. Therefore she could not have based her own 'hurry up' message on something Fairfield quoted from Chamberlain's. Her

She had contrived once again to get out of an awkward spot. '*Veldschoen*'s' messages to '*Telemones*' gave her less trouble. The incriminating words, 'Inform Chamberlain', were dismissed as the work of an officious Harris, not of an angry Rhodes. Graphically she pictured herself to the Committee, sitting at her desk, struggling with a mountainous pile of cables from all over the world. New ones keep pouring in, among them that of 30 December, 'Inform Chamberlain . . .' Dutifully she decodes it and then with the thought, 'That is Dr Harris, and not Mr Rhodes', promptly dismisses it from her mind.

The Committee were captivated once more by this summary treatment of their old enemy, particularly when she added: 'I attached to it exactly the amount of importance which I thought ought to be attached to Dr Harris's impression of the situation.' As Dr Harris was abroad and the Committee found it impossible to obtain his address, no one was ever able to check up on Miss Shaw's clever theory. It cannot now be accepted.

The next message – 'Unless you can make Chamberlain instruct High Commissioner' – she paradoxically assured them was genuine Rhodes. But she somehow managed to render this cable innocuous simply by saying she had not obeyed its instructions: 'It was just as well that Mr Rhodes should understand', said Flora cunningly, 'that Mr Chamberlain was not to be made to do anything; Mr Chamberlain's attitude was not exactly sympathetic to him at that moment.' (How her judges must have purred.) So she just got out the code book again and cabled back: 'Chamberlain awfully angry' – sharp and short, to save her woman's purse. In the end, Flora Shaw erected such a hedge of thorns, around both the Colonial Office and *The Times*, that no one dared to pry into either. She was never even

---

message must have been a piece of brilliant guesswork anticipating Chamberlain's probable attitude. On the other hand, Fairfield's 'hypothetical' remark which she quoted to the Tribunal was far too much like the real sentence in Chamberlain's 'hurry up' letter to be mere coincidence. Had Flora added to her many other gifts that of second sight? The explanation must be that she saw the 'hurry up' letter the day *after* she sent her cable to Rhodes, though in the excitement of fencing with the Tribunal, she inadvertently committed an anachronism, ante-dating by perhaps twenty-four hours a later conversation with Fairfield. In any case Fairfield had told his family that Miss Shaw's cable completely misrepresented him.

asked, for instance, why *The Times* alone had been accorded the equivocal distinction of publishing the 'women and children' letter. The editor of *Truth* was put once and for all into his proper place, in regard to the great 'Thunderer': 'It is not etiquette', said Miss Shaw in her most biting tones, 'to speak in public of what is done in the internal organization of any large paper.'

She used her last moments with Labouchere to deny again and most emphatically that she had ever carried communications between the Colonial Office and anybody else. Finally she thanked her inquisitor graciously: 'I am glad that you have given me the opportunity to make that statement, because there has been such a lot of talk and my name has had such liberties taken with it . . .' To which Labby, who had been the centre of so many storms, replied in his blandly ironic drawl: 'I am glad to be of any use.'

After her gruelling experience, Miss Shaw buried herself in the peace of Scotland, exhausted but triumphant. Her performance had been prodigious. She had kept hidden all that ought not to be revealed, but at the same time had never descended to the easy camouflage of rounding on Rhodes and Jameson. Congratulations showered upon her. Sir Herbert Stephen found her replies 'credible' as well as straightforward and satisfactory. Lord Loch joined in the praise. From her distant retreat, Miss Shaw could now look forward to a new, dazzling personality created in London, compact of maidenly charm and masculine vigour.

Only *The Times* decided to play down the whole proceedings. A surprisingly small number of peers and MPs, it stressed, turned up to hear the 'startling revelations' which the newsmongers were misguidedly expecting from Miss Shaw. The Colonial Secretary arrived late and left early. Most amazing thing of all, the room was not once cleared!

# 37

# Committee of No Inquiry

'Missing' was the keynote of the South Africa Committee: so much was missing from the evidence and the Report. Missing witnesses, missing telegrams, missing letters, missing signatories. Among the missing personalities were Rhodes and Harris, who both left the country when they left the box, and could not be recalled when needed. Fairfield was dead, Meade missing believed to be seriously ill, Rosmead missing believed to be on his deathbed. (Nevertheless, Stead considered a Commissioner of Oaths should have been sent to the bedsides of Meade and Rosmead, to take their evidence.) Earl Grey was missing; the possibility of seeing him was not even raised. Buckle and Bell were both mentioned by name; but who would dare to send for them after Miss Shaw's remarks about prying into *The Times*?

As for the missing documents, the 'Hawksley' telegrams represented the outstanding lacunae. Copies of many of them could have been produced from the Colonial Secretary's files; no one suggested this source. How and by whom they were spirited away was long a mystery. But thanks to the inspection by Lord Blake of a letter from Hawksley, now at Rhodes House, we know that Hawksley guessed, probably correctly, that the man who made away with them was Sir Robert Herbert, a director of the Telegraph Company and a former Permanent Head of the Colonial Office. Herbert had both the motive (loyalty to the old-boy network) and opportunity (a foot in each camp) to do the job.

Apart from the 'missing telegrams', there was other written evidence that the Committee failed to obtain, notably the Colonial Office correspondence. This included Chamberlain's letters to and from his staff in London and any secret documents which may have passed between London and Cape Town. Fairfield believed that the 'real hope' of Chamberlain's enemies was to 'get out the facts connected with his private correspondence with Sir H. Robinson commencing with some letter written from France or Spain'.[1]

(Evidently Fairfield had not seen this letter; it is not now among the *Chamberlain Papers*.) But there was never the slightest chance of this evidence seeing the light of day. Chamberlain said that it would be produced only over his dead body. His 'hurry up' letter to Fairfield of 18 December was specifically banned from publication by Salisbury.

There remained the High Commissioner's 'letter-book', mentioned by Bower who believed that the Colonial Office had made away with this evidence, together with other documents. It is unlikely, however, that Rosmead's letter-book, if it ever turned up, would prove a sensational find. Chamberlain, as Stead once put it, 'only winked', and he would avoid as far as possible putting his winks on paper.

At least one more document lay hidden, this time in the War Office files, which the Committee, if they knew of its existence,* could have demanded to see. This was Dr Jameson's covering note sent with Willoughby's letter from prison. If it had come to light the situation would have been awkward, for Jameson's letter flatly contradicted his evidence before the Tribunal. The War Office files, however, were not probed.

From the Report of the Committee, published on 13 July 1897, the whole of Part II was missing. The Committee, finding that the consideration of this part would run them into yet another parliamentary session, abandoned it. Two names were missing from the signatories of the final Report, those of Blake and Wyndham. The former refused to sign because Hawksley was too weakly handled, the latter because Rhodes was too strongly condemned. Labouchere confined himself to a Minority Report. Unable to accept the majority view that there were no stock-jobbing motives for the Raid, he wished in addition to lash out at the big names on the Company's board, especially the Dukes of Abercorn and Fife and the Earl Grey. 'It cannot be said that these noblemen fulfilled the object for which they had been appointed,' he wrote. Nor would he say that the

---

* Dr J. van der Poel believed that 'Chamberlain must have known it, and probably the other Ministers knew also'. If this was so, Chamberlain's audacity in himself suggesting that the War Office should be made to disgorge Willoughby's letter was immense. How could he be sure that Jameson's letter would not tumble out at the same time?

object for which the Colonial Secretary had been appointed was fulfilled. When Dr Harris made his 'guarded allusion', Chamberlain should have demanded to hear the whole truth instead of cutting him short. On the other hand, Labouchere joined with the majority in acquitting the imperial government of all complicity.

The conclusions of the majority were assembled under seven heads, occupying less than one whole page of the seven hundred and more pages of the Report. They described the Uitlanders' grievances which Rhodes had exploited and went on to blame Rhodes for the whole deceitful operation, with the exception of Jameson's final coup.* They saddled Beit and Maguire with shared responsibility. The other directors of the Company were neither excused nor blamed for their ignorance of what was going on, though they were censured in the body of the Report for laxity. The High Commissioner was completely exonerated on the grounds that he was the victim of 'a conspiracy to keep all information on the subject from him'. Bower and Newton were accused of 'a grave dereliction of duty'. No allusion was made to the position of *The Times*. The last paragraph but one was reserved for the expected exculpation of the Colonial Office. It came, in dignified and impressive plenitude:

Neither the Secretary of State for the Colonies nor any of the officers of the Colonial Office received any information which should have made them or any of them, aware of the plot during its development.

A sweeping condemnation of the Raid and of the preparations for it rounded off this tight-lipped summary of five months' work.

Harcourt, in sending his friend Chamberlain the draft of the Report, expressed the hope that he would find it 'satisfactory'. The word was a colourless one to describe the culmination of experiences as intense as those which had gone into the making of this Report. Soon after the Inquiry opened Chamberlain had a sharp attack of gout, which his wife described to Lord Salisbury as 'a great nuisance' – something of an understatement. Garvin was more

---

* *The Westminster Gazette* produced a cartoon entitled 'The End of the Game'. The Committee, blindfolded, and seated upon the prostrate body of the Colossus, are saying: 'Well, if we can't safely do anything else, we can all sit on Rhodes. That won't hurt anyone.' Two members are walking off in disgust.

revealing and said that throughout the sittings Chamberlain was on the rack. Yet despite his long-drawn-out anxiety, most of the witnesses and all the members of the Committee played the game. F. E. Smith was later to say of Joseph Chamberlain's son, Austen: 'He always played the game and he always lost it.' The father had a more trenchant personality. He could make others play his game and he nearly always won. In answer to Harcourt's question, the result was 'satisfactory'.

Foreign opinion, however, did not derive so much satisfaction from the Report. In Germany it was held that Chamberlain would be swept away by a violent outbreak of moral indignation, while an Austrian journal saw him branded as a criminal of the deepest dye. The French *Matin* described the Report as 'simply a hiding of the light to shield Mr Chamberlain and all his eminent co-operators in the scheme', while *Figaro* asked how Harcourt could have been so hoodwinked. 'Mr Chamberlain is laid bare at last,' it added, 'and the Colonial Office will not know him much longer.' (Only a mere six years . . .) The comment of *Le Temps* was the most succinct: 'It is the apotheosis of the Birmingham statesman; it is also the abdication of British conscience.' Kruger characteristically remarked that Britain had punished the dogs and let their masters go free.

The Report had its detractors at home as well as abroad. W. T. Stead turned violently against the Committee even before its Report was written. 'The Worshipful Company of White-Washers' was his nickname for Chamberlain and his friends, and he fulminated against 'this goose of a Committee whose foolish cackling has called attention to the very scandal it so clumsily attempted to conceal'. The Opposition lost no time in demolishing the Report. Lord Rosebery, not unmindful of the prominent part played by his detested rival, Harcourt, roundly declared: 'I have never read a document at once so shameful and so absurd. One would laugh, did one not cry.' Arnold Morley called it 'The Lying in State at Westminster', and to all of them it was a 'Committee of No Inquiry'.

# 38

# Jubilee and Gall

The contrast between Flora Shaw's triumph over the Committee and Graham Bower's torture is startling. This episode in Flora's career led to her becoming, five years later, the esteemed and influential wife of the future Lord Lugard. Bower's performance earned him the sack. Neither the fact that one admitted guilt while the other owned up to no more than a few peccadilloes, nor the difference between superb technique and painful collapse, can entirely explain it. Even the most censorious members of the Committee made allowances for Flora. Labouchere's Minority Report let her off with a couple of mild rebukes:

> The recollection of the lady was somewhat defective ... The relations of Miss Flora Shaw ... with the Colonial Office, were peculiar.

The Majority Report was 'satisfied' with her evidence. In the House of Commons, the ever-chivalrous Campbell-Bannerman was prepared to defend her in warmer fashion. 'The lady' must be forgiven, he said, because of her 'zeal and excited temperament'. He admitted that her telegrams contained 'many awkward expressions', but these were due to her innocence. When she talked about 'sealed instructions', she did not realize 'the very pointed meaning which such an expression would have when received in South Africa'. These benevolent words from the Liberal front bench must have caused much mirth both in Groote Schurr and in Printing House Square.

No doubt the fact that she was 'the lady' had something to do with it. But there were other factors at work. Bower followed immediately after Rhodes. The Committee, humiliated but still fresh, needed to draw blood. Bower laid himself upon the altar stone. Flora Shaw found her inquisitors shaken, exhausted and abased. She restored their self-respect.

Bower's interviews took place early in March; Flora's first cross-examination at the end of May. The *Annual Register* pointed out that the Queen's Diamond Jubilee began to engross the public mind long before the Whitsun recess, to the exclusion of all other business: 'Politics were neglected, debates disregarded, disturbing rumours discredited.' Among those discredited rumours were no doubt some concerning Flora Shaw's cables.

The public pageant and procession were held on 22 June, just ten days before her second cross-examination. The theme of the Diamond Jubilee was empire. It was in this very cause that she had sinned, if indeed she had sinned. Through her own sphere of influence, the press, she had endeavoured to further Rhodes's dream of an empire stretching from the Cape to Cairo. For the first time in Britain's history a splendid national pageant honoured colonial premiers above foreign princes. As the vast procession, led by the aged Queen-Empress, streamed over Westminster Bridge and past the Palace of Westminster at the end of its return journey along the south bank, it was noticed that the cheers of the crowds were loudest for the colonial troops, both white and coloured. 'I never dreamed of so stunning a show,' wrote Mark Twain. 'All the nations seemed to be filing by. It was a sort of suggestion of the Last Day, and some who live to see that day will probably recall this one, if they are not too disturbed in mind at the time.' Who cared about the Last Days of the South Africa Committee?

Mr Laurier, Canada's Prime Minister, blew the imperial trumpet as soon as he set foot in Britain. At a banquet in Liverpool he asked what was the true glory of the Victorian era. Was it art, science or the advance of civilization? No; more remarkable still was the wonderful grandeur, stability and evolution of the British Colonial Empire, exhibited 'to the gaze of an astonished world'. If the astonishment over Dr Jim's exploit was not altogether flattering, that did not worry the Jubilee crowds. Evolution had its 'sports' and the Raid was one of them.

Chamberlain gave a reception for the colonial premiers. The crowds were so enormous that Princess Maud was nearly torn to pieces and the Princess of Wales drove up in her carriage, took one look and drove away again, to the accompaniment of swearing footmen. Joe, noted Brett in his journal, was 'extremely wrathful' over this 'fearful bear-fight'. And the public were far more interested in his wrath at a social flop than in his possible relief at a Select Committee's fiasco.

The Spithead review, with its ironclads, torpedo-boats and swarms of small craft crammed with spectators, vividly called to mind the double network of iron guarding the Seven Seas; warships, and deep-sea cables sending out orders to them. Harris's messages, sent along those same cables, seemed so trivial as to be scarcely worth debating.

On the day of the Buckingham Palace garden party, 28 June, the ministerial benches were so empty that the Government's majority was at the mercy of the Opposition. The fortnight of celebrations following the pageant was still in full swing during Flora Shaw's second examination. On that very evening (2 July) was held the most dazzling and magnificent of all social events, the Duchess of Devonshire's fancy dress ball. For weeks beforehand society had been poring over family albums and visiting the National Portrait Gallery in search of historic costumes. The Print Room of the British Museum was full of dashing visitors. None of them wanted to look up the Transvaal Green book or the Cape Blue book to check Miss Shaw's answers.

Each guest at the ball was assigned to a famous 'Court': Maria Theresa's, Marie Antoinette's, the Empress Catherine's, Queen Guinevere's and many others. Ex-radical Joe found himself among the glittering supporters of Marie Antoinette's *ancien régime*. Perhaps the reason why he left the Grand Committee room early was in order to try on his wig and satin knee-breeches.

That same night a banquet was given at the Royal Colonial Institute. Sir Gordon Sprigg, 'caretaker' Premier of the Cape Colony, toasted the naval and military strength of the Empire. He went on to pay a significant tribute to the past fortnight's glorious exhibition of imperial *unity*. Should the South Africa Committee destroy this unity by striking at the very heart of the family circle – at the Colonial Office in Downing Street? Miss Shaw's engaging presence reminded the fifteen members of immediate rejoicings rather than of past errors. There were signs of a gentlemen's agreement not to pick holes in their only lady, nor to end their own labours and the Queen's Jubilee on an unpopular note.

*The Times*, as we have seen, gave Flora Shaw's final session only half a column; there were so many more pleasant things to report. Like other newspapers, it had been filled with articles on the Queen's reign from the time when the Committee was reaching its peak to the day it adjourned. The *Contemporary Review* had given a lead by allotting twenty-eight pages to little-known anecdotes from Her Majesty's past life. The Jubilee played a background part in the Inquiry similar to the Matabele rebellion in Jameson's trial. In each case the judicial procedure seemed inappropriate, if not downright unpatriotic.

The Committee of Inquiry, though it ran up so many blind alleys and drew so many blanks, did at least bring down two quarries: Bower, the Imperial Secretary for the Cape, and Newton, the Resident Commissioner for Mafeking. Both admitted their guilt. Both were dismissed the service, and though both were subsequently reinstated, Bower's distinguished career was blighted. Why did Bower confess?

Confession was not forced upon him. Rhodes and Jameson urged him not to confess, Rhodes telling him 'not to be a fool – no one will give you away'.[1] He did not 'save' the Colonial Office by confessing. Rhodes had already saved it when he withheld the 'missing telegrams' and testified, however ambiguously, to the innocence of Chamberlain and Robinson. Indeed, for the Imperial Secretary to admit collusion might well have proved dangerous to the Colonial Office. No, Bower's downfall (or heroism) lay in his loyalty to Rhodes. His 'naval standards', as he called them, prevented him from acting the part of St Peter and 'denying' his friend. He hoped against hope to avert an inquiry; but if it came he would tell the truth. Rhodes *did* tell him about the plot and he said so.

Could Bower have saved himself after admitting his complicity? It is probable that he could; but only by delating on Robinson and Chamberlain. In so doing he believed he would have 'caused South Africa to explode and set Europe in a blaze'.

Did Bower expect Chamberlain to save him? Certainly not by confessing to his own part in the affair. That, in Bower's view, meant war. But he did expect to be let off lightly. Instead, he was bullied unmercifully. He did expect Lord Rosmead and Lord Selborne eventually to concede, as man to man, their complicity. Yet up to the last neither of them would do so. Bower says that when all was over he challenged Lord Selborne point blank: 'Surely you must have intended to use those troops in connection with Johannesburg in some way?' Selborne answered: 'No, I give you my word I did not.' This statement was perforce accepted by Bower as final, but he could not resist adding: 'I thought, perhaps mistakenly, that he turned rather red . . . and looked into the fire.'

Bower did expect normal promotion after a decent interval. He never received it. Rosmead, indeed, had the bad taste, when he heard of Bower's dismissal, to beg him to get the vacant job for his own son-in-law. 'Those fellows are bound in honour to do anything you ask,' said Rosmead to the unfortunate Bower. But those fellows did next to nothing for him, though he went on asking for years afterwards. The collection of letters among his Papers tell a sad tale of hope deferred and heart-sickness. He could get nothing from his friends but sympathy.

By 1904 Bower was becoming impatient. He desired an inquiry into his case. Grey urged him against it: 'You have played a self-denying, self-sacrificing rôle in the interests of the Empire.' 1905 arrived and Sir Montagu Ommaney of the Colonial Office informed Bower that by this time it was too late for promotion. No one was left alive to challenge the Select Committee's findings. Bower replied that the great Dr Jameson himself (still alive as Prime Minister of the Cape Colony) had told Lyttelton, now Colonial Secretary, that he *did* discuss the plot with the late High Commissioner. Might not this alter the decision on promotion? 'I have only one life and the sands of that life are running out. I have spent ten years of it in the pillory from a sense of duty.'

Four more years went by; still no promotion. At long last Bower decided to bury the past, as the Colonial Office had devoutly hoped. But he went further and eventually buried it with his Trustees, until the far-off date of 1946. In December 1909 he applied for retirement on pension, and received a reply in which the word 'enjoy' has a distinctly ironic tinge: 'The Secretary of State [now Lord Crewe] trusts that you may be spared to enjoy many years of well-earned leisure.' One part, at least, of that friendly wish was amply fulfilled. The sands of Bower's life did not run out for another four and twenty years.

Bower's *Apologia*, written in 1906 to Sir Montagu Ommaney for
the perusal of Lord Elgin and Winston Churchill (the Colonial
Secretaries of State), is a document of over one hundred pages, from
which many of the facts of this story are drawn. Beginning in a mood
of detachment and stoicism, Bower wrote himself into one of
extreme bitterness. He concluded that three courses were open to
him when he faced the Select Committee. He could play the part of
Judas, betray his country and chief and save his own skin. He could
play the part of St Peter, repudiate Rhodes, Jameson and all those
standing in the pillory:

. . . throw mud at them and tell lies about them to the servant girls. St Peter
seemed to have produced many descendants. The breed of unctuously
rectitudinous liars was very numerous and conspicuous in England and
especially in official circles at that time but I could not enlist in their ranks.

He could, he said, play the part of a scapegoat: 'distinctly the
most honourable of the three. Therefore I chose it.' Bower believed
that it was the policy of Chamberlain and Robinson 'to sacrifice
subordinates as scapegoats for the sake of the peace of South Africa.
I had no faith in this policy. I did not think it honourable . . . but I
could not say they were wrong from the point of view of expediency.
Caiaphas the High Priest of the Pharisees is reported to have held
similar views . . .'

And so the *Apologia* comes to an end in mingled scorn and pride: 'I
have not only touched pitch. I have lived with pitch. But I claim
that I have not been defiled by it.'

In reading at last the story of Bower's silent endurance, it would
be wrong to assume that the consciences of his superiors were as
guilty as his own was clear. Flora Shaw, with her usual insight, put
this aspect of the affair in a letter to Bower:

In the frightful tangle of misapprehension in which this whole matter has
been involved, there may be, indeed I am disposed to think that there must
be some explanation possible on the other side . . .

Strictly speaking Bower was not a scapegoat; but he was a hero.
For his epitaph he might have found these words fitting: 'It is the

privilege of a gentleman to get the worst of any bargain throughout life.' They were favourite words of Flora Shaw's Irish grandfather.

One more harrowing item has been laid to Chamberlain's account. Early in November 1896, Bower says that he received a 'heartbroken letter' from his friend Edward Fairfield. At the coming Inquiry he was going to be disavowed by the Colonial Secretary. This, after a confident message to Bower by the previous mail that Chamberlain would protect both Fairfield and Meade. A day or two later Fairfield had a severe stroke. He never recovered.

If Fairfield was right, and he was indeed to be victimized for his part in the negotiations, it is a grim comment on the meaning of 'political necessity'. But was Fairfield right? Assuming that he had followed Chamberlain's line, there is no reason to think that the agents of Rhodes would have fatally mauled him at the Inquiry. Hawksley was his 'very great personal friend'. Chamberlain did protect Meade (though his illness somewhat altered the situation) as Fairfield said he had promised. Morals apart, it would have paid Chamberlain to protect Fairfield also. If Fairfield had been forced to confess to complicity, the strangeness of the parallel between the Bower–Robinson and Fairfield–Chamberlain combinations would have stuck out a mile. What an extraordinary thing that these two respected officials should each have agreed to share Rhodes's secrets and keep their principals in the dark! Who would have believed in the coincidence? Such a situation would have created more suspicion in the public mind than reassurance.

# 39

## Liberals in the Labyrinth

The Report was kind to the Colonial Secretary; astonishingly kind. Not a single member of the Committee, not even his political enemy Harcourt, nor his personal and political enemy Labouchere, qualified in the slightest degree the verdict of Not Guilty. Labouchere's behaviour seems inexplicable except on the assumption that he really believed Chamberlain to be completely innocent. It is possible, however, that he would have detected inconsistencies in Chamberlain's case had not his eyes been blinded by the glaring iniquities of 'Chartereds' – 'that gambling Company'. The millionaires whom Bower and Younghusband admired so much were his *bêtes noires*: to him the reformers' motives were sordid. Labouchere's crude lumping together of all the Uitlander millionaires did him no good with the public. People like Milner and Fitzpatrick were careful to distinguish between those 'with consciences and public spirit' (Beit, Wernher, Eckstein) and a millionaire of the J. B. Robinson type.* To expose the financial racket was Labouchere's obsessive interest. The Colonial Office was too far from the centre of villainy – the Stock Exchange – to deflect Labouchere's footsteps on to other, more relevant trails.

With Labouchere obsessed by the financiers, Harcourt was equally preoccupied in bringing to book the object of his special contempt, Cecil Rhodes. Harcourt was a man subject to 'bursts of violent enthusiasms and antipathies',[1] and both Rhodes and Bower suffered from his attacks. Joe, on the other hand, was his friend. Though Harcourt's son Loulou asserts that his father afterwards

---

* This gentleman had an unfortunate reputation for meanness. A story is told of him which, though it may be apocryphal, illustrates the kind of person Labouchere was universalizing. Robinson bought a concession for £100,000. He paid for it by counting out first one hundred and then one thousand sovereigns, saying briskly, 'Here are your hundred thousand pounds.' When Robinson urged upon Kruger (with whom he got on well) the need to introduce compulsory labour for Kaffirs, Kruger replied: 'That would be a breach of the Convention and we should have *Ou Ma* down on us again.'

came to doubt Chamberlain's complete innocence, Harcourt never saw reason to make his doubts public.

The Opposition did not oppose. How far and in what circumstances did they fail in their duty? It has been suggested that if the Liberals on the Committee of Inquiry had exposed the Colonial Office, far from a war resulting (as Bower and others feared), the Unionist Government would have fallen, the Liberals would have come into power and there would have been no Boer War.

This view is unrealistic. It ignores the desperate condition of the Liberal Party at that date. 'A complete wreck', 'a volcano in violent eruption', are two well-known descriptions of its parlous state. This chaos resulted from the bitter feud between Rosebery and Harcourt, who were often not on speaking terms, only conversing through third parties. Lord Rosebery called Harcourt 'a man I cannot trust';[2] this untrustworthy individual being leader of the anti-imperialist wing of the Party. Sir William was delighted when John Morley called Rosebery 'a dark horse in a loose box';[3] this ludicrous creature being leader of the imperialists inside the Party. It is inconceivable that in 1897, with the country rocked by the scandal which would have resulted from an exposure of the Colonial Office, the split fragments of the Liberal Party, itself torn on those very issues, could have smoothly floated together and formed a government capable of handling two continents, Europe and Africa, cock-a-hoop with Britain's enemies. A government of surrender, a government of imperial dissolution might have been possible; but who was prepared for that? As Graham Bower remarked: 'You can't keep Englishmen in a white sheet for an indefinite time – they would soon want to fight.'

The Liberals were in no state to take over from a disgraced Tory Party. Nor in their heart of hearts did they want to see such a *dénouement*. To them a disgraced Tory Party would have meant a disgraced Britain and there is no doubt that 'reasons of state' played a considerable part in determining their verdict. The Government were aware of the fact and suitably grateful. Speaking in Parliament, Her Majesty's Secretary of State for India, Lord George Hamilton, congratulated the Opposition on declining 'to push the Inquiry to a point which would endanger the supremacy of the British rule in South Africa'. The Liberals had been 'splendid' over this matter, said Lord George to the Primrose League. Harcourt, though Rhodes said he had not an ounce of patriotism in him, was not insensitive to British traditions of solidarity.

So far it is apparent that two factors, their own disunity and what might be called either 'reasons of state' or 'the spirit of the age', prevented the Liberals from attempting to expose the Government. It is possible that a third factor also was at work.

John Morley's *Recollections* contain the innuendo that both Rosebery and Harcourt were somehow entangled with Chamberlain: 'The two most important Liberal leaders allowed themselves to be drawn too closely with Chamberlain in this labyrinth.'[4] How much truth was there in this suggestion? Rhodes told a number of his intimates, including Flora Shaw, Dr Hans Sauer* and Graham Bower, that he had let Lord Rosebery into his secret. Bower told Chamberlain on 3 November 1896 (in response to an inquiry) that Rosebery then warned Rhodes not to move the border police until *after* the rising had begun.

In a second letter from Bower to Chamberlain, sent next day, there is a hint that Rosebery himself may have talked in a suspicious manner to members of the Government, perhaps apropos of the Jameson trial in which the Attorney-General, Sir Richard Webster, put the Government case against the raiders:

... It was not from me [wrote Bower] you heard the remark of Lord Rosebery that he was a bit of a filibuster himself. I myself heard it in the CO [Colonial Office] and believe you got it from Sir R. Webster.[5]

Either from this source or again from Rhodes's friends, rumours of Rosebery's and Harcourt's complicity reached the press. Chamberlain raised the matter in a letter of 1 January 1897 to Lionel Phillips. Phillips, it appeared, had seen the famous Harris–Rhodes correspondence, among which were the messages said to implicate the Liberal leaders. So Chamberlain asked him, 'Are you aware of any

---

* Hans Sauer relates in his memoirs how Rhodes explained to him after one of the sessions in Westminster Hall why he did not fear the Liberals' cross-questioning: 'we also have a cat in the bag,' said Rhodes, 'which, if we let it out, would show that one of their big men knew all about it [the conspiracy].' Forty years later Sauer felt it 'permissible' to reveal that Rhodes's cat was not Chamberlain but Rosebery. (*Ex Africa* . . . pp. 257–8.)

such communications, and, if so, do you know whether they will be produced before the House of Commons Committee?'[6] Was there another batch of 'missing telegrams' somewhere in the Hawksley dossier? Phillips's reply to Chamberlain's question, if he wrote one, is not among the *Chamberlain Papers*.*

Returning to Rhodes's own statement about Lord Rosebery, it is tempting to say, Why doubt it? 'Why should Rhodes have told a flagrant lie', asks a modern historian, 'to those who were in his confidence?'[7] It is clear, moreover, from the way Bower wrote about the matter on 3 November that he had no difficulty in believing Rhodes's story:

During the interview with Mr Rhodes he told me that he had told Lord Rosebery his plans and that he had thought it right to do so as the latter was making him a Privy Councillor.

Later on, after the raid, Mr Rhodes told me that Lord Rosebery had warned him that the Police must not move till after the rising.

I desire to add that Lord Rosebery's name was given to me in the strictest confidence and that in communicating the conversation to you in so far as it affects Lord Rosebery it is on the honourable understanding that it will only be used confidentially.[8]

Two months later, on 2 January 1897, Bower warned Meade that Chamberlain must on no account mention Rosebery's name when he interviewed Rhodes before the opening of the Inquiry. Rhodes was devoted to Rosebery and if his name were brought in Rhodes might go over to the Hawksley camp.

While Bower was in England, during the summer of 1896, he had told Meade the story of Rosebery's complicity. Meade got in touch with Lord Ripon, who broached the matter with his former Prime Minister, surely a delicate task. Rosebery denied the charge.

*Ripon to Meade. Confidential. 22 June 1896*
I have spoken to Rosebery about the matter which you mentioned to me the other day. He says there is no truth in the story.[9]

Other circumstances – the fact that Rosebery supported Hof-

---

* By 6 January 1897 Chamberlain had decided that the accusations against Rosebery were 'a mare's nest' and Colonial Office investigations had better be dropped. (Denis Judd, *Radical Joe*, p. 209.)

meyr's demand for an inquiry and denounced the Report as 'shameful' and 'absurd' – give weight to his denial of complicity. The truth may be that Rosebery, like others in this story, knew something of Rhodes's initial plans but nothing that he considered compromising. The mystery surrounding his name illustrates the difficulty in deciding exactly how much knowledge amounts to complicity. Was Rosebery's alleged degree of knowledge at all comparable with Chamberlain's? Without further evidence he must be given the benefit of the doubt, particularly as no evidence against him was found in the Rhodes Papers, when these were thoroughly inspected by C. M. Woodhouse.\*

As for Harcourt, some people believed that he had spared the Government in order to spare the Queen. In her efforts to soothe the truculent young Kaiser she had assured him that none of her Ministers was 'in it'. It would not be the part of a loyal servant to give Her Majesty the lie.

---

\*It is worth noting that Edward Hamilton, the political diarist, was profoundly shocked by the rumours flying about. On 21 February he wrote to Rosebery: 'There have been more foolish and more lying statements connected with the S. African business than I believe were ever current about any other matter. The latest I heard was that the late Government was implicated – that Rhodes has confessed to you as Prime Minister about his intentions on the Transvaal and made his confession when you offered him the Privy Councillorship, in case you thought he was with his intentions disqualified to receive the honour! . . .'

# 40

# *Last of the 'Missing Telegrams'*

The Liberals had their reasons for pulling their punches. But this was not to say that no blows at all were aimed at Chamberlain. A reply by Chamberlain in Parliament on 27 July 1897 caused many Liberals to pass from armed neutrality to the offensive. His speech began brilliantly. He did not merely rise to speak, said Sir Henry Lucy, he sprang to the dispatch box. How should he refute those 'anonymous assailants' who accused him of complicity in the Raid? His retort was that he had repudiated Jameson: 'My answer is my action. I was alone in London; I had no communication with my colleagues; I had to act at a moment's notice, and I did act . . . It is impossible . . . that I could have taken this step . . . if I had known about it, was myself a party to the Raid, and approved the policy of which the Raid was a part.' The question of his complicity was reduced to one simple choice which the House must now make. 'You have to believe my statement or the statement of those telegrams.'

But when Chamberlain came to the offence of Rhodes he summed it up as nothing more than 'one gigantic mistake' – an expression which to his audience seemed another gigantic mistake. He exonerated Rhodes of any personal dishonour and justified his deception of his colleagues: 'If a man goes into a revolution he must deceive other people.' There was a move to deprive Rhodes of his Privy Councillorship. 'Are we going to purge the Privy Council?' cried Chamberlain, to an accompaniment of loud cheers. (His enemies circulated the story that he looked across at another Privy Councillor, Sir Charles Dilke, who had been 'purged' from the House over the Crawford divorce but was now back in his place.*) Rhodes had been honoured, Chamberlain declared, 'for invaluable services which nothing can dim', not even that 'great mistake'.

If the reputation of Rhodes had not been dimmed, that of

---

* In August 1886 the Liberal ex-Cabinet met to consider whether Dilke should be struck off the Privy Council and decided against it. (Rosebery's Diary.)

Chamberlain certainly was. His words fell with the shock of hailstones in July. But instead of quickly melting away they had serious after-effects. For they made people put two and two together (the Report and the debate) and suddenly see many hitherto unnoticed facts in a sinister light. Chamberlain's part in the Raid, screamed Stead, was worse than Jameson's: it was Plato's 'lie in the soul'. A change indeed from Stead's earlier, 'He only winked'.

Chamberlain's 'whitewashing' speech, as it came to be called, was a major political blunder. He himself did not attempt to defend all his expressions: it was a 'last moment' effort made 'without any notes'.[1] It caused consternation among his friends and nausea among his foes; it lost the Government safe votes and lost Chamberlain the confidence of Harcourt. Was it also a moral lapse?

Chamberlain had worked with Rhodes, if only unofficially. No doubt it was an understood thing between them that if Rhodes failed he should be disowned; and because Jameson 'ran his side out', Rhodes certainly let down the Colonial Office. But that was no reason why his unofficial associate should go out of his way to throw mud. Chamberlain's conscience may well have pricked him when he signed the Majority Report. The reason there given for Rhodes's refusal to produce the 'missing telegrams' was an ignoble one: that he knew they were all lies. Chamberlain knew that was itself a lie. Rhodes withheld the 'missing telegrams' because the Colonial Office ordered him to do so. In making some restitution during the debate, Chamberlain, if not judicious, was not dishonourable.

There were further reasons why Chamberlain should speak up for Rhodes. Labouchere had frequently attacked the whole Rhodes group with 'infamous charges' and 'scandalous accusations'; while during the debate Philip Stanhope said that only the riches of Rhodes saved him from punishment. Chamberlain replied to Stanhope with a jest:

He thinks that a rich man can hardly enter into the kingdom of Heaven. [Laughter.] That may be so; at the same time I think it would press hardly upon many Members on both sides of the House. [Laughter.]

But to the graver allegation that Rhodes made the revolution for personal profit, Chamberlain replied with the famous 'certificate of honour':

There has been nothing proved – and in my opinion there exists nothing – which affects Mr Rhodes's personal position as a man of honour.

Above all Chamberlain defended Rhodes because he felt that Africa needed him. Sir Gordon Sprigg, stop-gap Prime Minister of the Cape, wrote to Chamberlain pleading, on behalf of the Colony, for Rhodes. Chamberlain read this letter to the House arguing that if the Cape lost Rhodes, Britain might 'lose South Africa', an argument he was to develop privately some months later.

These were the true reasons for the 'whitewashing' of Rhodes. But a colourful rumour soon began to circulate that something far more compelling lay behind Chamberlain's speech. It was an 'open secret', according to the *Annual Register*, that Chamberlain gave Rhodes his 'certificate of honour' under duress. This was the story:

In the pocket of a certain Liberal member, Mr D. A. Thomas, later Lord Rhondda, lay the 'missing telegrams'. Chamberlain, when he sprang forward so eagerly to speak, was well aware that they were in the House. He also knew that under certain circumstances they would be read to the members. Sitting under the clock was a confidential friend of Rhodes's. If this friend considered that Chamberlain was casting aspersions upon Rhodes, he would give Thomas the signal to read out the 'missing telegrams'. The confidential friend was of course none other than Bouchier Hawksley. He had often tried to use the telegrams as blackmail and failed. According to this tale, he succeeded at last.

Three years later the story was corrected by Hawksley himself. During the Khaki Election of 1900 he denied that Chamberlain knew the telegrams were in the House while he was 'whitewashing' Rhodes. But unless Chamberlain knew, there could be no duress.

At the beginning of the Boer War, with the Opposition out for Chamberlain's blood, an attempt was made upon the Colonial Office files. Philip Stanhope, MP, called upon Chamberlain to produce the Hawksley–Meade–Fairfield letters of 1896. The Colonial Secretary infuriated the Liberal back benches by retorting that he would show them only to two gentlemen on the front Opposition bench, Harcourt and Campbell-Bannerman, because they were honourable men as well as honourable members. But neither of the two honourable men had any wish to see the Gorgon's head.

Just over a year later, in January 1900, there was a last big effort to lift the lid off the Raid. This time all the trappings of melodrama were present. A number of letters from the Hawksley *dossier* were published abroad, in *L'Indépendance Belge*. (Some of them have already been quoted in this story.) As a result, D. A. Thomas, MP, moved to reopen the Inquiry into the Raid. The previous Inquiry, he said, was a farce: the front benches on the Committee stuck up for one another and the Colonial Secretary, as defendant-in-chief, should never have been on it. Thomas was seconded by S. T. Evans who ruthlessly exposed the weaknesses in Chamberlain's position, including a sonorous indictment of his 'whitewashing' speech:

... If these be the ideas of the Colonial Secretary with regard to public morality, it would be an evil day for this country if he were ever allowed to become the arbiter of our political ethics, or the compiler of our code of honour.

After the passage of so many years the excitement of Chamberlain's fighting reply and the hammer beats of his intense determination are as strong as ever. Let him tell the story of the Hawksley *dossier* and *L'Indépendance Belge* in his own words, as he told it to the House of Commons:

It appears a further inquiry is to be asked for on account of that precious collection of documents which was published in the *Indépendance Belge*.

Why, Sir, the hon. Gentlemen have been very scanty of information as to the way these documents were procured. They were stolen, apparently, from Mr Hawksley's desk by a clerk who was summarily dismissed, and they were then hawked about London to the newspapers holding different politics from my own, as well as those of my own side, and none of them would touch them, even with the tongs.

And then at last they found a customer, they found a customer in a well-known friend of the Boers.* He contrived to transmit them to Dr Leyds, and Dr Leyds paid, or promised to pay, £100 for them. Dr Leyds never made a worse bargain in his life than when he paid £100 for that rubbish ...

If this matter had been an ordinary case – if it had not been complicated by political motives and by personal animosities – not a man in this House

---

* An MP by the name of Dr Clarke.

would have said that there was a shadow of a shade of a ground for reopening the inquiry. They do not want an inquiry; they want an execution . . .[2]

The person who could have come forward to be Chamberlain's executioner was no more willing to do so now than he had been when he drafted the Report. Sir William Harcourt rose to support the motion; but only in order to reaffirm his previous position: obsessional hatred of Rhodes and his agents and belief in Chamberlain's innocence. He hoped that a fresh inquiry might expose 'these unscrupulous men' once for all.

There was one among the 'unscrupulous men' who wanted nothing better than a fresh inquiry. Hawksley had been driven on a tight rein for years. Ever since 1896 he had been straining to publish the 'missing telegrams'. Only the absolute veto of Rhodes held him in check. When the clerk first rifled Hawksley's desk his feelings must have been ambivalent. Now Harcourt's speech convulsed him with rage. Like Jameson, he wanted to bolt. It seemed at last as if Rhodes's solicitor would do what the Opposition had so long evaded: launch an all-out assault on the Colonial Office.

On 24 February Hawksley wrote to Rhodes's banker, Sir Lewis Michell, in South Africa: 'Surely it is not right to sit down under these charges and merely say that no one attaches any importance to Sir W. Harcourt's ravings. That won't do.' He knew that Harcourt's allegations were doing Rhodes 'and all of us' infinite harm. He begged Michell to point out to Rhodes the false position in which his policy of silence had landed them all. He ended with a threat: 'I am half inclined to publish everything on my own responsibility and don't think Rhodes would really be sorry . . .'

But there was to be no repetition of the Jameson bolt. The curb was applied to Hawksley for the last time and there were no more attempts from that source to disclose the secrets of the 'missing telegrams'. The wording of his grudging agreement not to publish suggests that he resented his own invidious position even more than that of Rhodes: '. . . no doubt from the view of the best interest of country and public policy generally it is right that the matter should be allowed to drop if others concur though it is somewhat hard upon the characters of private individuals.'[3]

The silencing of Hawksley did not mean that the Colonial Office was now safe. Only just over another year passed before there was a new crisis. Hawksley, acting for Wernher, Beit and Co., was faced with the problem of convicting a Member of Parliament (Arthur Markham) of slandering his clients while not protected by privilege, without using the essential evidence of the 'missing telegrams'. Markham had accused the firm, among other things, of 'instigating' the Raid; the 'missing telegrams' would furnish a strong presumption that someone else, even more powerful, had been involved. In the end the Court of Appeal established, to the satisfaction of all concerned, that the political aspect of the Markham case was 'irrelevant and embarrassing'; Hawksley no longer required the help of the 'missing telegrams', and the whole affair collapsed. But who could feel certain that next time the telegrams would not be relevant as well as embarrassing?

There was only one way to ensure that the lost should never be found: by their destruction. There is every reason to believe that Hawksley's copies of the 'missing telegrams' were finally obliterated even more effectively than they had earlier been expunged from the pages of Stead. If a date is to be assigned to this event it should be 1902, the year after the Markham case and following the death of Rhodes.*

---

*Bower, in letters to Sir James Rose Innes, said that Rhodes's trustees had been asked by Joseph Chamberlain to destroy the telegrams and had done so. His informant was Alfred Beit. (J. van der Poel, *The Jameson Raid*, p. 257.) C. M. Woodhouse, however, found the text of the first telegram, of 2 August 1895, in Rhodes House. See pp. 178 and 190.

# 41

# Verdict

Why did Chamberlain emerge unscathed from this, the most gruelling ordeal of his career? The Liberals did not press home their attack. Chamberlain himself combined clever defensive tactics with an indomitable will to survive. But these were not the main reasons. Ultimately, the result was due to an act of national solidarity. Without overt language, Chamberlain managed to convey to his compatriots the knife-edge on which he walked, and they approved. Edward Blake, who resigned from the Committee as a protest against the 'missing telegrams', made a penetrating speech in February 1900. The need to protect imperial interests in case of a Johannesburg rising had landed the Colonial Office, he felt, in 'a very delicate and critical position'. Between legitimate and illegitimate action 'there is a very thin partition wall . . . It is on this thin partition wall that the Minister must stand.'[1] He stood.

The unreal confusion and the equally unreal separation in the public mind between the Raid and the revolution afforded endless opportunities for tangled dialectics, of which many availed themselves, from Flora Shaw to J. L. Garvin. Chamberlain, when he summed up his case in a letter to Sir Robert Meade on 24 October 1896, himself fell into the trap: 'Meanwhile my case is that while I knew all about the revolution I knew nothing of anything so mad as Jameson's raid.' But to know nothing of the Raid was not to be innocent enough; and to know all about the revolution was to know far too much. It was indeed necessary to draw some line between Raid and revolution. But where should it be drawn? This difficulty undoubtedly impressed fair-minded critics like Blake and aided Chamberlain in his unspoken appeal to national solidarity.

Today, most of his judges would go much further in criticism. It is evident from this distance of time that Chamberlain and his friends were trying to play a game which should already have become out of date. It was all very well for Tudor princes to wink at merchant adventurers and repudiate them when they came to grief. It was all very well to say of the earlier Empire that it was acquired in a fit of absence of mind. But with the coming of democracy and other vast changes it was no longer possible for governments to affect the disguise of a split personality. They could no longer avoid commitment where plans for extending British territory were afoot.

The Jameson Raid, as was said in Parliament, lighted a brand which might take a hundred years to extinguish; and as the months passed into years the peoples of Africa did indeed plunge into deeper misfortune. Was there henceforth some nemesis hanging over the country? Sir William Harcourt came to wish that Africa did not exist. Sir Graham Bower longed to be quit of 'this infernal country with its intrigues and rascalities'. And Chamberlain asked: 'What is there in South Africa, I wonder, that makes blackguards of all who get involved in its politics?'

# 42

# Reckoning

Less than four years after Jameson and his troopers rode into the Transvaal its borders were again violated, this time in full-scale war. It was the terrible 'racial' conflict that friends of both Boers and British had long dreaded. Even the Uitlanders, despite all their confusions, were clear on this one point: their rising was on no account to be a racial war. But the Raid changed all that. New suspicions were planted in the Transvaal and grew apace. Kruger's armaments grew with them. The ease with which the burghers beat the raiders encouraged them to see in the whole might of the British Empire nothing but a multiplication of Johnny Willoughbys and Bobby Whites.

On the British side, two contrary impulses had equally unfortunate results. The jingoes, humiliated by the failure of Dr Jim's gamble, were only too eager for another, higher throw. The Poet Laureate buried the memory of *Jameson's Ride* under piles of new war poetry entitled *Songs for England*, which he distributed free to the troops as they embarked for South Africa. Verses like these, he hoped, would succeed at last in rousing the British lion:

> Slowly as stirs a lion from his bed,
> Lengthens his limbs and crisps his mane, She rose,
> Then shook out all her strength, and, flashing, said,
> > 'Where are my foes?'

Alfred Milner defended what he called 'the true jingo' in South Africa: 'The more I see of it the more proud and convinced I become of the great service which jingoism has rendered to humanity in these regions.'[1]

But over the Liberal forces in Britain a sense of shame was stealing that, beginning with the Raid and deepening after the Inquiry, flooded during the Anglo-Boer war into many unexpected corners of the national consciousness. It was reflected in the discreet part which the raiders played in the fighting: Jameson went through the siege of Ladysmith but kept himself to himself. The attitude of the military authorities towards him was not 'genial'.[2] It served to heighten Campbell-Bannerman's memorable denunciation of the concentration camps in which Boer civilians sickened and died. These were 'methods of barbarism'. And what was Jameson but an amiable barbarian, and what else but barbaric the code which shielded the Government and sacked its servants? Above all, it was reflected in the much-vaunted peace-terms which Britain granted to the defeated Boers. They have been hailed as generous, far-sighted, statesmanlike. Generous they certainly were, as only the compensation paid by a reformed character with a guilty conscience can be. But far-seeing? Looking back, it is at least arguable that they were generous to a fault. The British people at home, in their eagerness to experience the pleasant freedom which comes from a sin expiated, forgot that duty bound them to other races in South Africa besides the Boers.

In 1897 Milner described the situation of the blacks thus: 'All the Dutch and half of the English are slave-owners at heart, thinking that Natives are chattels with no rights, to be used, abused, taken on and made away with at pleasure.'

H. W. Nevinson was still more forthright. The only difference between a Boer and a Colonist, he said, in regard to the blacks was that the Colonist would hesitate longer before murdering one.[3]

Under the peace settlement the direct responsibility which the home government had hitherto felt for the Africans was allowed to slacken. Ashamed of the horror stories of war ('Kruger has a whip made out of the skins of Kaffirs'), they swung too far in the opposite direction, handing over to their defeated foes a dangerous degree of freedom in their internal affairs. Throughout this stage of the story an ominous phrase, 'Kaffirs' rights', flickers across the narrative, vanishes and flares again like distant lightning before a storm. Chamberlain remarked that the Afrikanders did not appreciate British methods towards Africans, but like the Israelites towards the Amalekites, 'they have a strong inclination to hew Agag in pieces before the Lord'. As an indirect result of the Raid they were soon free to hew Agag as they pleased. In 1910 the Union of South Africa came into being, steam-rolling into one homogeneous dominion the Dutch and English of the Cape Colony, the Free State, Natal and the Transvaal, the black serfs under the Boers and the potentially less under-privileged Africans among the British. It was not till the end of the Second World War that the dire nature of Africa's racial problem became clear. Then, fifty years after the Raid, just when Bower imagined that all its evil effects would have burnt themselves out, this most poisonous by-product burst into flame.

The new race war was to eclipse the earlier conflict between the two white races as the Anglo-Boer war eclipsed the Raid. Yet but for the Raid, the Boer war and the settlements that followed, the colour question might have been solved peacefully and piecemeal. The South African historian, Dr Jean van der Poel, wrote:

South Africa might today have possessed a slowly-matured federal constitution instead of an artificially constructed union . . . There is not much doubt that such a federation would have been able to accommodate the differences between the four provinces, particularly the colour differences, far better than the present, close union has been able to do.[4]

'Nature repairs her ravages – repairs them with her sunshine and with human labour.' So wrote George Eliot at the end of *The Mill on the Floss*. If sunshine and human labour are all that South Africa needs, there are abundant supplies of both. But where the ravages have been caused by man rather than by nature, the task of repair is harder. A clear understanding of what took place during the catastrophe is one of the human forces that can assist the process of healing.

What happened afterwards to those most intimately connected with the Raid is a story strangely overcast for the most part with shadows. Paul Kruger lived to see his people, the 'chosen people of the Lord', defeated in the war that he had not striven overmuch to avert. He died in exile in Switzerland before peace was signed. He was a Moses in reverse. Already his people were in the promised land. To drive out strangers from it he felt to be his divinely inspired mission. Instead he himself was driven out to die.

Rhodes never regained his power, though nine months after the Inquiry he was again a director of the Chartered Company. The speech he made to the shareholders in the Cannon Street hotel upon his restoration has an historic ring. He described the railway system which would soon cover his beloved country and ended with the resonant words: 'It gives you Africa – the whole of it!'

But the illness that had long threatened Rhodes struck him down only six years after the Raid. Sir Graham Bower believed he died of a broken rather than a diseased heart, though he made determined efforts to recover his old buoyancy.* Stead has left a very human account of Rhodes's private recipe for producing inner tranquillity. He believed in 'doing the comparative'[5]: telling himself how much worse things might be than they were. (One of the very worst things that happened to Rhodes towards the end of his life was his friendship with the Princess Radziwill, whose forgeries involved him in prodigious scandals.)

Before Rhodes passed from the scene that he had done so much to embellish and to ravage, he was able to make some spiritual amends to those coloured races who were to reap the worst results of the evil harvest. 'Equal rights for civilized men south of the Zambezi', became his creed. The cynic might say that Rhodes was simply after a coloured vote to replace the Dutch one which he had lost. That his feeling for Africa and its non-European races was genuine may fairly be deduced from his choice of a last resting place. He was buried among the tumbled boulders which a giant hand seems to have scattered over the Matopo Hills, close to the spot chosen by Moselikatze, King of the Matabele, for his own grave. Rhodes's tomb was cut out of the living rock and covered with a granite slab weighing over three tons.† Upon it rested a plain brass plate, with a plainer inscription: 'Here lie the remains of Cecil John Rhodes.' There was pride in this simplicity. Yet today 'his North' has become Zambia and Zimbabwe. Even the gift of his name has been rejected.

Joseph Chamberlain died a helpless cripple in the year that the First World War broke out. He had been living in a wheel chair for the

---

* On seeing the Duchess of Rutland's statue to her son who died in childhood, Rhodes wrote to her: 'I thought no man could suffer as I did about the Raid. I thought it was the biggest suffering ever meted out to man, but this beats it all.' (Diana Cooper, *The Light of Common Day*, p. 216.)

†Rhodes's most unsentimental biographer says that he was 'buried in a hole in the top of a hill'. (William Plomer, *Cecil Rhodes*, p. 159.)

past eight years, unable to play a part in politics, unable to speak except to his devoted family. It was a cruel life-in-death for a man who lived for politics. His last political activity had been to split in two the Conservative Party on which he himself had conferred the blessing of the Unionist wing. History has been less than kind to the memory of this daemonic statesman. When the name of Chamberlain crops up, there is said to be 'a smell of sulphur'.* To what does he owe this Mephistophelian reputation?

His contemporaries admired and feared in him a certain ruthlessness. Where born aristocrats of the old school, the Roseberys, Hartingtons, Spencers, Harcourts, retired with a shrug when thwarted in politics to the race-course† or the family home, Chamberlain would not take no for an answer. Politics were his life. Whatever the obstacles he meant to get his way. Some people came to believe that among the obstacles which he swept from his path were Charles Stewart Parnell and Charles Wentworth Dilke. Though these suspicions cannot be proved, they have undoubtedly contributed to the sulphurous impression.‡

His extraordinary force as a politician was not mitigated by public geniality. Among his intimates he could be the best of companions. But he chose to show to the outside world more of his cold deadliness in attack than any other quality.

Sir Graham Bower never recovered the position in the Colonial service which he had lost as a result of the Raid. His hope was to be appointed Governor of Gibraltar; he had to be content with Mauritius. He died in 1933 at the age of eighty-five in his Hampshire home, devoting himself to legal hobbies. He was a disappointed man.

Bower's colleague Newton fared less ill. He was reappointed to

---

* John Strachey. Sir H. Lucy (op. cit., p. 29) said that Labouchere adopted the watchword '*Cherchez Chamberlain*' when investigating any queer incident.

† When the Liberal Government fell in June 1885, Lord Hartington observed contentedly, 'Ascot week is a good moment for release.'

‡ There is a remarkable coincidence in the fact that both politicians were ruined by divorce suits and that Chamberlain's name was linked with a party to each suit: Mrs Crawford and Captain O'Shea. The theory, however, that he advised both Mrs Crawford and O'Shea to go ahead with the divorces, rests on slight evidence which can be explained in ways not damaging to Chamberlain.

the Colonial Service, knighted in 1919 on retirement and afterwards appointed by the Southern Rhodesians to be their High Commissioner in London.

Lord Rosmead retired to 42 Prince's Gardens, next door to Chamberlain. There he died of dropsy a few months after the Inquiry closed. The euphonious viscountcy, by which he set such store, is now extinct.

Sir Robert Meade could have retired in the normal way from the Colonial Service in 1896. Had he done so, his life might have been prolonged and his end happier. But Chamberlain persuaded him to remain at his post. At the end of 1896 he fell and broke his leg while trying to board a bus. With health impaired he overworked throughout the following year. He was too ill to appear before the Tribunal (a misfortune which must have had its compensations) and in 1898 he died of 'suppressed gout'.

Edward Fairfield died in tragic circumstances on 28 April 1897, two days before Dr Harris went into the box. His death at that precise moment was a merciful one, for he just missed Harris's disclosure of the 'guarded allusion', and the dragging in of his own name. Fairfield's brother Arthur was with him in San Remo when he died and shared his unfortunate relative's sense of victimization. Believing that their persecutors had followed them to San Remo, he wrote to the Colonial Office in 1899: 'I was always aware that we were being shadowed in San Remo – I believe by a lady of the Flora Shaw type amongst others. She was a relative of one of the directors of the Chartered Company.' In fact a woman journalist did try to meet them in San Remo, but with no ill intent.[6]

Only two of the chief actors in the drama had fairy-tale endings: Flora Shaw and Leander Starr Jameson. 'The lady' of the South Africa Committee married Colonel Sir Frederick Lugard in 1902. She travelled with her husband as much as her rather delicate health would allow. Although she had no children of her own, she was the much-loved aunt of many nephews and nieces. In 1918 she was created a Dame of the British Empire. In her portraits she seems to share that humane and level gaze so often found in the ladies who look down from the walls of women's colleges. When young, Flora Shaw had indeed been a warm supporter of the emancipation of women, but there was a curious quirk in her enthusiasm. Women, she said, must be trained to bear arms as well as babies before they could be admitted to equal citizenship. Perhaps there was a subconscious thought that had she commanded Jameson's troopers instead of merely abetting his plans, the results might have been different. Lady Lugard was thoroughly Victorian. She wore the voluminous gowns, laces and lockets of her period; but underneath her feminine charms lay the rock-like strength of the new woman. Labouchere and Chamberlain agreed on one point at least – to keep this woman voteless. Flora Shaw's performance before the Committee should have made them wonder how much longer they would succeed in doing so.

Twenty more years of life remained to Dr Jameson after the South Africa Committee completed its work. He spent it in making reparation for his moment of madness. A friend of Jameson's was once urging him strongly against a certain course of action. 'If you do that,' said he, 'you will be making the greatest mistake of your life.' 'No,' replied Jameson; 'it may be a mistake but it won't be my greatest mistake. I have made that already.' To his own circle Dr Jim was a hero though a human one: the embodiment of those pioneers celebrated in Kipling's *Poems of Empire*, 'Who are neither children nor Gods, but men in a world of men.'

The ill-health which first helped to drive Jameson from England and which broke him in prison, secured a permanent hold after the siege of Ladysmith. He fought it down. As long as the dying Rhodes needed him, he devoted himself to the friend whose career he had irretrievably damaged. From the departed Titan he turned to the peoples of South Africa, especially the Dutch, for whose miseries he felt largely responsible. His purpose was to reconcile the two white races. His almost incredible achievement was to become Prime Minister of the Cape Colony less than ten years after the Raid. He held the office from 1904 to 1908. But when he said of his last years that he had 'got square', he did not refer to any personal popularity. He had done what he could in the teeth of physical suffering to square the moral account. In 1911 King George V conferred on him a baronetcy (but like Willoughby's, it died out with him). Two years later, on the death of the Duke of Abercorn, Sir Starr became president of the Chartered Company. He died on 26 November

1917, the 'frail but intensely nervous frame' worn out by strains as violent as they had been conflicting.

The last five years of his life had been spent with his brother Middleton in England. Middleton has left a portrait of Sir Leander Starr Jameson which now hangs in the National Portrait Gallery. Can this be the man whose reckless action stirred all Europe and Africa to the depths? A quiet and agreeable little picture in cool tones of grey, white and violet, it is the likeness of an elderly professor rather than of a filibustering freebooter. The grey head is tilted back, the pince-nez nevertheless slipping down the nose. A pile of books is at his elbow and a small, fat volume (it may be his favourite Scott) is in his hand. Meditative and calm, this is a man who by the end of his life had indeed 'got square'.

Jameson and Rhodes, born in the same year, today lie side by side in the Matopo Hills. After the war Jameson's body was brought back to Africa. On 21 May 1920, in perfect autumn weather, the coffin of Rhodesian teak was mounted on a gun-carriage draped with the same Union Jack bearing the Rhodesian arms which had covered Jameson's friend. It was carried at sunset to the foot of the mountain which Rhodes called 'The View of the World' and lay all night in the light of camp fires guarded by sentries. Police, both black and white, dragged the gun-carriage to the crest, where a concourse of friends and admirers of Dr Jim were assembled: the Duke of Abercorn, Sir Otto Beit, representatives of the Government and Chartered Company and many of the old pioneers. General Smuts sent a telegram in which he described the dead man as a 'great South African'. A choir sang sweetly among the bare, ruined rocks. With due regard to symbolism, Dr Jameson was buried at Rhodes's right hand.

Thirteen years later a traveller visited the memorial to the Jameson Raid at Doornkop. It was a slab of granite ten feet square, surrounded by a rusted iron fence. Coarse veldt grass grew round and through the railings. Someone had used the monument for target practice, and the great stone was chipped.

# Notes

## Part I Façade

**1 A RAID TO REMEMBER**
1 J. P. R. Wallis, *Fitz: The Story of Sir Percy Fitzpatrick*, p. 169.

**2 THE COLOSSUS**
1 Basil Williams, *Cecil Rhodes*, p. 121.

**3 GOLDEN CITY**
1 J. P. R. Wallis, op. cit., p. 29.
2 Frank Harris, *Frank Harris: His Life and Adventures*, p. 496.
3 Edgar Holt, *The Boer War*, p. 46.
4 E. Moberly Bell, *Flora Shaw*, p. 108.
5 Sir Graham Bower to Sir Montagu Ommaney, 5 November 1906, *Bower Papers*.
6 J. P. R. Wallis, op. cit. p. 67.
7 Paul Kruger, *Memoirs*, Vol. I, p. 37.

**4 FERMENT**
1 Basil Williams, op. cit., p. 234.
2 Petition of Bathoen and Sebele, Colonial Office 417/145, 31 July 1895.
3 Edwin Lloyd, *Three Great African Chiefs*, p. 265.

**5 THE DRIFTS CRISIS**
1 Fairfield to Chamberlain, 4 November 1895.
2 Colonial Office, 417/144, 19911 and 20340.

**6 ONE MAN'S MADNESS**
1 J. van der Poel, *The Jameson Raid*, p. 98.

**7 REVOLUTION BY CONSENT**
1 J. H. Hofmeyr, *Life of Jan Hendrik Hofmeyr*, p. 489.
2 J. Rose Innes, *Autobiography*, p. 102.
3 J. P. R. Wallis, op. cit., p. 49.
4 E. Halévy, *History of the English People in the Nineteenth Century*, Vol v, p. 31.

**8 THE RAIDERS**
1 Ian Colvin, *Life of Jameson*, Vol. II, pp. 187–8.
2 J. B. Stacey-Clitheroe, *Letter* in *The Times*, 14 January 1931.
3 Michael Alexander, *The True Blue*, p. 180.
4 Sarah Gertrude Millin, *Rhodes*, p. 129.
5 *Illustrated London News*, February 1896.
6 Marquess of Crewe, *Life of Rosebery*, Vol. II, p. 565.
7 W. S. Blunt, *My Diaries: 1888–1900, 9 January 1896*.
8 Ian Colvin, op. cit., Vol. II, p. 272.

**9 'DELAY DANGEROUS'**
1 Bower to Ommaney, 11 December 1905 and 11 May 1906, *Bowers Papers*.

2 Bower to Meade, 4 November 1896. E. Drus, 'A Report on the Papers of Joseph Chamberlain relating to the Jameson Raid and the Inquiry', *Bulletin of the Institute of Historical research*, Vol. xxv (1952), p. 59.

3 H. W. Nevinson, *Changes and Chances*, p. 285.

**10 Caesarian Operation**

1 W. S. Blunt, op. cit., 1 October 1897.

**11 Into the Transvaal**

1 W. T. Stead, *Review of Reviews*, Summer 1896.

**12 'Ichabod'**

1 J. van der Poel, op. cit., p. 129.

**13 The Kaiser's Telegram**

1 *Cambridge History of the British Empire*, Vol. viii, p. 565.

2 Bower to Ommaney, 11 May 1906 (Bower's 'Apologia'), *Bower Papers*.

3 J. L. Garvin, *Life of Joseph Chamberlain*, Vol. iii, p. 92.

4 N. B. Crowell, *Alfred Austin*, p. 157.

5 Blanche Dugdale, *Life of Balfour*, Vol. i, p. 225.

**14 Prisoners in Pretoria**

1 J. Hays Hammond, *Autobiography*, Vol. i, p. 349.

2 J. P. R. Wallis, op. cit., p. 50.

3 Bower's 'Apologia', *Bower Papers*.

4 P. Fitzpatrick, *The Transvaal from Within*, pp. 231–2.

5 Colonial Office, 417/181,8400.

6 P. Fitzpatrick, op. cit., pp. 222–3.

**15 Trial of the Raiders**

1 W. S. Churchill, *My Early Life*, p. 113.

2 E. Moberly Bell, op. cit., p. 182.

3 J. van der Poel, op. cit., pp. 181–2.

4 Bower to Meade, 4 November 1896. E. Drus, op. cit., p. 59.

5 Chamberlain to the Duke of Devonshire. Garvin, op. cit., p. 114.

## *Part II Backstage*

**16 'The People's Joe'**

1 *Searchlight of Greater Birmingham*, Vol. i, No. i.

2 J. L. Hammond, *Gladstone and the Irish Nation*, Vol. ii, p. 650.

3 J. Green, *Jesse Collings*, p. 91.

4 *Searchlight*, Vol. i, No. i.

5 Viscountess Milner, *National Review*, 1934.

6 John Morley, *Recollections*, Vol. i, p. 362.

7 Blanche Dugdale, op. cit., Vol. i, p. 97.

8 Conor Cruise O'Brien, *Parnell and his Party*, p. 115.

9 H. W. Nevinson, op. cit., p. 86.

**17 Looking up the Files**

1 J. van der Poel, op. cit., p. 262.

2 Chamberlain to Wilson, 23 May 1897. E. Drus, op. cit., p. 61.

3 Garvin, op. cit., pp. 82–3.

4 Fairfield to Chamberlain, 5 January 1896. E. Drus, op. cit., p. 42.

5 Colonial Office, 537/128, 16 secret.

## 18 THE MATRIX
1 I. V. Lenin, *Imperialism: The Highest Stage of Capitalism*, p. 77.
2 Bower's '*Apologia*', *Bower Papers*.
3 E. Garrett and E. J. Edwards, *The Story of an African Crisis*, p. xxviii.
4 *Report of the Committee of Inquiry into the Raid*, 311 of 1897. Q.2518.
5 Lionel Phillips, *Some Recollections*, p. 140.

## 19 UNCONGENIAL OFFICIALS
1 W. T. Stead, *Joseph Chamberlain: Conspirator or Statesman?*, p. 62.
2 E. Moberly Bell, op. cit., p. 119.
3 Bower's '*Apologia*', *Bower Papers*.
4 Bower to Ommaney, 6 April 1905, *Bower Papers*.
5 Buxton to Bower, 22 May 1895, *Bower Papers*.
6 Ripon to Buxton, 21 May 1895, *Bower Papers*.
7 Bower's '*Apologia*', *Bower Papers*.

## 20 RHODES v. CHAMBERLAIN
1 J. L. Garvin, op. cit., pp. 32–3. B. Williams, op. cit., p. 136.
2 Bower's '*Apologia*', *Bower Papers*.
3 Colonial Office, 417/145, 6 August 1895.

## 21 THE 'GUARDED ALLUSION'
1 J. L. Garvin, op. cit., p. 39.
2 J. van der Poel, op. cit., p. 29.
3 311 of 1897, Q.8705.
4 E. Drus, op. cit., p. 48.
5 311 of 1897, p. 592.
6 J. L. Garvin, op. cit., p. 116. E. Drus, op. cit., p. 56.

7 E. Drus, op. cit., p. 41.
8 J. L. Garvin, op. cit., p. 116.

## 22 THE FIRST THREE 'MISSING TELEGRAMS'
1 Chamberlain to Salisbury, 1 August 1895, *Salisbury Papers*.
2 J. L. Garvin, op. cit., pp. 73–4 and 110–12. J. van der Poel, op. cit., pp. 42 and 49–50. E. Drus, op. cit., pp. 46–50.

## 23 GETTING ROUND THE CAPE
1 Bower's '*Apologia*', *Bower Papers*.
2 Bower to Meade, 3 November 1896. E. Drus, op. cit., p. 58.
3 Bower's '*Apologia*', *Bower Papers*.

## 24 FAIRFIELD IN THE TOILS
1 J. van der Poel, op. cit., p. 44.
2 Ibid., pp. 45–6.

## 25 THE 'FIREWORKS' TELEGRAM
1 J. L. Garvin, op. cit., p. 112.
2 E. Drus, op. cit., p. 49.

## 26 THE SICK MAN OF CAPE TOWN
1 J. L. Garvin, op. cit., pp. 59–62.
2 Ibid., p. 63.
3 Bower's '*Apologia*', *Bower Papers*.

## 27 HURRY UP! FOR PITY!
1 H. O. Arnold-Forster, MP, House of Commons, 19 July 1897.
2 *History of The Times*, Vol. III, p. 171.
3 Ibid., p. 210.
4 J. L. Garvin, op. cit., p. 70.
5 Ibid., p. 71.
6 R. H. Wilde, *Joseph Chamberlain & the South African Republic, 1895 to 1899*, Archives Year Book of South African History, 1956, p. 19.

7 J. L. Garvin, op. cit., p. 72.
8 E. Drus, op. cit., p. 35. J. L. Garvin, op. cit., p. 73.

**28 TORTOISE AND HARE**
1 *History of The Times*, Vol. III, p. 174.
2 311 of 1897. Q.7936.
3 Bower's *'Apologia'*, *Bowers Papers*.

**29 CATASTROPHE**
1 Bower's *'Apologia'*, *Bower Papers*.
2 *Report of the Cape Committee into the Raid:* 1896, p. 54, Q.668.
3 E. A. Walker, *W. P. Schreiner: A South African*, p. 71.
4 J. van der Poel, op. cit., pp. 91–2.
5 J. H. Hofmeyr, op. cit., p. 490.
6 J. L. Garvin, op. cit., p. 78.
7 Ibid., pp. 63 and 78, and A. L. Kennedy, *Salisbury: Portrait of a Statesman*, p. 268.
8 Ibid.
9 J. van der Poel, op. cit., p. 79.
10 J. L. Garvin, op. cit., p. 81.
11 Ibid., p. 79.

**30 THE PREMATURE DISPATCH**
1 Viscount Esher, *Journals and Letters*, Vol. I, pp. 194–7.
2 J. L. Garvin, op. cit., p. 109.
3 E. Drus, op. cit., p. 39.

**31 'WAR-MONGERING'**
1 E. Drus, 'Select Documents from the Chamberlain Papers concerning Anglo-Transvaal Relations, 1896–99', *Bulletin of the Institute of Historical Research*, Vol. XXVII (1954), pp. 160–1.
2 Ibid., pp. 161–2.
3 Bower's *'Apologia'*, *Bower Papers*. J. van der Poel, op. cit. pp. 160–1.
4 *L'Indépendance Belge*, 5 January 1900. Reprinted by W. T. Stead in *Joseph Chamberlain: Conspirator or Statesman*, pp. 89 et seq.

**32 BLACKMAIL**
1 J. L. Garvin, op. cit., pp. 113–16.
2 Chamberlain to Salisbury, 29 June 1896, *Salisbury Papers*.
3 Fairfield to Bower, 31 October 1896. *Bower Papers*.
4 F. Whyte, *The Life of W. T. Stead*, Vol. II, p. 97.
5 *L'Indépendance Belge*, and W. T. Stead, *Joseph Chamberlain*, pp. 139–40.
6 E. Drus, *Bulletins*, Vol. XXVII, pp. 164 and 168. J. L. Garvin, op. cit., pp. 139–40.
7 W. T. Stead, *The Last Will and Testament of Cecil J. Rhodes*, p. 180.

## Part III Probe

**33 EVE OF INQUIRY**
1 J. L. Garvin, op. cit., pp. 117–19.
2 Ibid., p. 116.
3 Sir Henry Lucy, *A Diary of the Unionist Parliament: 1895–1900*, pp. 123–4.
4 H. W. Nevinson, op. cit., p. 314.
5 Fairfield to Meade, 27 October 1896. E. Drus, *Bulletin*, Vol. XXV, p. 44.

**34 CROSS-QUESTIONING RHODES**
1 J. A. Spender, *Life, Journalism and Politics*, Vol. I, p. 81.
2 *L'Indépendance Belge*, and W. T. Stead, *Joseph Chamberlain*.
3 Sir Henry Lucy, op. cit., p. 129.

**35 TRIALS OF A TRIBUNAL**
1 *L'Indépendance Belge*, and W. T. Stead, *Joseph Chamberlain*.
2 W. T. Stead, *Review of Reviews*, Vol. xxv, p. 205.
3 E. Moberly Bell, op. cit., p. 184.

**36 LADY INTO FOX**
1 E. Moberly Bell, op. cit., p. 187.
2 Countess of Jersey, *Fifty-One Years of Victorian Life*, p. 324.

**37 COMMITTEE OF NO INQUIRY**
1 E. Drus, *Bulletin*, Vol. xxv, p. 44.

**38 JUBILEE AND GALL**
1 Bower's *'Apologia'*, *Bower Papers*.

**39 LIBERALS IN THE LABYRINTH**
1 Roy Jenkins, *Sir Charles Dilke*, p. 166.
2 Marquess of Crewe, op. cit., p. 512.
3 A. G. Gardiner, *Life of Harcourt*, Vol. II, p. 423.
4 John Morley, op. cit., Vol. II, p. 85.
5 E. Drus, *Bulletin*, Vol. xxv, pp. 58–9.

6 E. Drus, *Bulletin*, Vol. xxvII, p. 166.
7 E. Drus, 'Question of Imperial Complicity in the Jameson Raid', *English Historical Review*, October 1953, p. 592.
8 E. Drus, *Bulletin*, Vol. xxv, p. 58.
9 E. Drus, *English Historical Review*, October 1953, p. 592.

**40 LAST OF THE 'MISSING TELE-GRAMS'**
1 Chamberlain to John Ellis, MP, 14 October 1897. A. T. Bassett, *Life of John Ellis*, pp. 157–8.
2 House of Commons, 20 February 1900.
3 J. van der Poel, op. cit., p. 256.

**41 VERDICT**
1 House of Commons, 20 February 1900.

**42 RECKONING**
1 Sir Evelyn Wrench, *Alfred Lord Milner*, p. 106.
2 Ian Colvin, op. cit., Vol. II, p. 192.
3 H. W. Nevinson, op. cit., p. 319.
4 J. van der Poel, op. cit., pp. 261–2.
5 W. T. Stead, *The Last Will and Testament of Cecil J. Rhodes*.
6 E. Drus, *Bulletin*, Vol. xxv, p. 62; and information from Dame Rebecca West.

# Short Bibliography

Amery, J.: *Life of Joseph Chamberlain*, Vol. IV, 1951. Macmillan. (See below, J. L. Garvin.)

— *Great Contemporaries*, 1953, in which Amery has contributed a chapter on Joseph Chamberlain.

Bassett, A. Tilney: *The Life of John Ellis*, 1914.

Bell, E. Moberly: *Flora Shaw*, 1947. By the daughter of Flora Shaw's closest associate on *The Times*.

Bell, W. H. Somerset: *Bygone Days*, 1933. For chapters on the Raid and its sequel by a member of the Johannesburg Reform Committee.

Blake, Robert: *History of Rhodesia*, 1977.

— 'The Jameson Raid' in *History and Imagination*, 1981.

Blunt, Wilfrid Scawen: *My Diaries: 1888–1900*. Famous commentaries on the political and literary scene, with a caustic attitude to the establishment.

*Bower Papers*: All the original letters, reminiscences, etc., of Sir Graham Bower are in the South African Public Library, Cape Town, but there is a microfilm of select letters in the library of the Institute of Historical Research, London, and numerous extracts in Dr Jean van der Poel's *The Jameson Raid*. (See below.)

*Cambridge History of the British Empire*, Vols. VIII (1936) and III (1959).

Cecil, Algernon: *Queen Victoria and her Prime Ministers*, 1953. For essays on Salisbury and Rosebery.

Chilvers, H. A.: *The Story of De Beers*, 1939.

Churchill, W. S.: *Great Contemporaries*, 1937. For a chapter on Joseph Chamberlain.

Clarke, Sir Edward: *The Story of My Life*, 1918. Contains a contemporary account of the Raid's origins and sequel by one of Chamberlain's critics.

Cloete, S.: *African Portraits*, 1946. For vigorous accounts of Kruger, Rhodes and the Raid.

*Colonial Office Records*.

Colvin, Sir Ian: *The Life of Jameson*, 2 vols., 1922.

Creswick, Louis: *Life of Joseph Chamberlain*, 4 vols., 1904. Eulogistic.

Crewe, Marquess of: *Life of Rosebery*, 2 vols., 1931.

Drus, Ethel: The results of her researches into the *Chamberlain Papers* are published in the following articles: 'A Report on the Papers of Joseph Chamberlain relating to the Jameson Raid and the Inquiry', *Bulletin of the Institute of Historical Research*, Vol. xxv, 1952; 'The Question of Imperial Complicity in the Jameson Raid', *English Historical Review*, October 1953; 'Select Documents from the Chamberlain Papers concerning Anglo-Transvaal Relations, 1896–99', *Bulletin of the Institute of Historical Research*, Vol. xxvii, 1954. Indispensable material with very valuable comments.

Emden, P. H.: *Randlords*, 1935. Information on the South African magnates.

Ensor, R. C. K.: *England (1870–1914)*, 1936.

Esher, Viscount: *Journals and Letters*, 3 vols., 1934. Contains important letters relating to Rhodes and Chamberlain.

Fitzpatrick, Sir Percy: *The Transvaal from Within*, 1899. A lively account of the Johannesburg rising by one of the leaders.

Fraser, Peter: *Joseph Chamberlain*, 1966.

Gardiner, A. G.: *The Life of Sir William Harcourt*, 2 vols., 1923.

Garrett, E. and Edwards, E. J.: *The Story of an African Crisis*, 1897. Stimulating journalism, containing an interesting analysis of imperial complicity.

Garvin, J. L.: *The Life of Joseph Chamberlain*, 3 vols., 1932–4. (Vol. iv, with Vol. v to follow, are by J. Amery. See above.) The official biography and at present the main source for the *Chamberlain Papers*. Vol. iii deals with the Raid. Garvin writes powerfully but is not altogether objective.

Gross, Felix: *Rhodes of Africa*, 1956. Highly coloured and without references.

Halévy, E.: *A History of the English People, 1924–47*, Vol. v, or Pelican, Book i, 1926.

Hamilton, F.: Letter written 1937, in *English Historical Review*, April 1957.

Hammond, J. Hays: *Autobiography*, 2 vols., 1935. A contemporary account of the Johannesburg rising by another of the leaders.

*History of The Times*, 1935–47, Vol. iii. An account of the Raid and its origins from the angle of Printing House Square.

Hofmeyr, J. H.: *The Life of Jan Hendrik Hofmeyr*, 1913.

Hole, Hugh Marshall: *Old Rhodesian Days*, 1928. Reminiscences of the pioneers.

— *The Jameson Raid*, 1930. Detailed story; the best until Dr van der Poel's.

Holt, Edgar: *The Boer War*, 1958. Lucid and forceful. No references.

Jay, Richard: *Joseph Chamberlain: A Political Study*, 1981.

Jeyes, S. H.: *Mr Chamberlain: His Life and Public Career*, 2 vols., 1904. Informative but dull.

Judd, Denis: *Radical Joe*, 1977.

Juta, Marjorie: *The Pace of the Ox: Life of Paul Kruger*, 1937. A sympathetic portrait.

Kruger, Paul: *Memoirs*, 2 vols., 1902.

Lee, Sir S.: *King Edward VII*, 2 vols., 1925–7. For the story of the Kaiser's telegram.

Leslie, Sir Shane: *Men Were Different*, 1937. Chapters on Wyndham and Blunt.

Leyds, W. J.: *Kruger Days*, 1939. Reminiscences of Dr Leyds by Kees van Hoek. Interesting but slight and not always accurate about British politicians.

Lockhart, J. G.: *Cecil Rhodes*, Great Lives Series, 1933.

Lucy, Sir Henry: *A Diary of the Unionist Parliament (1895–1900)*, 1901. Lively anecdotes.

MacCarthy, Desmond: *Portraits*, 1931. Putnam. For chapters on Harcourt, Rhodes, Kruger and Blunt.

Mackail and Wyndham: *Life and Letters of George Wyndham*, 2 vols., 1925.

Michell, Sir Lewis: *Cecil John Rhodes*, 2 vols., 1910. Official biography by a close friend and colleague.

Millin, Sarah Gertrude: *Rhodes*, 1933. A balanced account in a baroque style.

Morley, Viscount: *Recollections*, 2 vols., 1917. For the best of all contemporary portraits of Chamberlain.

Pakenham, Thomas: *The Boer War*, 1979. Valuable new material including Prologue on the Raid.

Perham, Margery: *Lugard: The Years of Adventure, 1858–98*, 1956.

Petrie, Sir Charles: *Joseph Chamberlain*, Great Lives Series, 1940.

Phillips, Sir Lionel: *Some Recollections*, 1924. Account of the Johannesburg rising by another of the leaders.

Plomer, William: *Cecil Rhodes*, 1933. The most readable and astringent portrait of Rhodes; sketchy on the Raid.

Raymond, Harry: *Barnato: A Memoir*, 1897.

*Report of the British Committee of Inquiry into the Raid*: Blue Book 311 of 1897.

*Report of the Cape Committee of Inquiry*, 1896.

*Salisbury Papers*, Christ Church, Oxford.

Sauer, Hans: *Ex Africa*. A contemporary account by one of Rhodes's many doctor friends, 1937.

Spender, J. A.: *Life, Journalism and Politics*, 1927.

— *Life of Campbell-Bannerman*, 2 vols., 1923.

Stead, W. T.: *The History of the Mystery (Review of Reviews)*, 1896. Semi-fictional account of the Raid and its origins.

— *Blastus the King's Chamberlain*, 1898. An imaginary drama written round Chamberlain.

— *The Scandal of the South African Committee*, 1899. A pamphlet indicting Chamberlain and the Inquiry.

— *Joseph Chamberlain: Conspirator or Statesman?*, 1900. Pamphlet arguing that Chamberlain was the worst conspirator of them all.

— *Are We In The Right?*, 1900. Pamphlet denouncing the Boer War.

— *The Last Will and Testament of Cecil J. Rhodes*, 1902. Details on Rhodes's characters and beliefs.

Taylor, A. J. P.: *From Napoleon to Stalin*, 1950. For an essay on Lord Salisbury.

Thorold, Algar L.: *Life of Henry Labouchere*, 2 vols., 1913.

Trevelyan, G. M.: *British History in the Nineteenth Century and After, 1782–1919*, 1937.

van der Poel, Jean: *The Jameson Raid*, 1951. Contains indispensable material from the *Bower Papers* and is a brilliant if extreme statement of the case against the British Government.

Walker, E. A.: *W. P. Schreiner: A South African*, 1937. Personal data on Rhodes and the Raid.

— *A History of South Africa*, 1940.

Wallis, J. P. R.: *Fitz: The Story of Sir Percy Fitzpatrick*, 1955. Light and readable; from the Uitlander angle.

Whyte, F.: *Life of Stead*, 2 vols., 1925.

Williams, Basil: *Cecil Rhodes*. The most thorough and objective life of Rhodes.

Wolf, Lucien: *Life of the First Marquess of Ripon*, 2 vols., 1921. For Liberal policy in South Africa before the Raid.

Woodhouse, Hon. C. M. (with J. G. Lockhart): *Rhodes*, 1963.

— 'The Missing Telegrams and the Jameson Raid', *History Today*, June and July, 1962.

Younghusband, Sir Francis: *South Africa of Today*, 1898. Eye-witness account by *The Times* special correspondent.

# Index